ANTI-SEMITISM AND THE TREATMENT OF THE HOLOCAUST IN POSTCOMMUNIST EASTERN EUROPE

EDITED BY
RANDOLPH L. BRAHAM

The Rosenthal Institute for Holocaust Studies
Graduate Center/The City University of New York
and
Social Science Monographs, Boulder

Distributed by
COLUMBIA UNIVERSITY PRESS, NEW YORK

1994

EAST EUROPEAN MONOGRAPHS, NO. CDV

Holocaust Studies Series

*DS
146
E852
A57
1994*

Randolph L. Braham, Editor
The Institute for Holocaust Studies
The Graduate School and University Center
The City University of New York

Previously published books in the Series:
Perspectives on the Holocaust, 1982
Contemporary Views on the Holocaust, 1983
Genocide and Retribution, 1983
The Hungarian Jewish Catastrophe: A Selected and Annotated Bibliography, 1984
Jewish Leadership During the Nazi Era: Patterns of Behavior in the Free World, 1985
The Holocaust in Hungary - Forty Years Later, 1985
The Origins of the Holocaust Christian Anti-Semitism, 1985
The Halutz Resistance in Hungary, 1942-1944, 1986
The Tragedy of Hungarian Jewry: Essays, Documents, Depositions, 1986
The Treatment of the Holocaust in Textbooks, 1987
The Psychological Perspectives of the Holocaust and of Its Aftermath, 1988
Reflections of the Holocaust in Art and Literature, 1990
Studies on the Holocaust in Hungary, 1990

The Holocaust Studies Series is published in cooperation with the Institute for Holocaust Studies. These books are outgrowths of lectures, conferences, and research projects sponsored by the Institute. It is the purpose of the Series to subject the events and circumstances of the Holocaust to scrutiny by a variety of academics who bring different scholarly disciplines to the study.

The first three books in the Series were published by
Kluwer-Nijhoff Publishing of Boston

Copyright © 1994 by Randolph L. Braham
ISBN 0-88033-302-2
Library of Congress Catalog Card Number 94-67901

Printed in the United States of America

CONTENTS

INTRODUCTION

This volume–the fifteenth in the Holocaust Studies Series of the Rosenthal Institute for Holocaust Studies–is the outgrowth of lectures offered under the auspices of the Institute during the 1992 academic year. The lectures were devoted to an in-depth evaluation of a disturbing phenomenon–the reassertion of xeno-phobic nationalism and the concomitant rise of anti-Semitism in postcommunist East Central Europe. Following the dissolution of the communist regimes and the subsequent disintegration of the Soviet bloc, anti-Semitism, xenophobic nationalism, and ethnic rivalries resurfaced with a virulence often reminiscent of the interwar era. The end of the cold war notwithstanding, nationalist extremism has once again emerged as a major threat to the peace and security of Europe. Embraced by a variety of rightist groups and parties, ranging from sundry skinhead and neo-Nazi movements eager to resurrect the National Socialist system to chauvinists bent on ethnic cleansing, the rightist extremists have once again blended xenophobic nationalism with anti-Semitism as a core element of their ideology.

Following the collapse of the communist system, the nation-alist extremists of the former Soviet bloc nations, including those in the successor states of the USSR, openly adopted the ideologi-cal tenets of the anti-Semitism long practiced by their counter-parts in the West. A relatively large number of them are former communist officials and secret police agents eager to retain or regain their former privileges. The xenophobic extremists are actively supported–and often led–by fascists and even war criminals who repatriated from the West where they had been supported during the Cold War as vocal anti-communists. A common denominator of the ideological tenets of the newly emerged rightist extremists is the blending of traditional strains of anti-Semitism with the political-ideological strains that were developed by the Western "historical revisionists," the charlatans who specialize in the denigration and outright denial of the Holocaust. In pursuit of their objective, the xenophobic extremists take full advantage of the new political culture of their particular societies which–with the possible exception of the Czech Republic–lack a tradition of genuine democracy, let alone a liberal tradition of tolerance and pluralism.

As a rule the democratically elected leaders of the various countries, especially during their visits to the West, publicly condemn the views and actions of the extremists; they are more lenient with the nationalists-populists whose anti-Semitism is more covert and appeals to the traditional patriotic, national-Christian values of the non-westernized segments of their indigenous populations. For reasons of political expediency rather than from personal conviction, these leaders, along with other moderate political figures, condone the anti-Semitic messages of the nationalist-populists by their silence, even when they do not publicly support them.

The political influence and power of the populists and extremists vary from country to country. The variations generally reflect the social and political traditions of the specific former communist societies and the effectiveness with which they dealt–and are dealing–with the transition from a Soviet-style system to a market-oriented Western-type parliamentary democracy. The similarities and differences that characterize these countries' political and socioeconomic systemic evolution are reflected in the studies included in this volume. While many changes have taken place since the end of 1992 when these studies were completed, the essential features of the issues they analyze remain basically unaltered.

As is the case with all collective works, the studies included in this volume differ in approach and interpretation, reflecting the scholarly interests and specialization of the authors. Their views do not necessarily reflect those of the editor or of the Rosenthal Institute for Holocaust Studies.

I am indebted to the authors for their participation in the 1992 lecture series of the Rosenthal Institute for Holocaust Studies and for the expertise with which they prepared their papers for this publication. For its permission to reproduce my piece "Anti-Semitism and the Holocaust in the Politics of East Central Europe," scheduled to appear in issue 8 (2), 1994 of *Holocaust and Genocide Studies,* I thank Oxford University Press.

The publication of the Holocaust Studies Series would not be possible without the generous support of many friends. I am particularly grateful in this respect for the generous support of Elizabeth and Jack Rosenthal, the mentors of the Institute that bears their name, Gábor Várszegi, and the members of the Advisory Committee headed by Marcel Sand. I am also grateful to Dr. Frances Degen Horowitz, President, and Dr. Alan Gartner, Dean of Research and University Programs, of the Graduate School and University Center of the City University of New York, for their consistent support of Jewish and Holocaust-related studies. Last but not least, I am thankful to my wife, Elizabeth, who carried much of the burden of editing and proofreading.

Randolph L. Braham
March 1994

Anti-Semitism and the Holocaust in the Politics of East Central Europe

Randolph L. Braham

Anti-Semitism has always been a sensitive barometer in the politics of East Central Europe. It accurately reflected, for example, the gradual erosion of the democratic principles and institutions the states of the region adopted in the wake of the post-World War I settlements. Endemic in the area, anti-Semitism became particularly virulent during the interwar period when, under the influence of the Third Reich, its traditional religious component was strengthened by a more modern secular-racial content, paving the way to the destruction of the Jews during the Second World War.

Shortly after the war, the traditional and modern components of anti-Semitism were reinforced, and partially displaced, by new ideological-political strains. These evolved through the perversion of the two central factors in contemporary Jewish history, which were expected—naïvely in retrospect—to sound the death knell of anti-Semitism: the Holocaust and the subsequent establishment of the State of Israel. The perversion was first orchestrated by loosely organized extremist forces of the Right and then adopted—and exploited at various levels of intensity—by extremist forces of the Left, including the current and former communist states. Although guided by different ideological perspectives and conflicting political interests, these extremist forces embraced the new strains in contemporary anti-Semitism—anti-Zionism and its corollary opposition to Israel, and the distortion, denigration, or outright denial of the

1

Holocaust–with equal zeal. While the drive to distort and actually deny the Holocaust was begun by the Right, the campaign against Zionism and Israel was initiated by the Left during the late 1940s.[1] In the course of time, the two strains were fused with the more traditional religious and racial forms of anti-Semitism and used in various combinations by both extremes in accordance with their particular ideological and political needs.

In the Western world, the twin elements of contemporary anti-Semitism have been exploited with varying degrees of intensity and success primarily by sundry New Right, neo-Nazi, and white supremacist groups. By far the most pernicious and intellectually dishonest among them are the so-called "historical revisionists," the charlatans who specialize in the falsification of history, including the denial of the Holocaust.[2] The political-ideological underpinning for their nefarious positions was often provided by East European fascists who gained refuge in the West as champions of anti-communism. These former collaborators, many of whom had been actively involved in various aspects of the anti-Jewish drive during the Nazi era, provided, and continue to provide, the Holocaust deniers and their allies not only with "historical documentary substantiation" of their anti-Jewish positions, but also with ideological justification for their political agenda.

The leftist forces of the West, including the many formerly Moscow-oriented communists, Trotskyites, and New Left groups, focused their drive with almost equal intensity against Zionism and Israel. Although these leftist forces have differed in the course of time on their position on the Holocaust, they have nearly always ignored, denigrated, or distorted the tragedy that befell the Jews in accordance with their shifting political interests. The uses and abuses of anti-Semitism and of the Holocaust in the former Soviet bloc nations reflected the changing domestic and foreign policy requirements of the communist regimes. Since the end of the Second World War these policies underwent two fundamental shifts, each accompanied by systemic changes affecting political, governmental, and socio-economic structures. The first pertained to the formation, and the second to the dissolution, of the Soviet bloc during the post-1947 and post-1985 periods, respectively.

The Communist Era

The domestic and foreign policies of the Soviet bloc following its consolidation in 1947-48 had negative consequences for both the remnant Jewish communities in the area and Israel. This was particularly tragic because close to 90 percent of the six million Jewish victims of Nazism had lived in the countries that came under Soviet domination after the war. The hopes and aspirations of the relatively few survivors for communal revival were dashed by Stalin's anti-Jewish policies, which for all practical purposes continued until the mid-1980s.

The domestic anti-Jewish stance of the communist states was matched by their virulent anti-Zionist and anti-Israel position.[3] The latter was largely a consequence of the shift in Soviet foreign policy interests in the Middle East. Having first supported the establishment of the State of Israel and thereby also achieved a major objective in the Middle East, the withdrawal of the British from Palestine, the Soviet bloc nations shifted their foreign policy orientation. They embraced the Arab cause to advance, inter alia, their long-range strategic interests–the displacement of Western influence from the area. The pursuit of this geopolitical objective and the concomitant Stalinization of Eastern Europe coincided with the first major rift within the communist world, the Soviet-Yugoslav dispute over the character and leadership of the world communist movement. The anti-Titoist campaign that followed was soon intertwined with a relentless twin drive against Zionism and cosmopolitanism and against the State of Israel. Within a few years, Judaism and Jewish culture were severely curtailed and in some cases virtually obliterated. In the Soviet Union, for example, the leading figures of Jewish art and literature were arrested and many of them executed. Almost all communists of Jewish origin, who had been exploited during the consolidation of power, were purged from top decision-making positions in the state and party. Jews were gradually removed from leading positions in academia, and the admission of Jewish students into institutions of higher learning was drastically curtailed. "Bourgeois Jews," persecuted on the basis of both class and religion, were deported to penal camps. With emigration curtailed, many Jews tried to improve their chances by total assimilation and acculturation, concealing their identity even from their children. As a result many among the postwar generations grew up in ignorance of the Holocaust or of their religious and cultural heritage.

The Stalinist drive against Zionism and cosmopolitanism also brought about a radical change in official attitudes toward the Holocaust. The Holocaust-related documentary and scholarly works published during the first postwar years were removed from circulation.[4] The Holocaust became taboo and gradually sank in the Orwellian memory hole of history. While the communists never denied the horrendous crimes committed by the Nazis, and in fact often used them as justification for the preservation of their totalitarian rule, they systematically ignored or distorted the tragedy of European Jewry. The fact that the Nazis singled out the Jews for annihilation was simply overlooked and the millions of Jewish casualties were often routinely subsumed as losses incurred by their own nations. With the curricula and textbooks reflecting the party line, the pre-glasnost generations grew up virtually without any awareness of the Holocaust. The intensity of the anti-Jewish campaign and the extent to which the Holocaust was ignored or distorted varied from country to country. This will be illustrated with the policies that were pursued in the USSR, Romania, and Hungary, the three countries with relatively large Jewish populations.[5]

USSR

During the pre-glasnost era of the USSR, the Holocaust was perverted to suit the interests of the changing communist leaderships. Like the Jewish question as a whole, the Holocaust as a unique historical phenomenon was usually downplayed, distorted, or at best ignored in virtually all publications, including encyclopedias and textbooks. This tendency was evident in practically all the USSR republics.[6] The Soviet authorities prohibited the publication of books on the Holocaust and disallowed the distribution of those already available.[7] At the same time, they condoned, if not openly encouraged, the dissemination of obscenely anti-Jewish works and of distorted accounts of Nazism and the Jewish tragedy.[8] Crudely anti-Semitic works thinly disguised as anti-Zionist and anti-Judaistic tracts during the era of Stalin and Khrushchev were followed by perverted historical accounts on the Holocaust during the Brezhnev period. As part of their anti-Semitic and anti-Israel campaign following the 1967 Six-Day War, the historian-propagandists of the party placed much of the blame for the Holocaust on the Zionists. The Zionist leaders were accused not only of collaborating with the Nazis during the interwar and wartime periods, but also of pursuing, through Israel, a racist-imperialist policy after the war.[9] Following a twisted Marxist line of reasoning, many of these "historical" accounts were loaded with crude anti-Semitic overtones. Some attempted to "prove" that many Nazi leaders were in fact Jewish and that Jewish capitalists were actually behind Hitler.[10] Others aimed to demonstrate the linkage between Zionism and Nazism in the destruction of the Jewish masses. Perhaps the most obscene thesis was advanced by the leading Soviet "historical revisionist," Lev Korneyev, who not only questioned the number of Jewish casualties, but also suggested, along the lines of the Western neo-Nazis, that the Holocaust was one of "the myths of Zionist propaganda."[11]

Romania

Following the consolidation of communist power in Romania early in 1948, the official position on the Holocaust and the Jewish question in general underwent a radical change. The documentary and scholarly publications of the previous years[12] were replaced by general accounts that de-emphasized the anti-Jewish component of fascism and highlighted its alleged nonindigenous character. Conforming to the changing needs of the ruling communist elites, the historical accounts dealing with the fascist era, including indigenous Right radical movements and dictatorial regimes, took on an increasingly nationalist interpretation. The nationalist trend was initiated under the leadership of Gheorghe Gheorghiu-Dej and gained momentum during the dictatorial rule of his successor, Nicolae Ceauşescu (1965-89). While during their rule anti-Semitism was outlawed and the anti-Zionist campaign was devoid of its anti-Israel component–Romania was the only communist state that refused to break relations with Israel after the Six-Day War–the Ceauşescu regime launched its own "revisionist" program on the treatment of the Holocaust in general and the tragedy of Romanian Jewry in particular.

In accordance with its increasingly chauvinistic nationalist-socialist policies, including the desire to bring about the gradual rehabilitation of Marshal Ion Antonescu, Romania's wartime fascist dictator, the Ceauşescu regime embarked on a campaign to demonstrate that, in contrast to Hungary, there was no Holocaust in Romania. The broad historical policy guidelines were provided by Ceauşescu during the early 1970s in a statement in which he not only minimized and distorted the number of "persons" (the word "Jews" is not used) murdered in Jassy (Iaşi) and "interned" in the "occupied Soviet territory," but also conveniently overlooked the role the Romanians played in these mass murders. In contrast, he emphasized that "during the Horthyist and Nazi occupation, 170,000 citizens (sic) from Northern Transylvania were sent as forced laborers to Germany to concentration camps, and of these over 100,000 were killed."[13] Guided by these directives, the Party-supported "official historians" undertook to portray Antonescu's Romania as a country that not only prevented the Holocaust, but also afforded haven to thousands of foreign Jews. Consequently, the tragedy that befell Romanian Jewry was generally ignored in publications, including the press and the textbooks used at all levels of education. The relatively few Holocaust-related books that were published with the consent of the party authorities aimed either to portray crimes committed against the Jews by others, especially the

Hungarians,[14] or to demonstrate that the "tragic incidents" in Romania, including the 1940-41 massacres in Jassy and Bucharest, were primarily the consequence of Nazi instigation or direct German involvement.[15]

Throughout the Ceauşescu era, no objective historical accounts on the Romanian involvement in the Holocaust were allowed to be published. The participation of Romanian authorities and armed forces in the massacre of Jews in Bucharest, Jassy, and other cities and in the mass murder of Romanian (especially Bukovinian and Bessarabian) and Soviet Jews in Romanian-occupied Odessa and Transnistria was usually ignored, denied, or distorted.[16] The number of Jewish casualties was consistently minimized and the involvement of Romanian soldiers and gendarmes was usually explained as "unavoidable actions of self-defense against Jewish terrorists who sympathized with the anti-Romanian policies of the Soviet regime."[17] The officially sanctified historical tracts on the wartime era emphasized–and continue to emphasize–almost exclusively the positive aspects of Romania's role: that it was a country that refused to get involved in the "Final Solution" program, protected its Jewish nationals and served as a refuge to many persecuted foreign Jews.[18]

Hungary

During the Stalinist era, Hungary's record on the Jews and the treatment of the Holocaust was fundamentally the same as that of the other Soviet bloc nations. However, following the solidification of the Kádár regime that was established after the uprising of 1956, Hungary's record on these issues gradually changed. The transformation was due not only to the Kádár regime's liberal program of national communism, but also to the efforts of Jewish intellectuals in a community that numbered approximately 80,000 Jews–the largest in East Central Europe, excepting the Soviet Union. Although still strictly controlled, communal life experienced a slow but steady reinvigoration. The trend was interrupted in the wake of the Six-Day War, when Hungary, like the other communist countries, rekindled the anti-

Zionist and anti-Jewish drive with the vehemence of the Stalinist era. During the 1970s, however, Hungary reemerged as a "liberal" trendsetter, relaxing its controls not only over the economy, but also over the country's artistic and intellectual life. Hungary's literary, artistic, and scholarly output on the Holocaust remained unrivaled in the Soviet bloc. While a number of the Holocaust-related books were published by Christians,[19] the overwhelming majority of the scholarly and belletristic works were authored by communist Jewish intellectuals in academia and archival institutions.[20]

The Postcommunist Era

The policy of glasnost and democratization launched shortly after Gorbachev's acquisition of power in March 1985 brought about the second systemic change within the Soviet bloc. Hand in hand with the virtual dissolution of the world communist system and the disintegration of the Soviet bloc, this policy yielded two conflicting results with respect to the status of, and public attitudes toward, the Jews and the Holocaust. The restructuring of political life and the adoption of multi-party parliamentary systems in the former communist states brought about a resurgence of Jewish life, especially in the former USSR and Hungary. Keeping pace with the other ethnic-national groups, the Jews also experienced a revival of national consciousness and established a multitude of cultural, religious, and political organizations of their own. Jewish pride and self-assertion have been reinforced by the reestablishment of diplomatic relations with Israel and the consequent development of economic and cultural ties. Many assimilated and ostensibly acculturated Jews, especially children and grandchildren of Holocaust survivors, have reasserted their identity as Jews. Interestingly, many among these were the offspring of former top communist officials. Disillusioned with the theory and practices of communism and angered by overt and covert manifestations of anti-Semitism, they became eager to revive and preserve Jewish life and traditional cultural values. They have become particularly concerned with controversial issues that were treated as taboo in the past and have begun openly to confront the explosive issues of anti-Semitism, the discriminatory policies of the interwar and wartime fascist regimes, the hypocrisy of the communist parties and governments, and the many ramifications of the tragedy that befell European Jewry during the Nazi era.

Along with the establishment of parliamentary democracies and the restoration of civil liberties, however, democratization and the policies of glasnost also brought to the surface long-suppressed ethnic-national animosities. The political stresses and economic dislocations engendered by the dismemberment of the Soviet bloc and the jettisoning of the communist system revived the Jewish question and anti-Semitism as convenient instruments of domestic politics, even in countries with negligible Jewish populations. As the upheavals since 1989 clearly reveal, communist internationalism failed to stem the tide of nationalism in East Central Europe. Francis Fukuyama's thesis notwithstanding, the collapse of Soviet communism in 1989 has brought about neither "the end of history" nor the triumph of liberal democracy."[21] In fact, the many political, socioeconomic, and ethnic-national problems confronting postcommunist East Central Europe–all reminiscent of the pre-World War I and interwar periods–appear to denote, as Shlomo Avineri correctly observed, a "return to history."[22] Political liberalization and the accompanying marketization and privatization processes in an area basically devoid of any democratic tradition, let alone the tradition of tolerance and pluralism, have engendered a fierce xenophobic nationalist-populist reaction which not only poisoned relations between several of the former communist states, but also worsened the status of their indigenous ethnic-national minorities. The exacerbation of territorial and ethnic-national issues, including the spread of anti-Semitism–after many decades of "internationalist" education–provides a painful reminder of how deeply rooted xenophobia and intolerance are in the political culture, religion, and traditions of the people in the area.

The collapse of communism brought about the resurgence of conservative nationalist-populist fervor, reminiscent in its nuances of the 1930s. As under the Nazis, many of the newly established or activated xenophobic extremist groups have blended anti-communism and anti-Semitism in an explosive mixture. Ironically, among the most active members of these national chauvinistic groups are former leading communist officials, including secret police agents, eager to retain their power and privileges. Although operating only on the outer fringes of domestic politics, these groups periodically manage to focus public attention on the alleged linkage between Jewry and communism–a linkage that continues to be stressed with various degrees of passion in all former communist states.

The views expressed by xenophobic extremists, including the accusation that the Jews were responsible for all the evils of history–from the killing of Christ to the ravages wrought by communism and the ongoing problems of privatization and marketization–have tended to gain most credence and respectability among the less educated strata of East European societies.[23] Among the reasons are not only the hardships and social stresses caused by the economic dislocations, including inflation, unemployment, and a visible decline in living standards, but also the high political and governmental positions held by anti-Semites and Holocaust distorters in several of these states.[24]

The Nazi-style linkage of Jews and communism can be traced to several factors. For one thing, it was always a key component of anti-Semitic propaganda, especially since the end of World War I. The Right radicals exploited the embrace of communism by a relatively large number of secular Jews who, for a while at least, mistakenly believed that Marxism offered a solution to the age-old scourge of anti-Semitism. Moreover, they exploited the visibility of the proportionately large number of Jews who took on leadership positions in the Bolshevik movement and in the immediate postwar governments of several Soviet satellite states. Although communists of Jewish origin were, since the early 1950s, purged from virtually all leading party and state positions and the Jews suffered perhaps more than any other group under the communists since 1948, large segments of East European societies continue to cling to this nefarious linkage theory.

The political liberalization and economic reforms that followed the collapse of communism brought the Jewish question once again onto the front burner of East European politics. It was and continues to be exploited by a variety of extremist groups and parties whose number and influence vary from country to country.[25] Their propaganda campaign, incorporating traditional anti-Semitic and Jewish-conspiratorial themes, has been spearheaded by various groups of neo-Nazis, skinheads, and ultra nationalists, including a large number of opportunistic communists and secret police agents. The anti-Semitic drive is waged in the press and through the dissemination of both newer tracts that focus on the communist-Jewish linkage and traditional propaganda works. Among the latter, by far the most popular has been the *Protocols of the Elders of Zion,* the notorious forgery by the Tsarist secret police that was also used effectively by the Nazis in their war against the Jews. It has been disseminated in virtually all former communist countries and was serialized in newspapers and issued as a booklet.[26] The Jewish conspiracy theories of the *Protocols* have been "validated" by high-ranking officials, such as Metropolitan Johann of St. Petersburg, Russia, the second highest-ranking clergyman of the Russian Orthodox Church,[27] and reinforced by updated versions.[28] In several of the former communist states, Hitler's *Mein Kampf* was also reissued.[29] In Romania, the Nazi tract was published unabridged with the approval of the country's attorney general.[30]

The Jewish issue was also exploited during the elections of the post-1988/89 period, albeit in a shrewder manner, by vocal nationalist-populist elements. Subtle references to Jews as "the others," the alien ethnic minority group dominating the media and the professional fields, coupled with insinuations that Western-oriented liberal Christian politicians were of Jewish origin, punctuated the rhetoric of numerous candidates and their chief advisors in the right-of-center spectrum of postcommunist politics.[31] In Hungary, the debate has also revolved around the question of whether Hungarian Jews are Magyars of the Jewish faith, as the establishment Jewish leaders and their Christian supporters claim, or merely an ethnic-national minority, as asserted by both Jewish and Christian nationalists.[32] The issue became intertwined with the debate over the question of assimilation, launched by one of Hungary's most celebrated literary figures, who argued that in light of some major post-World War I experiences, that the Jews of Hungary, with a few exceptions, could not become truly assimilated.[33] Even more outrageous views about the Jews were frequently expressed by elements representing the right wing of the Hungarian Democratic Forum, Hungary's dominant Hungarian party.[34] The anti-Jewish diatribes are often joined by subtle attacks on liberals and antifascists who are disingenuously characterized as pro-Bolshevik.[35]

In Romania, the Jewish issue was intertwined during electoral campaigns with the drive to rehabilitate Marshal Ion Antonescu–*Conductor* (Leader)–during whose tenure close to 270,000 Jews were liquidated.[36] A taboo subject throughout the communist era, the Holocaust was brought into the turmoil of Romanian politics by Chief Rabbi Mozes Rosen early in 1990. In contrast to his earlier reticence, he courageously detailed the destruction of the Jews in the various parts of Romania and in the Romanian-occupied territories of the Soviet Union.[37] The Chief Rabbi has subsequently been subjected to a relentless attack by the neo-fascist, ultra-rightist press. Conveniently overlooking his services to Romania, he was–and continues to be–identified as an enemy of the Romanian people. The attack on Rabbi Rosen, spearheaded by ultra-chauvinistic rightist elements including a number of former Ceauşescu hagiograghers, has been intertwined with the denial of the Holocaust. The wartime fate of Jewry is often denigrated and compared to "the greater suffering" of Christians at the hands of "revengeful Judeo-Bolsheviks."

In Poland, where anti-Semitism was endemic, it was exploited as an effective political tool in various political campaigns, especially the presidential elections of 1990. Lech Wałsa courted popularity by exploiting the appeals of anti-Semitism.

Prime Minister Tadeusz Mazowiecki, a "pure" Pole, was tagged as a Jew, and Stan Tymanski, a previously unknown Canadian Pole, ran for the presidency with a program directed against the "Jewish enemies of Poland." In Yugoslavia, the civil war had a major impact on the Jewish community, splitting the leadership of Belgrade and Zagreb. While anti-Semitic writings appeared in both Serbia[38] and Croatia, anti-Jewish manifestations were more prevalent in Croatia.[39]

During the few years of postcommunist democracy in East Central Europe, the return to history incorporated the phenomenon of anti-Semitism without Jews.[40] Yet, considering the vehemence of the anti-Jewish rhetoric, overt manifestations of anti-Semitism in the area have, with a few exceptions, been generally minor. They involved the sporadic desecration of cemeteries and the toppling of tombstones, racist graffiti, and, rarely, the vandalizing of synagogues. The democratically elected regimes, moreover, provided for the punishment of anti-Semitic acts and assumed responsibility for guaranteeing full civil rights and equal protection under law to all their citizens.[41]

As previously noted, the anti-Jewish campaign and manifestations of anti-Semitism have generally been intertwined with distortions of the Holocaust. The destruction of European Jewry in general and the losses incurred in the various countries, along with the issues of collaboration and responsibility, emerged as sensitive and fiercely debated topics. The Holocaust, never a subject of serious and objective investigation in the region, has become intertwined with domestic power politics. Public attitudes toward the Holocaust varied—and continue to vary—in accord with the political-ideological positions of the individuals actively involved in the debate. These range from denigration or denial of the Holocaust by surviving fascists, neo-Nazis, and sundry indigenous "revisionists" to its distortion or generalization by xenophobic nationalists, and, finally, to admission of the Jewish tragedy as part of an overall European catastrophe by moderates.

Until 1989, East European Holocaust "revisionists," consisting almost exclusively of fugitive Nazi collaborators masquerading as anti-communists, were active primarily in the West, providing political-ideological support for their neo-Nazi colleagues engaged in Holocaust denial. It was the post-1985 glasnost policies that encouraged East European anti-Semitic elements to emulate their Western colleagues in testing the waters of Holocaust "revisionism" even before the communist system was jettisoned.[42] Taking advantage of the new freedoms of expression, self-styled Holocaust distorters emerged in virtually all parts of the former communist world. Again, the distortion and denigration of the Holocaust were usually intertwined with anti-Semitic, anti-Zionist, and anti-Israel diatribes.

The vilifying "revisionist" campaign gathered momentum during the post-1989 era. Self-styled chroniclers of the Second World War bent on protecting the "reputation and honor" of their countries hastened to emulate their Western "revisionist" colleagues, often reproducing the latters' writings.[43] These theses were fundamentally variations of those advanced earlier in the free world.

Revolting as the "revisionist" theses are, it is perhaps even more disturbing to witness the falsification of history by elites and public officials in power during the postcommunist era. They are engaged in a "history cleansing" process, aiming, among other things, at the gradual rehabilitation of their countries' wartime leaders. The drive in Romania for the official rehabilitation of General Ion Antonescu is a case in point. The sponging of Romania's historical record has been spearheaded not only by nationalist politicians who came to the fore since 1990, but also and above all by prominent intellectuals who had previously been in the active service of Ceauşescu's totalitarian system. The whitewashing of Antonescu's record aims not only at blurring Romania's involvement in the Nazi coalition, but also at glossing over the Romanian share in the mass murder of indigenous and Soviet Jews.

Another example of such official distortion is the "analysis of the Holocaust" provided by Franjo Tudjman, the President of Croatia.[44] In a highly controversial book, the former communist leader embraces a key element of the "revisionist" thesis, questing the number of Jews killed in the Holocaust. He also engages in a historical obscenity by drawing an analogy between the Nazi's treatment of the Jews and the Jews' treatment of the Palestinians, insisting that it represented "a historical step from Nazi-Fascism to Judeo-Nazism." His main objective is to minimize if not totally deny the role of the Croatian Ustaše in the mass murder of Serbs, Jews, and Gypsies, especially in Jasenovac, the notorious Croat concentration camp. He compounds the historical obscenity by claiming that the liquidation apparatus in the camp was largely controlled by Jews.[45]

In the former Axis states of East Central Europe–Bulgaria, Croatia, Hungary, Romania, and Slovakia–the "history cleansing" drive of the revisionists is supported by chauvinistic nationalists bent on upholding or restoring their countries' good names against the "accusations and lies propagated by the Jews." The scholarly and popular works dealing with the Second World War tend to distort the historical record in pursuit of particular national objectives. The tendency of their authors has been to absolve "the people" of all responsibility, without attempting to differentiate between the relatively large number of collaborators, the pitifully few righteous, and the overwhelming majority of those who witnessed the persecution of their Jewish neighbors with passivity. Another disturbing trend has been to portray the quisling leaders as patriots who did their best during the Nazi era to protect their national interests. In contrast to the vociferous pro-Antonescu drive in Romania, the endeavor to rehabilitate the wartime leaders in the other former Nazi satellite states is pursued in more subtle ways. The reburial of Regent Miklós Horthy's remains on September 4, 1993 will probably emerge as the first concrete step in that direction in Hungary. Attempts were also made in Slovakia to gradually rehabilitate Father Josef Tiso, the wartime president. Almost all blame for the "excesses" against Jews is placed on the Germans. The relatively few who admit the involvement of their own nationals in the anti-Jewish drive tend to explain it as the misguided actions of extremists, an aberration in an otherwise honorable historical record. These "patriots" usually review the alleged wartime suffering of the

Jews in the context of their nations' "just war" for the defense of Christian civilization against the Soviet Union and Bolshevism. They conveniently overlook not only the totalitarian nature of Nazism and the fascist system, but also the aggressive war the Axis powers initiated and waged against the Western democracies.

The Jewish losses, to the extent that they are admitted, are usually identified as the inevitable consequence of war in which casualties are incurred by all peoples involved. They point out that the Jews, after all, were associated with the anti-Axis coalition and were in fact Bolshevik terrorists against whom soldiers and gendarmes had to adopt defensive measures.[46] Moreover, these authors tend to balance the losses endured by the Jews against the suffering the Jewish survivors allegedly inflicted upon their nations during the communist era. The nationalists' distortion of the Holocaust is usually intertwined with the negation or minimization of the losses incurred by Jewry[47] and the accusation that the survivors embarked on a policy of vengeance after the war by embracing Stalinism.[48] These self-styled patriots also deplore the alleged preoccupation of "the Jewish-controlled media" with commemorating the Holocaust, questioning the loyalty of the Jews.[49] The Holocaust commemorative events are depicted as propaganda against the non-Jewish inhabitants. In Hungary, this depiction is usually coupled with the accusation that the Jews and their supporters fail to take a stand against the "genocidal policies" being pursued against the Hungarian minorities in the neighboring successor states. The stand of these right-wing pseudopatriots is often echoed at rallies by skinheads and neo-Nazis.

The nationalist-populist version of anti-Semitism, which is rather covert and appeals to the traditional patriotic, national-Christian values of the non-westernized segment of the indigenous populations, is condoned, if not always publicly supported, by the democratically elected leaders. This attitude is probably motivated more by political expedience than personal conviction.[50] Nevertheless, by failing to take a clear and unequivocal stand against their right-wing political supporters except during appearances before Jewish audiences at home and abroad, such leaders play into the hands of anti-Semites and Holocaust distorters.

With the exception of the short-lived free German Democratic Republic, none of the former Soviet bloc nations has fully come to grips with the Holocaust. They failed to accept responsibility for their own active involvement in the destruction of the Jews, let alone apologize for it. The exception was East Germany. After more than 40 years of official denial, the first freely elected parliament of East Germany admitted on April 12, 1990 the joint responsibility of the Germans for the expulsion and murder of the Jews, offered compensation, and asked the Jews of the world for forgiveness.[51] In contrast, the other newly independent states only expressed sorrow of the tragic fate of their Jewish communities, and, with the exception of Hungary, did not yet (1992) offer compensation.[52] There were only a few state leaders who showed remorse over the destruction of the Jews, but even these did so only during trips abroad or in general terms, without accepting responsibility for their nation's role in the Holocaust. For example, Lech Wałsa, who made some anti-Semitic remarks during his campaign for the presidency of Poland–remarks for which he apologized after the elections–asked forgiveness during his visit to Israel on May 20-23, 1991. Appearing before the Knesset, he declared:

> Though extermination was coming to us too, it was nevertheless not so terrible and not equal to the Shoah. We helped in the way we could....There were evildoers among us. I am a Christian and I am forbidden to weigh up the account of harm done to both nations in human scales. Here, in Israel, the country of your birth and rebirth, I ask for your forgiveness.[53]

On October 6, 1991, speaking at a memorial ceremony on the fiftieth anniversary of the mass murder at Babi Yar, President Leonid Kravchuk of Ukraine condemned the previous regime (of which he was a leading figure) for hiding the historic truth about the tragedy that the majority of the victims were Jews. He added: "This was genocide, and the guilt lies not only with the Fascists but with those who didn't stop the murderers. Part of it we take on ourselves."[54]

The new political elites, like the historians supporting them, have tended to sanitize the historical record by relativizing, generalizing or simply ignoring the Holocaust. The losses and suffering of the Jews are often acknowledged only in the context of their own wartime losses. It is difficult to determine how widely these theses are shared by the population at large. The "historical revisionists" and their sundry allies, including the neo-Nazis and skinheads, constitute but a tiny fraction of the population and operate only on the outer fringes of domestic politics. Should socioeconomic conditions continue to worsen under the impact of privatization and marketization, though, they could represent a potential threat to the fragile democratic systems.

While the leaders of the new democracies failed to come to grips with the Holocaust, they adopted a more resolute public stand than their predecessors in defense of Jewish rights and against the spread of anti-Semitism. They were supported in this endeavor by leading figures of the Christian churches who often provided the initiative and moral leadership. The campaign against anti-Semitism has occasionally been intertwined with the issue of Jewish-Christian reconciliation; the Holocaust continues to cast its shadow over the campaign. In Hungary, for example, one of the first to call for such a reconciliation was József Tornai, the noted poet. Speaking at the first national convention of the Hungarian Democratic Forum on March 12, 1989, Tornai declared that one cannot—and must not—enter into a debate over the Holocaust and that the time has come to share in the mourning for the victims torn from the national body politic. He dismissed the idea of an apology to the Jews, arguing that the current generation cannot assume guilt for the Holocaust any more than it can assume responsibility for the criminal acts that were committed against the Hungarian Jews by the wartime government. He expressed readiness to assume responsibility only for the failure to take appropriate steps toward reconciliation after the Holocaust.[55]

At its meeting of May 10, 1989, the Hungarian Parliament heard an impassioned speak by Mátyás Szűrös, its president, about the responsibility of nations to confront their historical past with courage and devotion to truth. He eloquently condemned all forms of prejudice and paid tribute to the memory of 600,000 Hungarian Jews and 30,000 (sic) Gypsies deported from Hungary.[56] However, even Szűrös found it necessary to generalize the Holocaust, lumping the martyrdom of those who perished on racial grounds–a people destined for total liquidation–with the suffering endured and the losses incurred by the Hungarian military during the war. The public statements of the newly elected leaders of Hungary are also relatively encouraging. During the July 8, 1990 unveiling of a monument dedicated to the victims of the Holocaust in Hungary, both President Árpád Göncz and Prime Minister József Antall were eloquent and forthright in their denunciation of anti-Semitism and commitment to the welfare of the Jewish community. While expressing no apologies, they commemorated the martyrdom of the Jews in words never before heard from Hungarian governmental leaders, identifying the Holocaust as a most shameful event in history.[57]

Perhaps even more encouraging is the position taken by some of the Christian church leaders. Recognizing the potential social dangers represented by anti-Semitism, they have taken measures to stem the tide. Reflecting their own democratic positions and their concern for their countries' image in the world, they followed the initiative of Pope John Paul II by condemning anti-Semitism as a crime against God and humanity. Particularly forceful in this respect were the leaders of the Hungarian Reformed Church and the Polish Roman Catholic Church. In its statement of June 12, 1990, the Synod of the Reformed Church of Hungary expressed its sorrow over the Holocaust and admitted that the Church "proved to be weak in faith and in action" during the war. While not clearly admitting

Hungary's part in the "Final Solution" program, the statement declared that in connection with questions pertaining to Jewish-Christian relations, the Church would "have to proclaim again and again responsibility and repentance."[58]

The bishops of the Roman Catholic Church in Poland adopted an even bolder position. In a pastoral letter on Jewish-Christian relations and anti-Semitism which was read in all Catholic churches in Poland on January 20, 1991, the bishops expressed their "deep conviction that all incidents of anti-Semitism are contrary to the spirit of the Gospel" and, echoing the words of Pope John Paul II, "remain opposed to the Christian vision of human dignity." While asking forgiveness for those Poles who had remained indifferent to the plight of the Jews or caused their death, the pastoral letter also reminded the parishioners of the injustices that were committed by the postwar communist authorities "in which people of Jewish origin also took part."[59]

These declarations represent courageous and important steps toward reconciliation and hopefully will be followed by others in all of East Central Europe. However, they may prove insufficient in the absence of concrete and forceful measures by the duly elected officials to protect minority rights and civil liberties. This is especially important since, with the exception of the Czech Republic, none of the former Soviet bloc nations had any tradition of real democracy and the concepts of pluralism and toleration are basically unknown. The failure to deal effectively with the scourge of anti-Semitism and to take resolute action against the Holocaust deniers may consequently have a direct impact on the future development of genuine parliamentary democracies in East Central Europe. The linkage between anti-Semitism, democracy and the Holocaust has been proved beyond a doubt. Just as unbridled anti-Semitism in the 1930s paved the way to the "Final Solution," the failure to confront the Holocaust honestly may once again encourage the spread of anti-Semitism with all its horrible social consequences in the post-communist era.

NOTES

1. It is generally agreed that the Soviet bloc's campaign against Zionism and cosmopolitanism was initiated by an article by Ilya Ehrenburg ("Po povodu odnogo pisma"; On Account of One Letter), which appeared in the September 21, 1948 issue of *Pravda*. The campaign was exacerbated during the early 1950s and after the Six-Day War of June 1967.

2. For some details on these ultra-rightist groups, see Randolph L. Braham, "Historical Revisionism and the New Right," in *Remembering for the Future. The Impact of the Holocaust on the Contemporary World* (Oxford: Pergamon Press, 1988), pp. 2093-2103, and idem., "Revisionism: Historical, Political, and Legal Implications," in Asher Cohen, et al., eds. *Comprehending the Holocaust–Historical and Literary Research* (Frankfurt am Main: Verlag Peter Land, 1988), pp. 61-96. See also Deborah E. Lipstadt, *Denying the Holocaust* (New York: The Free Press, 1993), and Pierre Vidal-Naquet, *Assassins of Memory* (New York: Columbia University Press, 1993).

3. The level of intolerance toward the Jews in East Central Europe varied from country to country. It is generally agreed that it was lowest in Bulgaria, a Slavic country with virtually no tradition of popular anti-Semitism.

4. This was the case, for example, with the three-volume work of Matatias Carp, the former Secretary of the Federation of Jewish Communities in Romania: *Cartea neagră* (Black Book) (Bucharest: Socec, 1946); *Pogromul de la Iaşi* (The Jassy Pogrom) (Bucharest: Socec, 1947); and *Transnistria* (Bucharest: Socec, 1948). In Hungary, the many documentary and journalistic-historical works published during the first postwar years, including those by Jenő Lévai and Ernő Munkácsi, became unavailable. See also footnote 7.

5. The situation in the other Soviet bloc nations was basically the same as in the three discussed in the text. For details consult Peter Meyer, et al. *The Jews in the Soviet Satellites* (Syracuse University Press, 1953).

6. For example, the Holocaust was treated more positively in Estonia, a union republic with relatively few Jews and virtually no tradition of anti-Semitism. For some details, see Zvi Gitelman, "History, Memory, and Politics: The Holocaust in the Soviet Union," in *Remembering for the Future*, pp. 2209-25. A revised version of the article appeared in *Holocaust and Genocide Studies* 5:1, 1990, pp. 23-37.

7. This was the case, for example, of *The Black Book*, compiled by Ilya Ehrenburg and Vasily Grossman. For some details on this campaign, see

William Korey, "In History's 'Memory Hole': The Soviet Treatment of the Holocaust," in Randolph L. Braham, ed., *Contemporary Views on the Holocaust*, (New York: Institute for Holocaust Studies of The City University of New York, 1983), pp. 145-56. *The Black Book* was published in English in 1981 (New York: Holocaust Library) and in Russian (*Czernya Kniga*) in 1980, Yiddish (*Dos Schwartze Buch*) in 1984, and in Hebrew (*Ha'sepher Ha'shachor*) in 1991, all by Yad Vashem in Jerusalem.

8.   See, for example, Trofim Kichko's *Judaism Without Embellishment*, which not only repeats archaic anti-Jewish cliches but also includes anti-Jewish cartoons reminiscent of the *Der Stürmer*.

9.   See in this category Yuri Ivanov, *Caution: Zionism!* (Moscow: Progress Publishers, 1970). The same grotesque thesis was advanced by Vladimir Bolshakov, a leading propagandist, in his two-part article in the February 1971 issue of *Pravda*.

10.   This obscene thesis was advanced, among others, by M. S. Gus in his *The Madness of the Swastika* (1972). For a brief analysis of this propaganda work, see Korey, "In History's 'Memory Hole'."

11.   Korneyev's work, *The Class Essence of Zionism*, was published in 1982. For further details, see William Korey, "Soviet Treatment of the Holocaust: History's 'Memory Hole'," in *Remembering for the Future*, pp. 1357-65. See also Alfred D. Low, *Soviet Jewry and Soviet Policy* (Boulder, CO: Social Science Monographs, 1990), and Theodore Freedman, ed., *Anti-Semitism in the Soviet Union. Its Roots and Consequences* (New York: Anti-Defamation League of B'nai B'rith, 1984).

12.   See note 4.

13.   Nicolae Ceauşescu, *România pe drumul construirii societăţii socialiste multilateral dezvoltate* (Romania on the Road of Building the Multilaterally Developed Socialist Society), vol. 11 (Bucharest: Editura Politică, 1975), p. 570.

14.   This category includes, for example, the books by Oliver Lustig dealing with the tragedy of the Jews of Northern Transylvania, which was under Hungarian occupation from September 1940 through the fall of 1944. See also, Mihai Fătu and Mircea Muşat, eds. *Horthyist-Fascist Terror in Northwestern Romania. September 1940-October 1944* (Bucharest: Meridiane Publishing House, 1986). This is also the case of the single Holocaust-related booklet published by the Jewish leadership of Romania during the Ceauşescu era: *Remember. 40 de ani de la masacrarea evreilor din Ardealul*

de Nord sub ocupaţia horthystă (Remember. Forty Years Since the Massacre of the Jews of Northern Transylvania Under Horthyist Occupation) (Bucharest: Federaţia Comunităţilor Evreieşti din Republica Socialistă România, 1985).

15. An example of this kind of historical treatment is *Zile însingerate la Iaşi, 1941* (Bloody Days in Jassy, 1941), by A. Kareţki and M. Covaci (Bucharest: Editura Politică, 1978). For a fully documented overview, see Radu Ioanid, "How Romania Reacted to the Holocaust, 1945-1990," in *The World Reacts to the Holocaust* (Baltimore: Johns Hopkins University Press, 1994). See also Bela Vago, "The Destruction of Romanian Jewry in Romanian Historiography," in Yisrael Gutman and Gideon Greif, eds., *Historiography of the Holocaust Period*, (Jerusalem: Yad Vashem, 1988), pp. 405-32, and the following studies by Jean Ancel: "Foreword," in *Documents Concerning the Fate of Romanian Jewry During the Holocaust* (Jerusalem: The Beate Klarsfeld Foundation, 1986), XI, pp. 5-46; "Plans for Deportation of the Romanian Jews and Their Discontinuation in Light of Documentary Evidence (July-October 1942)," in *Yad Vashem Studies*, XVI, 1984, pp. 381-420; and "The Romanian Way of Solving the 'Jewish Problem' in Bessarabia and Bukovina, June-July 1941," *Yad Vashem Studies*, XIX, 1988, pp. 187-232.

16. For some details on Romania's involvement in the Holocaust, consult Raul Hilberg, *The Destruction of the European Jews* (Chicago: Quadrangle Books, 1961), passim. See also Randolph L. Braham, *The Politics of Genocide* (New York: Columbia University Press, 1981), pp. 902-05; and I. C. Butnaru, *Holocaustul uitat* (The Forgotten Holocaust) (Boston: The Author, 1985).

17. This explanation was given to this author by many top-ranking Romanian officials during numerous visits to Romania both during and after the Ceauşescu era.

18. There is, of course, considerable truth to these assertions. While Marshal Ion Antonescu consented to the deportation of many tens of thousands of Romanian Jews, especially from Bessarabia, Bukovina, and the Herta Region, to Transnistria where more than half of them were killed, he rejected the Nazis' demand for the implementation of the "Final Solution" program in late August 1942. In 1944, during the deportation of the Jews of Hungary, Romania also was a haven to several thousand Jews who dared cross the border. For some details see Braham, *Politics of Genocide*, pp. 902-13.

19. Among the works authored by non-Jews one must include György

Száraz, *Egy előitélet nyomában* (In the Footsteps of a Prejudice) (Budapest: Magvető, 1976), and István Nemeskürty, *Requiem egy hadseregért* (Requiem for an Army) (Budapest: Magvető, 1972).

20. For references to the many scholarly, belletristic, and documentary works published in Hungary during the pre-glasnost era, see Randolph L. Braham, *The Hungarian Jewish Catastrophe. A Selected and Annotated Bibliography* (New York: Institute for Holocaust Studies of The City University of New York, 1984). See also Randolph L. Braham, "Hungary Reacts to the Holocaust" in *The World Reacts to the Holocaust* (Baltimore: The Johns Hopkins Press, 1994).

21. Se Francis Fukuyama, *The End of History and the Last Man* (New York: The Free Press, 1992).

22. Shlomo Avineri, "The Return to History and the Consequences for the Jewish Communities in Eastern Europe," in Yehuda Bauer, ed., *The Danger of Antisemitism in Central and Eastern Europe in the Wake of 1989-1990* (Jerusalem: The Hebrew University, 1991), pp. 95-101.

23. See, for example, Lev Gudkov and Alex Levinson, *Attitudes Toward Jews in the Soviet Union. Public Opinion in Ten Republics* (New York: American Jewish Committee, 1992), and Renae Cohen and Jennifer L. Golub, *Attitudes Toward Jews in Poland, Hungary, and Czechoslovakia. A Comparative Survey* (New York: American Jewish Committee, 1991).

24. During the Gorbachev era of the Soviet Union, for example, two recognized anti-Semites, Valentin Rasputin and Venyamin Yarin, served on the 15-member Presidential Council. In Hungary, István Csurka, a noted literary figure who played a leading role in the Hungarian Democratic Forum (*Magyar Demokrata Fórum*), the country's dominant political party, emerged as a vocal spokesman for an influential group of anti-Semites. In Romania, President Ion Iliescu, a former Ceauşescu supporter, appointed Paul Everac, the author of the highly anti-Semitic and Holocaust-denying work *Reacţiona-rul* (The Reactionary, Bucharest, 1992) as head of Romanian Television. Croatia, to cite a last example, is headed by President Franjo Tudjman, the author of *Bespuca povijesne zbljnosti* (Wastelands of Historical Truth, Zagreb, 1990), a work that distorts the Holocaust in general and Croatia's role in the mass murder of Gypsies, Jews, and Serbs in particular.

25. In contrast to Bulgaria and Serbia, where few if any of the newly emerged nationalist groupings had a specifically anti-Jewish platform, in the former USSR and Poland a relatively large number of nationalist fringe

parties adopted one. In the former USSR, by far the best known of these parties are the *Pamyat* and Vladimir Zhirinovsky's ultra-nationalist Liberal Democratic Party; in Poland, the most influential anti-Jewish parties are the National Party and the Polish National Community-Polish National Party. In the other former communist states of East Central Europe, the chauvinistic nationalist organizations and parties opted, for a variety of domestic and international reasons, to underplay, though not ignore, the Jewish question and the theme of anti-Semitism. Among such larger organizations and parties one can include the Slovak National Party first in Czechoslovakia and then in independent Slovakia; the Christian National Union-Hungarian National Party, the Hungarian National Socialist Action Group, and the National Federation of Hungarians in Hungary; the Greater Romanian Party and the Party of Romanian National Unity in Romania; and the Croatian Democratic Union and the Party of Rights in Croatia.

26.   For further details see *The Danger of Anti-Semitism in Central and Eastern Europe*. In Bulgaria, anti-Semitic articles have appeared primarly in *Duma* (The Word); *24 Chasa* (24 Hours); and *Zora* (Dawn). In the Czech and Slovak republics, such articles have appeared in *Stredocesky Express; Zmena; Hlas Slovenska;* and *Slovenské Ozveny*. In Hungary, the major anti-Semitic organs are *Szent Korona* (Holy Crown) and *Hunnia* (Hunnia). Romania has a relatively large number of publications, including *Europa; România Mare* (Greater Romania); *Gazeta de Vest* (Western Gazette); *Mişcarea* (The Movement); *Totuşi Iubirea* (Love, Nevertheless); *Vremea* (Time); and *Noua Dreaptă* (The New Right).

27.   William Korey, "Genocidal Hoaxes, Czarism's Evil Echo," *Jewish Week*, June 18-24, 1993. The article also analyzes the publication by *Pravda* (May 5, 1991) of an article on ritual murders that stressed that such murders were systematically practiced by Hasidim.

28.   Miroslav Dolejsi, for example, attributed the collapse of communism in Czechoslovakia to a conspiracy involving "the Jewish-Masonic world mafia." See his *Prevrat 1989 alebo História sa opakuje?* (1989 Coup, or History Repeating Itself?) (Bratislava: Agres, 1991). Similar interpretations are being advanced in the other former Soviet bloc nations as well.

29.   Excerpts from *Mein Kampf* were serialized, for example, in *Voenno-Istoricheski Zhurnal* (Military History Journal), an organ of the Soviet Ministry of Defense edited by Major General Viktor J. Filatov. For some background information see *The New York Times*, January 7, 1991. See also

Vladimir Nosenko, "The Upsurge of Anti-Semitism in the Soviet Union in the Years of *Perestroika:* Background and Causes" in *The Danger of Anti-Semitism in Central and Eastern Europe,* pp. 83-93; and Walter Laqueur, *Black Hundred. The Rise of the Extreme Right in Russia* (New York: Harper Collins, 1993).

30. See the protest letter addressed by Rabbi Mozes Rosen and Th. Blumenfeld to Attorney General Vasile Manea Dragulin, who approved the publication and circulation of *Mein Kampf* in Romania. *Revista Cultului Mazaic,* 760, June [I] 1993.

31. In Hungary, for example, this view was articulated by István Csurka (see note 24). On his radio talk of January 14, 1990, for example, he appealed to Hungarians to "wake up" to the dangers represented by a "dwarf minority" threatening to retake control of the country–a clear reference to the Jewish intellectuals, including former communists, associated with the rival Alliance of Free Democrats (*Szabad Demokraták Szövetsége*).

32. For details consult Istvan Deak, "The Danger of Anti-Semitism in Hungary" in *The Danger of Anti-Semitism in Central and Eastern Europe,* pp. 53-61.

33. In the second installment of his semi-biographical account ("Nappali hold"; Daytime Moon) published in the September 5, 1990 issue of *Hitel* (Credit), Sándor Csóori, the Kossuth-Prize-winning poet stated, inter alia: "The possibility for a spiritual-psychological welding [of Jews and non-Jews] came to an end with the Soviet Republic, the Horthy era, and especially the Holocaust. Naturally there always were and will be [Jews such as] Antal Szerb, Radnóti, György Sárközi, István Vas, György Harag, Ottó Orbán, György Konrád, György Faludy, and Tamás Zala, but one feels ever more strongly nowadays that reverse assimilationist tendencies are surfacing in the country: liberal Hungarian Jewry wishes to 'assimilate' the Maygars in style and thought." For a critical analysis of the Csóori case, see László Karsai, "A Shoah a magyar sajtóban," in Mária M. Kovács, et al., eds., *Zsidóság–identitás–történelem* (Jewry–Identity–History), (Budapest: T-Twins, 1992), pp. 59-80.

34. The chief representatives of this wing were István Csurka, István Balas, Izabella B. Király, and Gyula Zacsek. Their outrageous anti-Semitic views were long tolerated by the leadership of the Hungarian Democratic Forum, including Prime Minister József Antall, Jr., as "private opinions." However, their apparent drive to acquire power within the party, and the

negative impact of their activities on Hungary's image abroad, induced the party leadership to oust them in June 1993.

35. Jenő Fónay, a member of Parliament and Vice President of the World Association of Hungarians, declared early in September 1992: "Anyone who condemns fascism in 1992 is an outrageous communist traitor." Among those who concurred with Fónay's views was István Csurka. *Budapest Week,* September 24-30, 1992.

36. See Raphael Vago, "Anti-Semitism in the New Romania," in *The Danger of Anti-Semitism in Central and Eastern Europe,* pp. 63-74.

37. Throughout the communist era, Chief Rabbi Rosen failed to raise publicly the issue of Romania's involvement in the destruction of close to 270,000 Jews and dealt almost exclusively with the Holocaust of the Jews in Northern Transylvania during the Hungarian occupation of the region (1940-44).

38. In May 1989, the Serbian authorities seized the copies of the *Protocols of the Elders of Zion* that were being sold near Belgrade University. An anti-Semitic article by Olivera Erdeijan ("Jews Crucify Christ Again"), which appeared in the January 15, 1992 issue of *Pravoslavje* (Orthodoxy), the official journal of the Serbian Orthodox Church, was condemned by most Serbians, including Patriarch Pavle. Jennifer Golub, *The Jewish Dimension of the Yugoslav Crisis* (New York: American Jewish Committee, 1992), pp. 2-3.

39. The most serious anti-Jewish incident in Croatia took place on August 19, 1991, when the Jewish Community Center of Zagreb and the Jewish cemetery were bombed. The bombing, committed by right-wing Croat extremists, was condemned by many segments of Croatian society and by President Tudjman.

40. With the exception of Hungary and the former USSR, relatively few Jews were left in East Central Europe. In 1990, Bulgaria had from 5,000 to 8,000 Jews; in Czechoslovakia the estimates ranged from 5,000 to 15,000, and in Poland from 4,000 to 10,000; in Romania there were approximately 17,000; and in the former territory of Yugoslavia approximately 5,000. "Anti-Semitism in Central and Eastern Europe. A Current Survey." *Research Report* (Institute of Jewish Affairs), London, no. 4-6, 1991, 51 pp. For a somewhat journalistic but useful overview, see Charles Hoffman, *Gray Dawn. The Jews of Eastern Europe in the Post-Communist Era* (New York: Harper/Collins, 1992).

41. Provisions to this effect are included in all the constitutions of the states in East Central Europe. In addition, some states established separate institutions to protect the rights of ethnic minorities. Romania, for example, set up a National Committee on Minorities in April 1993. Critics of Romania's ethnic politics argue, however, that the Committee will have no impact on the country's treatment of indigenous minorities and that it was established primarily to counterbalance the country's image of intolerance abroad.

42. See, for example, Josef Sebesta's *V-zemy zaslibene?* (In the Promised Land?) (Prague: Melantrich, 1987).

43. In Hungary, *Hunnia* and *Szent Korona* are among the most active vehicles for the dissemination of "historical revisionist" theses. See, for example, Viktor Padányi's "Néhány szó a zsidó katasztrofáról" (A Few Words About the Jewish Catastrophe). *Hunnia*, Budapest, April 25, 1991, pp. 2-9. The article was excerpted from the author's *A nagy tragédia* (The Great Tragedy) that was originally published in Australia (Minerva Books) in 1977. *Hunnia* also reproduced articles by western 'revisionists,' including Marc Weber.

44. For reference to his work, see footnote 24. For a highly slanted account of the Holocaust in Croatia aiming to place much of the blame on the Serbs, see Jakov Gumzej, *Victims of War in Croatia and BiH* (Zagreb: The Croatian Association for the Protection and Development of Human Rights, 1993). The 16-page brochure was disseminated at the 1993 Vienna Conference on Human Rights.

45. For a perceptive review of Tudjman's book, see Robert D. Kaplan, "Croatianism," *The New Republic*, November 25, 1991, pp. 16, 18. During his trip to the United States as President of Croatia, Tudjman claimed that his book was inaccurately translated and the alleged anti-Semitic sections were used out of context. He also indicated that he was never an anti-Semite and would fight against all manifestations of anti-Semitism. The Jewish leaders of Croatia also defended the Tudjman government against charges of anti-Semitism. Golub, *The Jewish Dimension of the Yugoslav Crisis*, p. 6. Whatever the motivation–expediency or genuine regret–Tudjman reportedly changed his views on the Holocaust. In a letter transmitted to the B'nai B'rith by Kresimir Cosic, the Croatian Ambassador in Washington, Mr. Tudjman expressed his apologies for the book and pledged "to work for greater understanding between Croatia and the world's Jews." *The New York Times*, February 15, 1994.

46. See note 17.

47. The minimization of the losses incurred by Jewry is advanced not only by historical revisionists, but also by respectable individuals. A *Hunnia* article alleged that of the 60 million victims of the Second World War, only 1.5 million were Jews and of these 1.2 were murdered by the Soviets and only 300,000 were killed by the Germans. George Hodos, "Anti-Semitism in Hungary," *Midstream*, April 1993, p. 25. The more brazen revisionists and nationalists insist that most of the Jews survived and returned after the war or emigrated to other countries, including Australia, Canada, Israel, the United States, and Western Europe.

48. This thesis was advanced, among others, by József Szendi, a former Hungarian gendarme, who published his memoirs with the aid of the Miskolc office of the Hungarian Democratic Forum. While silent about his role during the ghettoization and deportation of the Jews in 1944, he practically boasts about his involvement in the apprehension of Jews and anti-Nazi Hungarians. See his *Csendőrsors. Hernádnémetitől Floridáig* (Gendarme Fate. From Hernádnémetitől to Florida). (Miskolc: A Magyar Demokrata Fórum Miskolci Szervezete, 1990). A former resident of Tennesse, Szendi was denaturalized and left America in June 1993, following an agreement with the Justice Department.

49. See in this category the writings of István Benedek. Many of his articles were collected in his memoiristic work titled *Hetvenhét* (Seventy-Seven) (Budapest: Szent Molnár Társaság, 1991).

50. This probably explains the appointment of Paul Everac by President Ion Iliescu of Romania (see note 24) and István Csurka's tolerance by Prime Minister József Antall, Jr. until June 1993 (see note 34).

51. For the text of the East German apology for the Nazi's crimes, see *The New York Times*, April 13, 1990. Important as this declaration was, it had no practical consequence, inasmuch as East Germany was soon integrated into the new unified Germany.

52. In April 1991, the Hungarian Parliament adopted a law providing for the compensation of property losses incurred during the 1949-1967 period, i.e., the communist era. On April 7, 1992, a new law was passed covering material losses incurred between May 1, 1939 and June 8, 1949. Another law, adopted on May 12, 1992, provided for the compensation of those who, for political reasons, were illegally deprived of their lives and liberty between March 11, 1939 and October 23, 1989. For most survivors of the Holocaust,

the benefits to be derived from these laws will appear as "too little too late."

53. "Anti-Semitism in Central and Eastern Europe," *Research Report*, London, 4-6, 1991, p. 33. See also Robert Cullen, "Report from Ukraine," *The New Yorker*, January 27, 1992, p. 52. Similarly, in his April 1993 (*Yom ha'Shoa*) speech in the Choral Temple of Bucharest, President Iliescu of Romania spoke about the Holocaust of European Jewry in general without making any reference to Romania. In a Christmas 1990 resolution the Slovak Parliament acknowledged and expressed regret over the deportation of the Slovak Jews.

54. József Tornai, "A kiengesztelés pillanata," (The Moment for Reconciliation), *Magyar Nemzet* (Hungarian Nation), Budapest, March 25, 1989.

55. According to László Karsai, the number of Gypsies deported from Hungary did not exceed 5,000. See his *A cigánykérdés Magyarországon, 1919-1945* (The Gypsy Question in Hungary, 1919-1945) (Budapest: Cserépfalvi, 1992), p. 7.

56. For excerpts from their speeches, see *Új Élet* (New Life), Budapest, July 15, 1990.

57. For the text of the declaration, see *Új Élet*, August 1, 1990. For the English version, consult *Christian-Jewish Relations*, London, 23, no. 1, 1990, pp. 43-45. The Reformed Church planned to issue a similar statement in 1946, but was vetoed by Bishop László Ravasz, the head of the Church. The initiative of the Reformed Church was followed up by the Catholic Church, Hungary's main Christian denomination.

58. *The New York Times*, January 20, 1991.

Anti-Semitism and the Treatment of the Holocaust in Postcommunist Bulgaria

Frederick B. Chary

Jews have lived in Bulgaria several centuries longer than Bulgarians;[1] the oldest Jewish monument is the second-century synagogue at Nikopol on the Danube. At the earliest, the South Slavs arrived in the fourth century A.D.; the Bulgars are said to have come in the seventh. However, the bulk of Bulgaria's Jews are descendants of the great Spanish migration that took place after the expulsion from Iberia in the fifteenth century. While the Sephardic expellees settled chiefly in Constantinople and Thessaloniki, they also established communities in Sofia, Plovdiv, Burgas, and Varna. Because of the relative tolerance of the Ottoman Empire, in succeeding centuries Ashkenazi immigrants escaping anti-Semitism arrived in Bulgaria too. Some of these later immigrants adopted the Sephardic rite, but Ashkenazi communities remained in Ruse, Varna, and Sofia. By the end of the nineteenth century there were 30,000 Bulgarian Jews, 90 percent of whom were Sephardim.

This was not a large portion of the population–somewhat under one percent. Furthermore, for a Balkan, indeed an Eastern European country, Bulgaria is rather homogeneous. Turks and other Moslems (who traditionally grouped themselves together by religion rather than ethnicity) were the largest minority in the land, approaching 10 percent, after the liberation from the Ottoman Empire in 1878.[2] Greeks, Armenians, and Gypsies also appeared in significant numbers but all between 1 percent and 2

31

percent of the population. (The 1920 census of Bulgaria listed over a hundred different nationalities living in the country, counted by self-identification, native language, and religion. The census even included three Japanese Buddhists!).[3] The Jews of Bulgaria were mostly city dwellers, making up 12 percent of the urban population, while the majority of Bulgarians lived in the countryside.

Jews in Bulgaria were organized in official community institutions, consistories, under the administrative authority of the Ministry of Foreign Affairs and Religious Cults–a policy dating back to Ottoman times and continued after 1878 in independent Bulgaria. At the time of Bulgarian independence the Jewish community numbered about 14,500, of whom 5,000 lived in Sofia, the capital of the new state. Another 8,000 lived in the province of Eastern Rumelia that was not joined to Bulgaria until 1885. The Bulgarian population of these two areas was about 3,000,000. The Russo-Turkish War of 1877-78 and Bulgarian independence brought some anxiety to the Jews because of Russia's infamous anti-Semitism, but in fact despite a few incidents there was no great animosity by the Christians toward the Jews. The latter generally had little interest in the Bulgarian national movement. However, the Jewish community of Sofia played a key role in preventing the destruction of the city by fire during the Turkish retreat of 1878–an incident duly noted by the new Bulgarian monarch Prince Alexander Battenberg. Despite the clear stipulation in the constitution of the new Bulgarian state that the Orthodox confession was its official religion, all other creeds that did not offend the public order were permitted. The constitution as well as an international treaty guaranteed that the Jewish community would not suffer legal discrimination. Bulgarian society and the government generally honored this commitment in practice. By virtue of his office, the grand rabbi selected by the central consistory established in Sofia sat in the constitutional convention along with the chief mufti of the Bulgarian Moslems and the Bulgarian Orthodox Christian metropolitans.

From 1878 to 1939, Jews generally stayed aloof from Bulgarian politics and were not well integrated into society, although there were several prominent individual exceptions. While there were some Bulgarian merchants in the new land and a growing native Bulgarian capitalist class, most Bulgarians were farmers. All were but one or two generations away from the land. Jews along with Greeks and Armenians were historically the country's merchants and accepted as such. Trade in various branches fell to the various ethnic groups; for example, Jews specialized in import-export and the tobacco trade. At that time, Bulgaria was a country of small and mid-size farmers with few large landowners. Aside from the monarch and isolated individuals in the cities, there were very few really wealthy Bulgarians, Christian or Jewish. Bulgaria was in a state of nascent modernization, and its cities were the domains of small shopkeepers, artisans, and entrepreneurs. There was enough opportunity to go around. Ethnic hostility based on economic competition was rare. Furthermore, the one growing exploitation problem–the merciless taking advantage of peasants by usurious village innkeepers and money lenders–was exploitation of Bulgarians by Bulgarians. Table 1 presents the proportion of Jews among the population of Bulgaria according to various censuses between 1887 and 1934.[4]

TABLE 1

Census of Jews in Bulgaria

Census Date	Total Population	Bulgarians		Minorities, Total		Jews	
		Number	Percent	Number	Percent	Number	Percent
1877	3,154,375	2,326,250	73.75	828,125	26.45	24,352	0.77
1892	3,310,713	2,505,260	75.67	805,453	24.33	28,307	0.86
1900	3,744,283	2,887,860	77.13	857,423	22.87	33,633	0.90
1905	4,035,575	3,210,502	79.56	825,073	20.44	37,656	0.93
1910	4,337,575	3,523,151	81.23	814,424	18.77	40,067	0.92
1920	4,846,971	4,041,276	83.38	805,695	16.62	43,232	0.89
1934	6,077,939	5,128,890	84.39	1,064,530	15.61	48,398	0.80

At the time of Bulgaria's liberation from the Ottoman Empire in 1878 the Bulgarian Jews were as backward as the rest of the country. The traditions of the Turkish *millet*[5] dominated the thinking of the community. Over the next decades, in large part through the efforts of the French *Alliance Israelite Universelle* (AIU), the Jews modernized. They adopted French and Bulgarian as languages of communication. In the first census of 1887 almost all the Jews identified the medieval Spanish Ladino as their native language; in 1934 less than 60 percent did so.[6]

After the First World War the younger generation of Jews became ardent Zionists. Sofia lay on the route from Vienna to Istanbul, and many Zionist leaders including Theodor Herzl and Baron Maurice de Hirsch visited the Bulgarian capital on their journeys to negotiate land sales in Palestine with the Turkish Porte. After World War I the young Zionists ousted the conservative "notables" from leadership positions in the central consistory. The "notable" German-born Grand Rabbi Marcus Ehrenpreis was driven back to Sweden and his position taken by the Bulgarian-born Asher Hannanel–a war hero to boot–who had served in the crown prince's cavalry regiment. Even when, after World War I, the crown prince became King Boris III and Hannanel thus had a relationship to the King, the Bulgarian foreign office failed to recognize the unusual rabbinical election. The office remained officially vacant.

Other Jews served in the Bulgarian army as well, some even reaching high officer rank. There were three Bulgarian Jewish colonels. Like other ethnic and religious communities, Jews traditionally had their own schools. Modernization, while not ending these, brought about their decline as more and more Jews sent their children to the state-run schools which, by the way, included religious instruction.

Males represented 85 percent of the Jewish work force. Twenty percent of the community lived below the poverty line. Jews held a variety of occupations before World War II, as shown in Table 2.[7]

TABLE 2
Fields of Employment of Jews
Between the Two World Wars

Branch	Active Population	Self-employed		Employees	
		Number	Percent	Number	Percent
1926					
Business, banking, credit, insurance	7,373	4,665	63.3	2,708	36.7
Industry, crafts, transportation	4,729	1,736	36.7	2,993	63.3
Professions, civil service, domestic service	1,342	231	17.2	1,111	82.7
TOTAL	13,144	6,632	49.3	6,812	50.7
1934					
Business, banking, credit, insurance	9,381	5,243	55.9	4,138	44.1
Industry, crafts, transportation	5,165	1,616	31.3	3,549	68.7
Professions, civil service, domestic service	2,582	999	38.7	1,583	61.3
TOTAL	17,128	7,858	45.9	9,270	54.1

While in fact as well as law Bulgarian society after the 1878 liberation demonstrated a tolerance toward minority groups not often found in Eastern Europe, anti-Semitic attitudes were not unknown. We find mild ethnic prejudices, but also a few pogroms stemming from rumors of blood-libel. However, we do not find any politicians rising to prominence on an anti-Semitic program. Quite the contrary, calls to traditional Bulgarian tolerance and liberalism became stronger as the century moved on, even into the period of fascism.[8]

Of the handful of Jews who participated in national politics or influenced culture, the most prominent were the Radical Party lawyer Iosif Fadenhecht, the journalist Iosif Herbst, and the poet Dora Gabe. Few Jews were elected to Parliament. One of the most famous Bulgarian Jews in the world today is Nobel Laureate Elias Canetti of Ruse. He did his major writing, however, after the had left Bulgaria and cannot really be considered part of Bulgarian culture.

As elsewhere in the world, the rise of Hitler and Nazism in the 1930s was accompanied by a new rise in anti-Semitism in Bulgaria. Fascism, nevertheless, still did not find much fertile ground in the kingdom. It was international events that drew the Balkans into the German orbit and brought the vile disease promulgated by Hitler to Bulgaria. The most virulent anti-Semitic organizations in the country were the National Union of Legions and the Defenders of the Bulgarian Spirit (*Ratnitsi*). In the thirties these groups had a significant following, but they never gained a majority and were unable to come to power even during World War II.[9]

Initially Bulgaria, like the other countries of southeast Europe, declared neutrality in World War II, but economically it was linked to Germany. In February 1940 Boris appointed the pro-German art historian and Minister of Education, Bogdan Filov, Prime Minister in order to outmaneuver strong-minded politicians seeking to cut into his power. Filov appointed Petur Gabrovski, a man with *Ratnik* connections, Minister of Internal Affairs.

With Gabrovski as supervisor of police functions, anti-Semitic actions began, although no actual discriminatory legislation had yet been introduced into the country. However, many foreign Jews hoping to find passage to Palestine had come into Bulgaria in the wake of the war's beginning; now Bulgarian authorities expelled several hundred over the Turkish border or deported them on unseaworthy vessels. Gabrovski also sent a lawyer in his department, Alexander Belev, to Germany to study the Nuremberg racial laws.[10]

The fall of 1940 brought the war into the Balkans and Bulgaria closer to the Reich. Under pressure from Germany, the government pushed anti-Semitic legislation, modeled on the Nuremberg laws, through Parliament.[11]

Many sections of the law did not apply to the Bulgarian community. Furthermore, the small number of Bulgarian Jews, their relative isolation, and many loopholes made the law easy to evade. In the Parliament the major debates over its provisions were arguments among rival Bulgarian politicians, both between those on the left and the right and among the various leaders of the right itself.

Bulgaria's active participation in World War II on the side of the Axis beginning in April 1941 brought more severe legislation regarding the Jews. The government introduced special confiscatory taxes and restrictions on movement. In the summer of 1942 a major new decree prepared the community for deportation to the death camps in Poland.[12]

The government hoped to avoid the outcry that had come from opposition members of the Assembly and certain parts of the public when the first law had been debated. Therefore a new law charged the government "to take all measures for solving the Jewish question."[13] The decree based on this law, issued in August 1942, bypassed parliamentary debate and established a Commissariat for Jewish Affairs.[14]

The head of the new office, the Commissar, was the same Alexander Belev who had been instructed earlier by the Reich in anti-Semitic legislation. The new law required Jews to wear the identifying yellow star and to live in ghettos. Its real intent was to prepare for deportation and that fall Belev and Theodor Dannecker, from Adolf Eichmann's office on Jewish matters in the SS, worked out a schedule. The same Dannecker was the official who had previously arranged for deportations of Jews from France.[15]

The plan called for the Jews to be deported in three groups of 20,000 each. The first deportations were envisioned to include about 12,000 Jews living in Bulgarian-occupied Greece and Yugoslavia as well as 8,000 Bulgarian citizens–the leaders of the Jewish community and all Jews living in the southwestern part of the country, chiefly Macedonia, where temporary relocation camps were to be established. Belev and Dannecker arranged for this first deportation to occur in March and April 1943.

Even though the Commissariat tried to keep its plans secret, news of the deportations leaked out and public protests including some prominent persons in the government, society, and the church prevented the deportation of the Bulgarian Jews, although it could not prevent the deportation of those from Greece and Yugoslavia. There was even a debate over the issue in the Parliament, where a sizable portion of the ruling majority objected to the plans.[16]

Furthermore, the change in the German fortunes of war in the spring of 1943 gave Sofia second thoughts about cooperation in this matter. Belev proposed a new plan for expelling the Sofia Jews from the capital as a first stage for complete deportation. He argued erroneously that it was the large number of Jews in proximity to the crown, Parliament, ministries and Holy Synod offices that had prevented the March action from taking place. The expulsion of Jews from Sofia took place in May but brought even further protests.[17]

However, during the summer of 1943, which witnessed the death of the King, the fall of Italy, and the German retreat from Soviet Russia, the government gave up its plans to deport the Bulgarian Jews. Because of corruption in his office, Belev was replaced by a bureaucrat. The end of the next summer, 1944, saw the Red Army march into Bulgaria (Moscow had declared war five days before) and the communist-led Fatherland Front take power. Many Jews who had fought as partisans participated.[18]

Over the next months the task of restoring Jewish life began. On the one hand, Bulgaria had switched sides and was now fighting with the Allies in Yugoslavia and Austria; over 30 Jewish soldiers were killed in action in these campaigns. On the other hand, the new government held war crimes trials of people who had participated in the pro-Axis government. The courts handed out numerous harsh sentences to government leaders and politicians; even members who had signed protests on behalf of the Jews or spoke out against anti-Semitic actions were executed. The people's courts also sentenced to prison members of the last pre-communist government who had opposed the Axis but did not join the Fatherland Front. However, the trials of those involved in anti-Semitic acts ended with comparatively lenient sentences. Only Belev, one of his assistants, and a third person involved in anti-Semitic propaganda but who did not take part in the deportations received capital sentences; these were precisely the three accused who had managed to disappear before the Fatherland Front came to power. Other officials of the Commissariat and the leaders of the Jewish forced labor units were acquitted or given comparatively light sentences.[19]

The years following the war presented the Fatherland Front government with a number of problems regarding the Jews. Initially the communist leaders wanted the Jews to remain in Bulgaria, but most of the Jews themselves were anxious to emigrate to Palestine. This was encouraged by Zionist organizations and supported by some of the partners of the communists in the Fatherland Front. As the full horror of the Holocaust became known, the "miracle" of the Bulgarian Jewish survival began to play a role in the developing political struggle of East and West. By 1947 the communists changed their views and supported the emigration of Jews to Palestine. The new government's attitude stemmed partially from a misguided hope that a new Jewish state would be an ally of the Soviet Union rather than the West and that it would present an opportunity to embarrass Great Britain, which was then preventing the partition plans before the United Nations. Emigration also solved a number of economic and national questions for Sofia, but Jews would not be able to emigrate there until after the state of Israel existed. When given the opportunity, 80 percent did so. Table 3 shows the year by year statistics.[20]

TABLE 3
Jewish Emigration from Bulgaria, 1918-1967

Period	Emigrants	Period	Emigrants
1918-1938	2,658	1949	19,100
1939-1945	3,220	1950-1951	2,076
1946-May 15, 1948	1,179	1952-1960	1,380
May 15-December 31, 1948	13,681	1961-1967	337
		GRAND TOTAL	43,361

This emigration represented one of the largest *aliyahs* to the new Jewish state. It also represented one of the largest communities of Bulgarian emigrants in the world. As the horrors of the anti-Semitic legislation dimmed with time and the story of their survival was glorified, most although not all of the Israelis of Bulgarian background looked back fondly on their and their parents' homeland.[21] The Bulgarians came to Israel just after the Arabs of Palestine had fled, and the old Arab towns of Jaffa, Ramala, and Akko took on a distinctive Bulgarian character reminiscent of the west side of Sofia.[22] Correspondingly, the Jewish population remaining in Bulgaria shrank as shown in Table 4.[23]

TABLE 4
Decline in Jewish Population of Bulgaria, 1934-1965

Census Date	Total Population	Jews	
		Number	Percent
December 31, 1931	6,077,939	48,398	0.796
December 31, 1946	7,029,344	44,209	0.629
December 1, 1956	7,613,709	6,027	0.062
December 1, 1965	8,227,868	5,108	0.062

Immediately after the war, i.e., before the emigration, a lively Jewish life was restored including theaters, newspapers, choral groups, and reading rooms.[24] Communists formed the Jewish Anti-Fascist League, whose titular head was the noncommunist Avram Tadzher, an ex-colonel of the Bulgarian army who had served with Crown Prince Boris in World War I. The League organized an active political and social life for the Bulgarian Jews. It invited Russian author Ilya Ehrenburg to the country. Communist leader Georgi Dimitrov himself gave the opening speech at its first congress. However, there was also an active Zionist life which in fact attracted more Jews than the communist associations.[25]

Quite naturally these activities diminished with emigration. The Jews who remained in Bulgaria integrated into the secular life of the country. In 1957 they established the Social, Cultural, and Educational Association of the Jews of the People's Republic of Bulgaria. The number of newspapers dropped from eight (previously published in Hebrew, Ladino and Bulgarian) to one–the Bulgarian *Evreiski Vesti* (Jewish News). The Jewish Scientific Institute with its well-preserved library and archives became part of the Bulgarian Academy of Sciences. Religious activities all but disappeared. Rabbi Hannanel, a hero at first, was arrested and jailed on charges of speculation. By the 1960s there was no practicing rabbi in Bulgaria.

The Jews remaining in Bulgaria were directed into the golden ghettos of education and culture, although they also filled other professions including the diplomatic and civil service. The latter but not the former seems to have been unusual in communist countries.[26] Table 5 describes the trade or profession of the Jews,[27] and Table 6 their employment,[28] in 1965.

Table 7[29] illustrates the increase of Jews in the professions requiring higher education between 1936 and 1965. (The 1936 statistics were compiled by the Jewish consistory of Sofia for the capital alone.)

TABLE 5
Jewish Occupations in 1965

Occupation	Number of Jews (includes families)
Worker	1286
Non-cooperative craftsman	60
Cooperative craftsman	4
Office worker	3302
Professional	52
Private tradesman	87
Cooperative farmer	220
Non-cooperative farmer	4
Clergy	3
TOTAL	5108

Federick B. Chary

TABLE 6
Jewish Employment in 1965

Category of Employment	Jews Employed	
	Number	Percent
Management at national and district level in state and cooperative enterprises and public organizations	226	9.7
Science, education, culture, and the arts	416	17.9
Accounting, planning and trade	520	22.4
Engineering and technology	302	13.0
Medicine	145	6.3
Metallurgy	134	5.8
Clothing industry	91	3.9
Law	36	1.6
Other fields	449	19.4
TOTAL	2,319	100.0

TABLE 7
Increase of Jews in the Professions

Profession	Sofia, 1936*		Bulgaria, 1965*	
	Number	Percent	Number	Percent
Engineers and draftsmen	25	0.10	126	2.47
Architects	2	0.01	38	0.74
Physicians	66	0.27	83	1.62
Dentists	60	0.25	14	0.27
Pharmacists	40	0.17	6	0.12
Lawyers	53	0.22	23	0.45
Teachers	37	0.15	84	1.64
Employed in university and higher education	0	0.00	68	1.33
Research scientists	0	0.00	49	0.96
TOTAL	283	1.18	491	9.61

* The total Jewish population of Sofia in 1936 was 24,071; the total Jewish population of Bulgaria in 1965 was 5,108.

In Bulgaria Jews became exceptionally prominent in the universities, academies, the theater, and the arts. Jewish literacy, always higher than that of their Bulgarian neighbors (who by the way had a higher literacy rate than their Balkan Christian and Moslem neighbors) now became universal. In 1965 only a handful of Jews over seven years old, mostly elderly persons, were unable to read and write. Bulgarian replaced Ladino as the Jews' native language (see Table 8).[30]

TABLE 8
Native Language of Jews in 1934 and 1965

Year	Number of Jews	Language			
		Bulgarian		Ladino	
		Number	Percent	Number	Percent
1934	48,398	19,263	39.8	28,002	57.9
1965	5,108	4,974	97.4	133	2.6

The educational status of the Bulgarian Jews in 1965 is shown in Table 9,[31] while the 1965 breakdown of academic/professional status for Jews with higher educational degrees is show in Table 10 for 1965 and Table 11 for 1972.[32]

TABLE 9
Educational Status of Jews in 1965

Educational Level	Active Population	Non-Active Population	Total
University	726	95	821
Vocational institute	339	164	503
High school	514	492	1,006
Middle school	592	934	1,526
Elementary school	98	517	615
Some elementary school	17	223	240
Semi-literate	2	11	13
Illiterate	2	341*	343*
Unknown	29	12	41
ALL LEVELS	2,319	2,789*	5,108

* Includes 269 children under seven years of age.

TABLE 10
Ranks of Jews with Higher Education, 1965

Rank	Bulgarians		Jews	
	Number	Percent	Number	Percent
Academician	31	0.0004	1	0.0196
Corresponding member	56	0.0007	1	0.0196
Professor	452	0.0055	14	0.274
Associate professor or senior researcher	1,585	0.0055	56	1.0196
Other graduate degree holders	6,801	0.0829	32	0.626
Total university degree holders	129,469	1.579	804	15.74
Total graduate degree holders	8,925	0.109	104	2.04
Total population	8,201,400		5,108	

TABLE 11
Ranks of Jews with Higher Education, 1972

Rank	Bulgarians		Jews	
	Number	Percent	Number	Percent
Academician	30	0.0003	1	0.02
Corresponding member	42	0.0005	2	0.0392
Professor	1,774	0.021	22	0.431
Associate professor or senior researcher	3,003	0.035	69	1.35
Other graduate degree holders	11,784	0.137	57	1.12
Total university degree holders	183,307	2.14	n.a.	n.a.
Total graduate degree holders	16,573	0.193	151	2.96
Total population	8,576,200			

Jewish activity in the theater and the arts and letters during the postwar years has also been impressive. The best known of the Jewish Bulgarian intellectuals (aside from Nobel Laureate Elias Canetti, whose connection with Bulgaria is tenuous) is the playwright and novelist Valeri Petrov. Many Jews had been involved in the theater and other aspects of arts, i.e., films and radio, before the Second World War. There were a handful of established Jewish writers in Bulgarian, most notably the poet Dora Gabe, and some painters. After World War II they represented a larger fraction of the total, considering the size of the remaining community. Part of this must be viewed from a negative perspective, as the arts were one of the few avenues open to Jews in postwar Eastern Europe. Furthermore, as in the Soviet Union, many Jewish children were encouraged to become musicians–although it must be said that, as elsewhere, this was a profession which both Jews and Bulgarians eagerly pursued. In fact, the *per capita* number of Jews in the arts and letters is only slightly more than that of Bulgarians–3.6 percent compared to 2.1 percent of the population as a whole.

As alluded to above, some degree of anti-Semitism, nevertheless, remained in postwar Bulgaria. It generally took the form of the mild prejudices held in other societies: "All Jews have money," "Jews are clever at languages and sciences," etc. There were also some quite scandalous instances, such as the trial of Rabbi Hannanel. In 1974 the economist Heinrich Shpeter was given a capital sentence for espionage, but international pressure on Sofia led the government to allow him to emigrate to Israel.[33] Other aspects of anti-Semitism included hidden quotas in various government and economic departments.[34]

In post-World War II Bulgaria, the story of the Holocaust itself became a major political issue. Royalists in exile, both Jews and Christians, began to publish books and articles claiming that the resolute action of the King had brought about the survival of the community. Except for a few notations in various reference books, the government and historians in Bulgaria did not enter into the debate until the late 1950s. There were, however, some anti-monarchists in Israel who challenged the royalist interpretation of the events.[35]

In 1957 the Association of Bulgarian Jews stated as its goal an emphasis on friendship between Jews and Bulgarians in the country, and the survival of the community became the chief means of demonstrating success. The new "official" interpretation not only denied the efforts of the King, but claimed that he had been an active agent in promoting deportations. "The saving of the Bulgarian Jews" was accredited in the first place to the Bulgarian Communist Party's leadership of the Bulgarian people in opposition to deportations. In fact, Todor Zhivkov, who by that time had emerged as the leader of the state, was given credit personally for organizing the resistance. This claim was based on the coincidence that during the war he had been a communist functionary in the Gypsy quarter of Sofia, which the Filov government had designated as the Jewish ghetto in 1942.

Over the years the official interpretation was somewhat modified as a result of new documentation, the partial liberalization of historical research in Bulgaria, and the work of foreign scholars. By the end of the communist period Sofia's interpretation maintained that all layers of Bulgarian society, including anti-communist officials who had been executed or imprisoned in 1945, as well as members of the church, the judiciary, and the bourgeoisie had played significant roles in the survival of Bulgarian Jewry. Until his ouster in November 1989, however, Zhivkov was still given major credit. The King's role was reduced from one of active agitator for deportation and execution of the Jews to one of passive inaction. One of the reasons for this more realistic portrayal of events, undoubtedly, was that the more official histories claimed major or complete credit for the communist party, the more the Bulgarian people–who trusted nothing that was communicated officially–believed erroneously that the King must indeed have saved the Jews. The debate continues to rage even now.[36]

The ouster of Zhivkov in November 1989 led to the establishment of a reformist government, although one that was still composed of communists. While a significant portion of the population supported the new government and the communist reformers, a majority most likely did not. Nevertheless, two years passed before a non-communist government came to power. Indeed during that period the Communist Party, renamed the Socialist Party, won the first round of free and fair elections. However, the country fell into political and economic stagnation because of the nearly equal division between the socialists and the main opposition coalition–the Union of Democratic Forces

(UDF). The Socialists agreed to choose Zheliu Zhelev, a UDF leader, as president of the country.

In November 1989 the leadership of the Bulgarian Jewish Social, Cultural and Educational Association immediately backed the socialist reform government. Commenting in *Evreiski Vesti,* Dr. Iosif Astrukov, the president of the Association, promised that the Jewish community would help in rebuilding Bulgaria "in a just socialist way." He referred to mistakes of the era before November 10, the day Zhivkov resigned, but did not go into detail. There was little change in the bland articles in *Evreiski Vesti* except that more items about Israel and other world Jewish communities appeared. (Such articles, in fact, had been published even before November 10.) The Jewish leadership's illusion that they could continue in power, however, did not last long.[37]

At the customary New Year's Party at the Association's social hall ushering in 1990, young Jews staged a demonstration demanding that the Association adopt a more ethnic-centered posture. They demanded that Jews in Bulgaria be permitted to celebrate Hanukkah and Purim and that Hebrew be taught. One of the ironies of these protests was that these were the children of Jewish communists who had elected to stay instead of migrating to Israel. Even those who had only one Jewish parent (and since this was really a demonstration of ethnic pride rather than religious commitment, it did not matter which parent that was) joined in the protests. The seeds of the demands for a change of direction had been maturing for some time along with the growing movement for civil liberties and freedom of expression as well as the opposition to the *status quo* among all of Bulgaria's ethnic groups. The Jews of Bulgaria had been unhappy with the anti-Israeli positions of their government going back to the crisis of 1967. In more recent years there has been some revival of traditional Jewish customs including attendance by young people at Sabbath services, and even the departure of a few young men to the Jewish seminary in Budapest. Also notable as an example of the trend is one case which gained attention in the West, when Maxim Koen, the son of communist professors, attended Yeshiva University in New York at the request of Bulgarian folklorists, to relearn Sephardic chants.[38]

Although the protests had Zionist overtones, initially the Jews did not have migration to Israel as a goal; in fact they insisted that they wished to remain Bulgarian Jews loyal to the new Bulgarian state. The model to which they specifically pointed was France. Yet, despite the secular nature of the community and of the protests, one of their first demands was for the formation of a religious committee within the Association. They identified with the supposed lack of anti-Semitism in Bulgaria–one of their criticisms of the Association's leadership was that it did not protest against Zhivkov's dictatorship, in contrast to the protests which the Bulgarian community had carried out against the fascist government in the Jews' hour of need in 1943.

The established Jewish leadership responded. Dr. Astrukov, in a front page article entitled "The Truth" in *Evreiski Vesti* (January 8, 1990), the same issue which reported the protest, defended his tenure. Astrukov said that the truth could now be told. Courageous people in the Association had been able to meliorate the harsh atmosphere and even threats of the Zhivkov years. Astrukov claimed that almost as soon as he became president, he had become aware of the quota system for Jews, and along with Isak Fransez, the former president, and Matei Iuzari, the Association's secretary, had prepared a report about it which he had submitted to the Central Committee of the Communist Party. These complaints had brought some positive results. Astrukov pointed to the permanent exhibit on "the saving of the Bulgarian Jews" in the Association's offices, the scholarly annual published by the Association, and various other publications. His efforts had also helped gain permission for the Jewish choir. He admitted, however, that little was done about the quotas. Also, he had been unable to prevent the limiting of Jewish activities in the provinces and the ending of contacts with the international Jewish associations. The president asserted that despite official censorship he assiduously saw to it that *Evreiski Vesti* served the interests of the Bulgarian Jews. He described the struggles with the responsible politicians in the Central Committee as brutal. He intimated, without giving names, that some of them were anti-Semites, but instead he was able to bring the attention of the government and the Central Committee to the problems of the Jews: the unofficial quota system, the neglect of the central synagogue and Jewish graves, etc.

Dr. Astrukov, in the same article, insisted that he was still a committed Marxist and that his activity on behalf of the Jews was in accord with the ideals of communism. With the advent of *glasnost,* he writes, and the decision in 1987 by the Bulgarian Central Committee to permit liberalization, he had hoped to reorganize the Association, but had never received a response to his proposals. Even a meeting with Zhivkov in 1989 had brought no results. However, the communist leadership had agreed to look at the status of Jews and Armenians in Bulgaria.

Despite Dr. Astrukov's efforts to defend the Association's communist leadership, the community's opinions were now turned against them. One of the old leaders committed suicide. On January 13, 1990, the Jewish Association held an open meeting of its Executive Committee. The Committee agreed to promulgate a new constitution and restructure the Association. The Committee then ousted the communist leadership and replaced them with members committed to fundamental change, and changed the Association's name to "*Shalom,* the Association of Jews in Bulgaria." The new executive committee, headed by Edi Shvarts, stated its basic principles: political independence and representation of all Jews in Bulgaria. *Shalom* would be democratic and progressive, "leading an uncompromising battle against racism and anti-Semitism, fascism, and chauvinism." The Association planned to represent the Jews in their relations with the Bulgarian government and maintain contacts with Jewish organizations around the world. It promised to work for the social, cultural, and economic benefit of the Jews of Bulgaria, and to conduct scholarly research as well as publish information for non-Jewish Bulgarians about the Jews and their contributions to Bulgarian society. Above all, the Association believed that the fate of Bulgarian Jews was linked to that of Bulgaria as a whole.

The Jews also elected a central Jewish spiritual council under Iosif Levi to revive religious education and services in Bulgaria. Levi stated that one of his main goals was finally to finish the repair of Sofia's central synagogue.

The synagogue had been a victim of arson earlier in the year, but Levi disclosed that the perpetrator was a juvenile thief, and the act had not been anti-Semitic vandalism. However, a few reports of definite anti-Semitism appeared in the press. For example, a gang of hooligans attacked and cut off the hair of a school girl whose poetry in support of democracy and *Ekoglasnost*, the ecology movement that started the revolution against Zhivkov, received national attention, and unknown persons painted a Star of David on her family's apartment door. There were other incidents but really no widespread anti-Semitism. On the other hand the prominent communist film director Angel Wagenstein, who was being criticized for his continuous support of Zhivkov's policies by both Jews and non-Jews, publicly raised the specter of anti-Semitism as a factor in the criticisms although it is clear that it was his communism and not his Judaism which brought opposition.

Evreiski Vesti also reported the appearance of some anti-Semitic articles by Bulgarians. These were remarkably few. One was a translation of the work of Nikolai Nikolaev, a Bulgarian American monarchist, who wrote a book claiming the history of revolution in the world since the French Revolution was a conspiracy of the Rothschild family. Another was an article by a socialist newspaper in the provinces complaining about investment in Stara Zagora by a Jew who had emigrated. The comment of *Evreiski Vesti* was that more such foreign investment was needed. We might note here that Todor Zhivkov was personally acquainted and had friendly relations with at least two prominent Jewish millionaires–Armand Hammer and Robert Maxwell–who had invested in Bulgaria during his tenure.

Evreiski Vesti also began to publish informational articles on Jewish holidays as they occurred and on Jewish customs. In March the Jewish community celebrated Purim for the first time in years. In August the Joint Distribution Committee, which had been in Sofia in the years after World War II, returned to Bulgaria to reestablish an office. Sofia reestablished relations with Israel, and the Bulgarian-Israeli Friendship Association was formed. The first foreign head of state to visit the new Bulgaria was President of Israel Chaim Herzog. A delegation of English parliamentarians led by Labor MP Greville Janner came to Sofia; Janner attended Sabbath services.

One aspect of the new Bulgaria involved the exoneration of returning exiles who had been under sentence by the communist government for fascist activity during World War II. The Parliament passed a law quashing these sentences without reviewing individual cases. Because of the circumstances of the survival of the Bulgarian Jewish community, no returning persons had actually been involved in direct war crimes; however, some people involved in the anti-Semitic campaigns of the 1930s and active in fascist organizations have returned.

It was not anti-Semitism but the harsh economic conditions of postcommunist Bulgaria that spurred renewed emigration to Israel. By 1992 about 2,000 of the remaining 5,000 Jews had joined the mass migration from Eastern Europe. The *Shalom* Association met the changing conditions with new approaches. It has tried to become an avenue for international business, informing Bulgarian Jewish emigrés that *Evreiski Vesti* is "a key to the Bulgarian market." *Shalom* also wishes to become an international scholarly center of Sephardic Judaism, using the rich Bulgarian Jewish archives. The Bulgarians participated in the 1993 International Sephardic Conference in Barcelona.

In conclusion, it can be stated that since 1989, while some incidents have occurred, anti-Semitism has not been a major problem in Bulgaria. Jews who remain in the country are as integrated into the general society as are those in the countries of the West; ethnic hostility in Bulgaria still focuses on the Moslems and to a lesser extent the Gypsies. It should be noted, though, that anti-Moslem politics also has been successful only in a minor way in Bulgaria. A few openly anti-Turkish parties were successful in the 1991 elections by running in a coalition with the socialists, but the most blatant parties failed to get even a single seat. On the other hand, the Turkish Rights and Freedom Party gained 15 percent of the seats although Turks constitute only 10 percent of the population. After the elections the Rights and Freedom Party held the balance of power in the country. With its support the UDF formed the first non-communist Bulgarian government since 1946, although no members of the Party joined the cabinet. In the fall of 1992 the Rights and Freedom Party, dissatisfied with the UDF's economic and minority rights positions, switched its support to the Socialists, who backed a new government at the end of the year. The Jewish vote is split between the Socialists and the UDF. Despite the small number of Jews in the country six Jews were elected to the new Parliament in 1991–three are Socialists, three are UDF–and the history of the Holocaust in Bulgaria continues to be a point of argument between right and left.

NOTES

1.   A good impartial complete history of Bulgaria still needs to be written. In the meantime Bulgarian Academy of Sciences, *Istoriia na Bulgariia* [History of Bulgaria], ed. Dimitur Kosev et al. (Sofia: "Nauka i izkustvo," 1962-1964) and the Academy's more recent but incomplete edition begun in 1979 [Bulgarian Academy of Sciences, *Istoriia na Bulgariia v chetirinadeset toma* (History of Bulgaria in fourteen volumes), ed. Velizar Velkov (Sofia: Bulgarian Academy of Sciences, 1979-) are useful. For the period 1870-1920 see the excellent study by Richard J. Crampton, *Bulgaria 1878-1918: A History* (Boulder: East European Monographs, 1983). For the Bulgarian Jews see Saul Mezan, *Les juifs espagnols en Bulgarie* (Sofia: n.p., 1925) and Frederick B. Chary, *The Bulgarian Jews and the Final Solution: 1940-1944* (Pittsburgh, University of Pittsburgh, 1944). Volume ten of the *Aintsiklopediyah shel galut* [Encyclopedia of the Diaspora] deals with Bulgaria: A. Romano et al., eds., *Yehudot Bulgariyah* [The Bulgarian Jews] (Jerusalem: The Encyclopedia of the Jewish Diaspora Co., 1967). The Social, Cultural and Educational Association of the Jews in the Peoples Republic of Bulgaria's *Godishnik* (Annual) (hereafter, *OKPOE Annual*) published yearly since 1966 has valuable articles. Almost all volumes have an English translation.

2.   Bulgaria, Direction Générale de la Statistique, *Annuaire Statistique* (Sofia, Government Press; annually).

3.   Ibid., 1920.

4.   Bulgaria, *Annuaire Statistique*, 1887-1934.

5.   *Millets* were the various religious communities, Moslem, Orthodox, Jewish, etc., through which the Ottoman government carried out the day to day administration of its diversified population.

6.   Salvator Izrael, "Bulgarskite evrei v godinite na narodna vlast" [The Bulgarian Jews in the Years of People's Power] in *OKPOE Annual*, 1971, p. 124.

7.   Ibid., p. 117. (The calculations have been corrected for accuracy.)

8.   See Mezan for anti-Semitic incidents. For tolerance see *Bulgarskata obshtestvenost za rasizma i antisemitizma* [Bulgarian Public Opinion on Racism and Anti-Semitism], ed. Buko Piti (Sofia: n.p., 1937).

9.   See Chary, pp. 7-9.

10.   Ibid., p. 36.

11.   Ibid., pp. 37-41.

12.   Ibid., pp. 41-55.

13.   Ibid., p. 53.

14.   Ibid., p. 54.

15.   Ibid., pp. 69-84.

16.   Ibid., pp. 90-100.

17.   Ibid., pp. 129-52.

18.   Ibid., pp. 152-57; Marshall Lee Miller, *Bulgaria During the Second World War* (Stanford: Stanford University Press, 1975), pp. 135-216; Nissan Oren, *Bulgarian Communism: 1934-1944* (New York: Columbia University Press, 1971), 230-31.

19.   Chary, pp. 178-80.

20.   Izrael, pp. 114-15.

21.   See the friendly addresses of Shulamit Shamir, the wife of the former Israeli prime minister and a native of Sofia, and of Abraham Melamed, secretary of the Israel-Bulgaria Society, delivered at the conference in Bulgaria on the survival of the Bulgarian Jewish community in Sofia in November 1988. Mrs. Shamir delivered her speech in Bulgarian. These are reprinted in *OKPOE Annual*, 1989, pp. 225-33, 242-43. For contrast see the unfriendly account by Bulgarian-born Israeli Viki Tamir, *Bulgaria and Her*

Jews: The History of a Dubious Symbiosis (New York: Sepher-Hermon Press for Yeshiva University, 1979).

22.   Personal observation by the author in 1965.

23.   Izrael, p. 114: Bulgaria, *Annuaire Statistique, 1934-1966.*

24.   A type of library very popular in Bulgaria and traditionally used as a center for cultural, political and social meetings and education.

25.   Chary, pp. 175-83.

26.   Because of his Jewish ancestry the Soviets did not permit one Bulgarian whose father was a Christian Bulgarian and hero of the resistance as well as a member of the Central Committee of the Bulgarian Communist Party, but whose mother was Jewish (her father also a hero of the resistance) to attend the diplomatic school in Moscow. The Soviet government offered him instead admission into any other educational institution he cared to attend. During the communist period, however, Bulgarian Jews in the sciences had little difficulty in getting appointments to Soviet universities.

27.   Izrael, p. 120.

28.   Ibid., p. 121.

29.   Ibid.

30.   Ibid., p. 118.

31.   Ibid., p. 124.

32.   *OKPOE Annual,* 1988.

33.   See the following 1974 issues of *The New York Times:* June 6, 2:4; June 7, 14:1, 14:3, 2:5; July 5, 2:8, August 15, 4:5; August 23, 5:1.

34.   Iosif Astrukov, "Istinata" [The Truth] in *Evreiski Vesti* [Jewish News], Sofia, 57, 1 (January 8, 1990), pp. 1-2.

35.   Among the most prominent works are Benjamin Arditi, *Roliata na tsar Boris III pri izselvaneato na evreite ot Bulgariia* [The Role of King Boris III in the Deportation of the Bulgarian Jews] (Tel Aviv, n.p., 1952) and *Yehudi bulgariyah bishanot hamishpat Hanatsi: 1940-1944* [The Jews of Bulgaria in the Years of Nazi Occupation] (Tel Aviv: Israel Press, 1962); Khaim D. Oliver, *We Were Saved: How the Jews in Bulgaria Were Kept from the Death Camps,* 2d ed. (Sofia: Sofia Press, 1978); Haim Kechales, *Korot Yehude Bulgaryah* [The Rescue of the Bulgarian Jews] (Tel Aviv: Davar, 1969).

36.   See for example Christo Boyadjieff, *Saving the Bulgarian Jews in World War II* (Singer Island, Fla: Free Bulgarian Center, 1989) and "Tsar Boris, koito kaza 'ne' na Hitler" [King Boris, Who Said "No" to Hitler] in

Kultura, Sofia, September 7, 1990, reprinted in *Evreiski Vesti*, Sofia, vol. 57, no. 17 (October 9, 1990), p. 1.

37.   The events since 1989 have been published in *Evreiski Vesti* .

38.   *The New York Times*, December 3, 1988.

Anti-Semitism and the Treatment of the Holocaust in Postcommunist Czechoslovakia (The Czech Republic)

Fred Hahn

Historical Background

In the first Czechoslovak Republic the Czechs generally respected T. G. Masaryk's principles of humanity and morality. He believed that morality was based on the commandment to love one's neighbor as oneself, e.g., that one should not hate but love.[1]

Humanity, Masaryk claimed, is the Czech national program. Humanity does not consist in daydreaming about the whole of mankind but in always acting humanely, justly and decently.[2] The veneration of Masaryk, "the president liberator" as he was called, was general. He fought anti-Semitism and the superstition of ritual murder. By the turn of the century he was hated by the Czech people, maligned as a traitor, and accused of having been bought by the Jews.

The history of anti-Semitism and violent outbreaks against the Jews in the Czech lands goes back to the eleventh century. Jews were held in contempt, hated, separated and mistrusted. They were exposed to extortion and theft of their wealth by taxation, the nobles, and the court. Jews were not allowed to reside in the royal cities, and were repeatedly expelled, the last time in 1754 by Maria Theresa. Despite all the hardship, Prague became a center of Jewish learning and culture. It was known as "mother in Israel." Milestones of Jewish emancipation were in 1781 the *Toleranzpatent* of Joseph II and the 1848 and 1849 abolishments of intolerable restrictions: the *Familianten* law which provided that only the first born sons of Jewish families were allowed to marry, and the *Freizuegigkeitsgesetz* which restricted the Jews in their movements.

The revolution of 1848 promised better prospects for the Jews, but their hopes were soon dashed by violent anti-Jewish riots in Prague and renewed political reaction. Complete freedom from restrictions seemed impossible and the burden of prejudice was very heavy. The Jews were excluded from the National Guard, anti-Semitic leaflets were distributed, and the city council ordered all Jews living outside the ghetto to return into it.

The harassment of the Jews continued well into the 1860s. The constitution of March 1849 had legalized for the first time Jewish acquisitions of real estate outside of the ghetto, and many Jews took advantage of this opportunity. This constitution, however, was abolished by the so-called Sylvester Patent of 1851 which reinstated absolutism in Austria. With the invalidation of the constitution all legislative provisions it contained also lost their force. The exclusion of Jews from ownership of real estate outside of the ghetto was therefore reinstated. The consequences were sometimes tragic. If the petition to the emperor for exemption from the rule was not granted the real estate had to be sold at great loss or was confiscated by the authorities. The 1867 constitution finally gave the Jews full equality. The new freedom of the Jews was not greeted with joy by the Czechs.

Anti-Semitic books and pamphlets of the most vicious kind flooded the market and were eagerly read by all strata of the population. Generally Jews were portrayed as repulsive and as usurers who ruined the Czech people. Many of the anti-Semitic writers such as Jan Neruda described only "bad" Jews. Neruda went so far as to write, in an article entitled *Velikonoční rozprava o Židech* (Easter Discussion About the Jews): "I had hoped that this year something really festive would happen, for instance a little killing of Jews."[3] Anti-Jewish feeling remained very strong, especially in the countryside.

In 1897 Eduard Gregr, one of the most important leaders of the Czech people, noted that "all Prague is anti-Semitic today," and Jan Herben, a writer and friend of Masaryk, added: "The whole Czech people, except for a few, is anti-Semitic."[4] Anti-Semitism and bigotry were widespread.

Masaryk was taught to fear the Jews and he believed that they needed Christian blood. He remembered that in the 1850s every little boy in southern Moravia was raised to hate the Jews. At home, at school, and in the church they were practically taught anti-Semitism. In church the priest's sermons were anti-Jewish and in school the teacher admonished the children not to come near a Jew. In a short biographical essay, *Our Mr. Fuchsel,* Masaryk describes the anti-Semitic and superstitious conditions in a small Moravian village. Each child was raised to hate and to fear the Jews. His mother forbade him to see or to visit the Lechners because the Jews needed the blood of Christian children. The superstition about the Jewish search for Christian blood was so deeply ingrained that young Masaryk looked at the fingers of Jews to see whether there was blood on them. He remarks that he kept this foolish habit for a long time. One day, Masaryk relates in his essay, his anti-Semitism was undermined when a Jewish classmate was overheard praying by the joking class, but it was not yet completely overcome. At the end of this short story Masaryk speculates why the Czechs have no theoretician of anti-Semitism. The old primitive anti-Semitism came to the fore in the Hilsner affair in 1899. "It was then that I perhaps atoned for all the ugliness into which anti-Semitism had misled me."[5]

Masaryk's intervention in the Hilsner affair, the famous blood libel trial in Polna (1899), made him world famous but hated by the Czechs. Actually, Masaryk's real reason for expressing his views on the Hilsner trial seems to have been not to protect the Jews or Hilsner but to eliminate the terrible superstition of ritual murder from the beliefs of the Czech people.

In Masaryk's republic (1918-1938) anti-Semitism was socially unacceptable (even though it lingered on and reemerged with fascism). Jews of all convictions enjoyed equal rights not only by law but also in practice. The Czechs generally accepted Masaryk's aphorism as a guideline: "A nation's attitude toward the Jews is the measure of its cultural maturity."[6] Masaryk's leadership, his fight for justice and truth and his humanism reassured all Jews. President Eduard Benes also adhered to the principles of Masaryk. With the rise of fascism and Nazism, however, a small fascist party spread anti-Semitic propaganda. The painter Karel Relink published a book, *Spása světa, ubozí pronásledovani židé* (The Salvation of the World, the Poor Persecuted Jews) which can easily compete with the infamous *Stürmer* of Julius Streicher in terms of inflammatory statements.

In the second republic Masaryk's principles were very quickly forgotten. Immediately after the Munich conference (September 1938) when Czechoslovakia was forced to give up the Sudetenland (northern Bohemia), anti-Semitism and anti-Jewish propaganda was in full force. First of all, Nazi and anti-Jewish propaganda was published by the Czech fascist press. Professional organizations joined the professional anti-Semites to eliminate Jewish competition, and a *numerus clausus* was proposed. The humanitarian principles and traditions of T. G. Masaryk and of the first republic were rapidly abandoned. Nazi propaganda, of course, was in full swing after the German occupation on March 15, 1939 and even made some impression on many workers.

Of the 118,000 Jews in Bohemia, Moravia and Silesia in 1939 only 26,000 were able to emigrate and about 77,000 perished in the Holocaust.

The Postwar Era

In 1945 President Beneš returned to Czechoslovakia; in 1948 the communists took over the government. First friendly to the new state of Israel, they supplied it with weapons and airplanes for its war with the invading Arab states. The friendly attitude toward the Jews and toward Israel, however, changed rapidly when the Soviet Union unleashed a violent anti-Semitic campaign. The highpoint in Czechoslovakia was the so-called Slansky trial which eliminated all Jews from the top communist leadership by executing them. This trial went on for a long time and many Jews were sent to prison as Zionist spies. In 1968 socialism with a human face brought a short reprieve. Masaryk's ideas were again extolled–but only for a short time. After the Soviet invasion anti-Zionism became another name for anti-Semitism.

From that time onward, the Jewish communities were under strict government supervision and were often used to spread propaganda. A government official was always present at the council meetings of Jewish communities and they were no longer free agents. It is no wonder that many Jews avoided being seen at the offices of the community or at religious services. The latter were permitted, but those who attended were in danger of job discrimination for themselves and disadvantages in the education of their children. Therefore, services were mostly attended by old people and many hesitated to register with the Jewish community. Many even refused to acknowledge their Jewishness and even kept it secret from their children.

The contribution of the Jews to the war effort was minimized by pointing out that only a few Jews were killed in the war operations. The regime also tried to ignore that most of the victims of the Holocaust were Jews. The Charter 77 group, in a document of April 5, 1989, states that from 1939 through 1945, according to statistics, textbooks, and speeches, 360,000 Czecho-slovak citizens were murdered or executed by the Germans or fell in battle. The document then continues: "Only rarely, how-ever, and practically never when the relevant text is aimed at wider audiences, do we encounter information that 240,000 to 255,000 of the total number of victims were persons of Jewish origin who constituted the majority of the Jews of the pre-war republic."[7]

For many years no mention was made of the fact that the famous children's pictures from Theresienstadt were painted by

Jewish children. The Theresienstadt memorial and the planned Ghetto Museum there were to be used for propaganda purposes. Emphasis was on the small fortress; many visitors believed that the ghetto was not in the city but in the fortress. Typical is an article by the chairman of the North Bohemian National Council which administered Theresienstadt. He wrote: "We still have many serious tasks. One of the most important is to build the Ghetto Museum whose use is especially urgent at this time of growing Zionism which threatens world peace with its aggressions....The memorial should endeavor to shape the profile of the new socialist man, constantly struggling with rightist opportunism. The memorial must serve as a warning that Nazism and the era of the exploiters must never return to our fatherland."[8] Only in 1991, after the demise of communism, was the Ghetto Museum established. It has become a dignified memorial for the 153,000 Jews who passed through Theresienstadt. The history of the ghetto is not yet completed because research under communism was limited and the information could not be compared with that in the West or in Israel. The new and efficient director of the memorial and the museum, Jan Munk, pointed out that many teachers from Western Europe who visit Theresienstadt with their students are better able to explain its history than the guides who were trained by the communists.[9]

In 1991, 141,000 people visited the memorial. Not all came to pay homage to the victims. In the visitors' book there were also swastikas and inscriptions of *Sieg Heil*.[10]

Official anti-Semitism and disregard for the Jews and their suffering during the Holocaust manifested itself in the way the communist authorities dealt with the Pinkas Synagogue in Prague. Between 1954 and 1959 part of the interior of the synagogue was transformed into a memorial to the 77,297 Jewish victims from Bohemia and Moravia who perished as a consequence of Nazi persecution. The names of all the victims were very impressively displayed on the walls of the synagogue and thus a very dignified monument to their memory was created. In 1968 the synagogue was closed as its walls were threatened by rising ground water. From that time to 1992 the synagogue was closed to the public. For purely ideological and anti-Semitic reasons, the restoration proceeded at a snail's pace. The memorial to the perished Jews was destroyed in the course of the restoration. The names of the Holocaust victims will again be restored. This work will also take a long time but at least the synagogue will be open to the public as a historical monument and as a memorial to the martyred Jews of Bohemia and Moravia.

Another act of anti-Semitism and disrespect for the Jewish suffering in the Holocaust was the refusal of the communist authorities to authorize the installation of a plaque commemorating the site where the Jews of Prague were gathered before their transfer to Theresienstadt and other camps.

A sad chapter was—and is—the desecration of Jewish cemeteries and synagogues which the Nazis did not destroy. Many cemeteries were abolished by the communists but those that remained were often vandalized; tombstones were stolen and sold to stone masons or even exported.

Jewish religious and cultural life was impeded under communist rule. Religious services and the meetings of the Jewish communities had to be held under the watchful eyes of the authorities. The teaching of Hebrew was not authorized and was discontinued in the 1980s even in the School of Languages. Those who learned Hebrew privately had to worry about discrimination in their further education if it became known.

It is interesting that in 1986 an anti-Semitic history of Bohemia even appeared in *Samizdat*. It claims that all misfortunes that happened in Czech history were caused by forsaking the true faith and by the Jewish/Hungarian/Great German liberal clique. The book is full of fantastic fabrications; for instance, the assassination of Archduke Franz Ferdinand in Sarajevo in 1914 is said to have been the work of Freemasons and the murderer to have been a Jew. The author also claims that Masaryk was the illegitimate son of a Jew and therefore acted in the service of Freemasons and the Jews.[11] Anti-Semitic literature was normally not published in *Samizdat;* this history was an exception. On the other hand, anti-Zionist and anti-Semitic books and articles were published under communism, and since nothing could be printed without government approval these publications must have expressed the opinion of the government. For example, the communist regime awarded the title of National Writer to Alexej Pludek, whose work included a few anti-Semitic novels published in the 1970s and 1980s. In 1986 the long-established publishing house Melantrich published the anti-Semitic, anti-Israel and anti-Zionist book by Josef Šebesta, *V zemi zaslibené?* (In the Promised Land?).

The attempt of the few Jews who returned from the camps to regain their property caused widespread resentment and even riots. It is no wonder that the return of the Jews was often viewed with misgivings. In Prague there had been 35,425 Jews in 1938 but only about 3,000 returned from the concentration camps. Thus a tremendous amount of property remained that had belonged to victims of the Holocaust. However, those who returned demanded their property back and encountered many difficulties. The proceedings quite often dragged on until 1948, when the communists took over and nationalized the property.

Constant Nazi propaganda and the claims for restitution created an adverse climate for the returning Jews. This anecdote is typical of the feelings of the average man toward the returning Jews: After liberation from Theresienstadt a lady bicycled happily toward Prague. She did not know yet that her whole family had been killed by the Nazis. She was happy until she heard the first Czech words: "For heaven's sake, they are here again." This anecdote was written down only after the "velvet revolution" of 1989; the author believes if the lady were still alive she would be happy but afraid.[12]

Official anti-Semitic actions and propaganda came to an end on November 19, 1989. For fifty years, first by the Nazis and then by the communists, the Jews were discriminated against and maligned. Their suffering during the Holocaust was ignored, their presence in Theresienstadt was used for propaganda purposes, and their contribution to the well-being of the country simply overlooked. The official historiography devoted no attention to the thousand-year history of the Jews in the country and practically none to the Holocaust. After the war the young generation had no opportunity to learn about or study the fate of the Jews except for a few books which were published by survivors–if they were available. Most textbooks mentioned the Holocaust only in just a few sentences.

Had discrimination against the Jews under communism not been so sad it would have sometimes bordered on the ridiculous. In 1991 a broadcaster recalled: "For four years I was not allowed to come to the radio station because I looked Jewish. A certain Dr. Dolejši judged that I was Jewish, which unfortunately I am not. When one of my coworkers confirmed that I was not Jewish the good doctor just said: Maybe he is not a Jew but he looks like one."[13]

The communist regime was certainly not propitious for Jews. Government pressure inhibited cultural activity, restricted Jews in the free exercise of their religion, and promoted atheism. Because of the communist surveillance many Jews feared to acknowledge their Jewishness and thus they and their children, who often did not know that they were Jewish, were alienated from Judaism. Cemeteries and synagogues were liquidated. The latter were often used for storage or as laundries and in a few cases as apartments.

The leaders of the Jewish communities were forced to cooperate with the authorities; if they became too independent or had too many connections abroad they were unceremoniously dismissed. The suffering of the Jews during the Holocaust–even their presence in Theresienstadt–was ignored and their contributions to the country were minimized.

The Velvet Revolution changed all that. The intellectuals, and especially the young generation, reacted with disdain to everything that the communists did or suppressed. Even the communist newspaper *Rudé Právo* changed its tone and wrote in June 1992: "Despite the fact that the Jews have been living in our land since the tenth century, our knowledge about them is very scant....The political break with Israel in the beginning of the 1950s only deepened our ignorance about the thousand-year-old development of Jewish culture in our land."[14] After the Velvet Revolution the Czech press has discovered the Jews: they seem to have become a favored topic. It almost seems as if the press wanted to make up for something they were now allowed to do before.

Nowadays–in 1992–articles of Jewish interest abound in the press. Many extol the great merits of the Jews for the country and remember their great suffering on its territory. Teaching about anti-Semitism and the Holocaust is planned. The students are to be taught that the history and culture of the Jews in Bohemia and Moravia is an indivisible part of the history and culture of the country. Articles with titles such as "Who Are the Jews?," or "Life with the Star" or about anti-Semitism try to inform the public objectively.

In May 1992 the Kafka Society organized a four-day conference on anti-Semitism in the former communist countries. One of the participants claimed that anti-Semitism in Czechoslovakia had its roots in an "anti-liberal fiction" and was mainly advocated by left-wing groups who were frustrated by the social transformation, were afraid of the open society, and did not trust the parliamentary system.[15] This of course is true, but it is only part of the problem. The secretary general of the Federation of Jewish Communities of the Czech Republic attributes anti-Semitism in the Czech lands to xenophobia, atavism, and superstition. He believes that anti-Semitism in the Czech lands is only marginal and insignificant.[16] President Havel's assistant, Petr Oslz, agreed that anti-Semitism in the Czech lands is only marginal but warned against underestimating it, declaring that every kind of racism is dangerous and that anti-Semitism is one of the most dangerous ones.[17] Thus the respectable press tries to inform the public sympathetically and objectively about the Jews and tries to rebut the slanderous allegations of the Nazis and neo-Nazis and the superstitious claims of the anti-Semites. For example, a very informative article entitled *Diabolic Talmud* knowledgeably explains the contents and character of the Talmud and condemns those who try to use the Talmud against the Jews. It continues: "The Talmud and the Torah contributed most significantly to the fact that in the inimical environment of exile, the Jews preserved their national, religious, and cultural identity.

Mainly for this reason the Talmud became the target of anti-Semitic attacks....Slanderous attacks against the Talmud did not stop to this day."[18] Another newspaper, in an article entitled, "Anti-Semitism Yesterday, Today...and Tomorrow," emphasizes that the Jews were always a loyal, economically and cultural mature group in the country, as they proved by their outstanding participation in Czech and German culture. "This better tradition of our history...must continue in the present along with the fight against anti-Semitism, that relic of barbarity and stupidity and remnant of the dictatorial regimes, not for the sake of the Jews but for the sake of a healthy, moral development of our nation."[19]

Of course there are exceptions–it cannot be otherwise. They appear to be remnants of communist propaganda about the Jews or successors of the old Czech fascist press. The circulation is small but their anti-Semitism is violent. *Týdenik Politika* (Weekly Politics) can easily be compared with Streicher's *Stürmer*. The responsible press, however, often attacks this anti-Semitic paper, demands criminal prosecution–which unfortunately has constantly been delayed–and tries to educate the public, as mentioned above. The mainstream press generally points out that the Jews were always loyal citizens who contributed greatly to the cultural and economic development of the country. Masaryk's statement that anti-Semitism does not belong in a democratic society is often cited.

Since 1990 many books of Jewish interest are being published and avidly read. Many authors who previously were banned are able to publish their old works as well as new ones. Right now there is no publisher of anti-Semitic literature in the Czech republic. However some anti-Semitic books, among them the *Protocols of the Elders of Zion,* are being distributed by Agres Publishers in Bratislava. Efforts have been repeatedly made by legal means to stop the distribution but so far they are to no avail. A few newsstands still sell them, despite the fact that according to the criminal code all incitement to racial hatred is a criminal offense, as a by-product of the new freedom of expression.

Quoting the criminal code, the Jewish community complained in September 1991 to the federal prosecutor about the distribution of the *Protocols*. The book continued to be sold in Prague and the authorities did not do anything about it, despite the fact that the Bratislava prosecutor had initiated criminal proceedings against Agres, the publisher, and had banned the sale of the book. In Bratislava, 1497 copies of the book were confiscated and in Olomouc (Olmütz), during the book fair, another 939. The confiscation was ordered by the Bratislava prosecutor who held that the book promoted a movement aiming at the suppression of the civil rights and freedom of citizens. Many exhibitors and visitors at the book fair, however, condemned the action of the police as a dangerous precedent for freedom of the press and civil rights. According to the co-owner of Agres, the criminal proceedings against it had already been quashed but they had been reopened on the occasion of the visit of the Israeli ambassador to Bratislava; he intended to appeal to the constitutional court.[20]

As incredible as it seems, after fifty years of anti-Jewish propaganda and restriction, in the post-1989 Czech Republic, Masaryk's principles are again being applied and the presence of President Havel is reassuring. As in the first republic, Jews are enjoying all the rights of free citizens. A large number of organizations have been established, including the Kafka Society, the Christian-Jewish Society, B'nai B'rith, Maccabi, the Union of Jewish Youth, and many others. The leaders of the Jewish community are optimistic, and do not fear anti-Semitism.[21] Are they not too optimistic?

The condition of the Jewish cemeteries is a sad chapter. It was bad under communism and it did not change much since, despite the fact that many articles in the newspapers condemn the situation and demand the protection and saving of the cemeteries. Vandalism and stealing of tombstones–if any are left–are still going on without interference by the authorities. Some cemeteries are bare of tombstones. An example: in Puclice I had had the tombstone of my great-grandfather repaired. In 1990 it was still standing in its place. When I visited the cemetery in

1991 it had disappeared. The responsible press denounces the neglect and the willful desecration and destruction of the Jewish cemeteries and synagogues. The *Prague Post* of April 1992 quotes *Lidové Noviny* as writing: "...the Jewish cemeteries are for the most part deserted, unattended, belonging to nobody. But these Jewish graves *do* belong to somebody. They belong to us! We have survived the Holocaust....Taking care of the deserted graves should be an absolute duty for us."[22]

A periodical commented: "Legally these cemeteries and synagogues belong to the Jewish community, but morally they belong to the Czech people. Now, in the atmosphere of freedom, it is up to us whether they will be forgotten or become a living heritage worthy of steady honor and care.[23] Unfortunately, all the good will of the newspapers is of no value if the authorities do not support it by deeds.

In 1990, former citizens of Czechoslovakia were still excluded from reacquiring their property if it had been seized by the state between February 25, 1948 and January 1, 1990; only Czechoslovak citizens residing in Czechoslovakia could claim such property. The wording of the restitution law caused great disappointment among the emigrants who had to leave the country for political or religious reasons; since all Jewish emigrants had left the country between 1938 and 1989, they were virtually excluded from reacquiring their property. While this law was being discussed in the Federal Assembly, it was proposed to extend restitution to religious communities and to return their seized property. Two deputies opposed the inclusion of religious communities into the law because the Jewish community, which would only squander and export cultural memorabilia, would then be eligible.

One of the deputies added that, along with the Deputy Premier, they had come to the conclusion that a real danger existed on account of an agreement between the Jewish Museum, the Jewish community, and the Israeli embassy. This plainly anti-Jewish action provoked a storm in the Federal Assembly and in the press. The excuse for the attack were tentative proposals and negotiations between the Czechoslovak and Israeli governments for a transfer of part of the collections of the Jewish Museum in Prague to Israel. The fact is that the Jewish community was not involved and that its president had opposed the transfer. *Lidové Noviny* commented that at the moment when the two deputies spoke, the old slogan passed over the head of the assembly like a cloud: "Der Jud ist schuld, Heil und Victoria." (It's the Jew's fault; glory and victory!).[24] The Federation of Jewish Communities in the Czech Republic protested against the suspicion that it would administer its property in violation of the law. "It is a dangerous attempt to brand this group (the Jews) as a group of citizens of second order whose rights have to be restricted by a special law. The Federation of Jewish Communities emphatically protests against this and demands that both deputies revoke their statements and apologize publicly....At the same time we demand that the Deputy Premier declare whether the claim concerning his personal actions is correct."[25]

In discussing the same law, one deputy proposed to return the property seized by the Germans from the Jews to their rightful owners. The motion was defeated. One newspaper noted that the property thus was seized a second time.[26] *Lidové Noviny,* however, asserted that the Jewish property was seized three times: the first time by the Nazis, the second time by the communists, and the third time by the Federal Assembly.[27] According to a 1945 decree by the President of the Republic and a 1946 law, property seized by the Nazis was supposed to have been returned to the Jews who came back from the camps or to their heirs. When the communists took over the government, however, they disregarded the law and nationalized the properties. The Federal Assembly, in turn, made it very difficult for the Jews to get their properties back, and as mentioned above those who reside outside the country are excluded anyway. An additional law passed in 1992 regulates the restitution of the property of Germans and Hungarians who reside within the republic, but not the restitution of Jewish property.

While the responsible press attacks and condemns anti-Semitism, most people have a friendly attitude toward the Jews and if they are anti-Semitic their anti-Semitism is subdued. There are of course individuals, groups, and publications that malign and hate the Jews. As against the about 118,000 Jews in the Czech lands in 1939, only about 3,000 are now registered. In Prague, 1,000 registered before 1989 and 400 more came out of hiding after the Velvet Revolution. In the Czech Republic there may be about 7,000 Jews altogether, and still there are some people who hate the Jews, denying their suffering and the Holocaust. On February 26, 1992, Norwegian television showed a film about Slovakia in which the deputy of the Federal Assembly, Stanislav Panis, declared that he does not believe that six million Jews died in German concentration camps. Nobody in his party reprimanded him, despite the fact that the press called him a neo-Nazi and the whole affair was discussed with great disgust. Panis was accused of being a fascist who denied the Holocaust and claimed that Auschwitz is just a matter of policy for the advantage of Israel.[28]

More serious are attacks against Jews and the sensational revelations about them in the gutter press. The well-known anti-Semite Alexej Pludek mostly has his stories about Jewish-Masonic conspiracies published in the *Špigl* (Mirror) which also publishes a lot of trash involving non-Jews. The worst anti-Semitic neo-Nazi publication in the Czech Republic is *Týdenik Politika* (Weekly Politics), edited by Josef Tomas and printed and distributed in Prague. It imitates the infamous *Stürmer*. It is sold at newsstands and has a circulation of about 5,000 copies. The editor and his aide Jaroslav Voříšek boast openly of their Nazi-type anti-Semitism.

For example, the headline of the issue of June 16, 1992 reads: "The Influence of the Jews is Unbearable, We Are a Colony of Tel Aviv."[29] The paper argues that it is not anti-Semitic but anti-Jewish: the Arabs are also Semites, therefore it is incorrect to call anti-Jewish attitudes anti-Semitic.[30] Another headline, "Gojims for Sale, How We Became Merchandise" is self-explanatory.[31] Every issue offers anti-Semitic literature for sale, including the *Protocols of the Elders of Zion*. Theories about Jewish world conspiracies abound, revisionist material about the Holocaust is reprinted, and Jean-Marie Le Pen, the French neo-fascist, is adored. So far Tomas has been able to publish his anti-Semitic venom and propagate Nazism with impudence. The Federation of Jewish Communities in the Czech Republic sent a letter on August 29, 1991 to the President of the Federal Assembly, complaining about racist anti-Jewish Nazi publications. "It is not encouraging that we did not receive an adequate reaction from any of the higher institutions, beginning with the office of the president and ending with the Federal Assembly." Proposing a change in the criminal law, the Federation believes that a consistent and fast procedure would be in the interest not only of the Jews who have had a sad experience but also of the whole society of the state, and of democracy.[32]

Changes in the criminal law were passed by the Federal Assembly on December 11, 1991. The new Paragraph 260 of the Criminal Law declares: "Whoever supports or propagates movements which demonstrably are directed toward the suppressing of rights and the freedom of citizens or declare national, racist, class, or religious hate (as for instance fascism or communism) will be punished by loss of freedom from one to five years." Thus the law is here, but Josef Tomas was able to publish without impediment or punishment. On April 15, 1992, the Federation of Jewish Communities sent a complaint to the prosecutor of the city of Prague demanding the prosecution of the publishing house Agres and of the responsible editor of the periodical *Týdenik Politika*. The Federation argued that both committed criminal acts by systematically insulting the Jewish nation and race, inciting hatred for the Jewish nation, and demanding the suppression of its rights and freedoms. The complaint also claimed that both expressed sympathy with fascism and that *Týdenik Politika* published inflammatory anti-Semitic articles and therefore both were committing criminal acts according to the abovementioned law.[33]

At the same time, the newspaper *Respekt* tried to find out why anti-Semitic books including the *Protocols* were still available at newsstands in Prague despite the fact that the prosecutor in Bratislava had banned them and had ordered them confiscated. No one wanted to take action on the matter; the police sent the reporters to the prosecutor and the prosecutor sent them back to the police. They finally were received by the spokesman of the general prosecutor, whose point of view in this matter was quite peculiar. He said: "Are you concerned with respecting the law as such or only with one particular magazine or book and the people behind it? I find it surprising that you are only concerned with the problems of the Jewish nation." The newspaper commented: "This is the standpoint of a representative of an office that, as he himself put it, not only supervises investigations but also, according to the law, makes sure that laws are respected."[34] A deputy questioned the general prosecutor in the Czech National Council about the Federation's complaint and the report in *Respekt*. According to *Roš Chodeš* the tone and content of his answer were unsatisfactory. The periodical concluded that the matter did not interest the general prosecutor.[35] On July 14, 1992, Josef Tomas was finally indicted for slander.[36]

Finally, in December 1992 criminal charges were filed against *Týdenik Politika* for printing a list of 168 prominent Jews in contemporary Czech culture and attacking them as "Slavs from the Jordan river" who made Prague "their secondary world center" and displayed their characteristic physiognomies everywhere. The Jewish Telegraph Agency reported that several cultural organizations had put out a joint declaration in which they accused *Týdenik Politika* of discrediting the country's democracy and openly taking up the traditions of *Der Stürmer*.[37] The publisher of *Týdenik Politika* suspended its publication for the duration of the criminal investigation. The press and the Jewish community were watching the proceedings carefully.

After the Velvet Revolution, "skinheads" also appeared in the Czech lands, mostly young people who imitate similar movements in Germany and Great Britain. Most of them do not know the goals of the movement or what fascism is and have no idea why they claim to be against the Jews.[38] More important was an attack on the Jews in the now defunct newspaper of the Christian party, *Mladá Demokracie,* on May 24, 1990, which claimed: "The Jews are exceptional because after all the pogroms, including the Nazi one, they are still here, and are mightier than they ever were before."[39]

One has to remember against whom this vicious anti-Semitism is directed. Whom can this tiny remnant of a once proud Jewish community hurt? There are only nine Jewish communities left of what used to be several hundred. Prague, Brünn (Brno), Pilsen, Ostrava, Olomouc (Olmütz), Usti nad Labem (Aussig), Carlsbad, Liberec (Reichenberg), and Teplitz have religious services, sometimes with difficulty. Despite the fact that most Jews feel reasonably safe and most of the media are on their side and condemn anti-Semitism, it should not be underestimated and should be fought by all means.

According to an opinion poll of 1992 conducted by the Independent Institute of Social Analysis, five percent of Czechs believed that Jews had too much influence in society, four percent thought they endangered political development, and 15 percent did not like the idea of having Jews as neighbors. (They liked Gypsies, Arabs, and Russians even less as neighbors.)[40]

In conclusion, it can be said that in the Czech Republic open anti-Semitism exists, but only at the fringe of society. If one considers that at the turn of the century the Czech people were superstitious and very anti-Semitic and that they have been subjected to fifty years of anti-Jewish propaganda, it seems that the teachings and the humanism of Masaryk and the liberalism of Havel have prevailed and a remarkably low record of anti-Semitism has resulted. It is possible that reaction against the oppression and ideas of communism also played a certain role. Caution is necessary, but education might minimize the danger. President Havel had this in mind when he declared: "...we have to remind ourselves time and again of the horrors that befell the Jewish people, chosen to rouse the conscience of humanity through their suffering....Therefore it is necessary to talk about the suffering of the Jewish people even if it is so difficult to do so."[41]

NOTES

1.   T. G. Masaryk, *Ideale der Humanität* (Ideals of Humanity) (Prague: Deutsche Buchgemeinde, 1935), p. 119.

2.   Karel Čapek, *Conversations with Masaryk* (London: George Allen & Unwin, 1944), p. 213; T. G. Masaryk, *Česká Otázka* (The Czech Question) (Prague: Čin, 1936), p. 218.

3.   Oskar Donath, *Žide a Židovstvi v České Literatúře* (Jews and Judaism in Czech Literature) (Brno: The Author, 1923).

4.   J. Herben, "T. G. Masaryk über Juden und Antisemitismus" (Masaryk about Jews and Anti-Semitism) in *Masaryk und das Judentum* (Masaryk and Jewry), Ernst Rychnovsky, ed. (Prague: Marsverlaggesellschaft, 1931), p. 289.

5.   T. G. Masaryk, "Unser Herr Fuchsel" (Our Mr. Fuchsel) in *Boehmische Dorfjuden* (Bohemian Village Jews), Oskar Donath, ed. (Brünn: Max Hickel, 1926).

6.   Quoted in *Czechoslovak Jewry, Past and Future* (New York: Czechoslovak Representative Committee, 1943), p. 5.

7.   "The Tragedy of the Jews in Post-War Czechoslovakia, Charta 77, Document No. 29/1989," *Soviet Jewish Affairs*, London, vol. 20, no. 1, 1990.

8.   From a letter of April 1, 1973, and a concept of an article for *Hlas revoluce* (Voice of Revolution) written by Maximilian Pergler, Chairman of the Commission of the Council of the North Bohemian National Committee.

9.   "Ve světě vědi víc" (In the World They Know More), *Lidové Noviny* (People's Newspaper), April 23, 1992.

10.   Ibid.

11.   "O jednom kuriosním samizdatu" (About Curious Samizdat), *Lidové Noviny*, May 11, 1991.

12.   "Návrat z ghetta" (The Return From the Ghetto), *Respekt* (Respect), no. 8, May 2-8, 1990.

13.   *Reflex*, no. 49, December 2, 1991.

14.   "Židovská kultura u nás" (Jewish Culture in Our Country), *Rudé Právo* (Red Light), June 12, 1992.

15.   ČSTK # 19920522D00870. May 22, 1992.

16.   "Překonat povery o Židech" (Overcoming Superstitions About the Jews), *Metropolitan*, April 25, 1992.

76   *Fred Hahn*

17. "Nepodcenujme antisemitismus" (We Do No Underestimate Anti-Semitism), *Metropolitan,* May 14, 1992.

18. "Diabolský Talmud" (Diabolic Talmud), *Respekt,* October 21-27, 1991.

19. "Antisemitismus včera, dnes...a zítra" (Anti-Semitism Yesterday, Today, and Tomorrow), *Forum 11,* February 20, 1991.

20. "Proti zabavení knih" (Against the Confiscation of Books), *Mlada Fronta* (Young Front), March 16, 1992.

21. "Překonat pověry o zidech" (Overcoming Superstitions About the Jews), *Metropolitan,* April 25, 1992.

22. "Czechoslovak Press Survey," *Prague Post,* April 7-13, 1992.

23. "Zapomenuté dédictvi" (The Forgotten Heritage), *Reporter,* no. 19, September 20-October 4, 1990.

24. "Basik bolševik" (Basic Bolshevik), *Lidové Noviny,* February 1991.

25. "Stanovisko FŽO" (The Point of View of the Federation of Jewish Communities), *Roš Chodeš* (Beginning of the Month), March 1991.

26. "Týden ve F. S." (The Week in the Federal Assembly), *Respekt,* September 30-October 6, 1991.

27. "Do třetici všeho zlého" (Bad Things Come in Threes), *Lidové Noviny,* October 3, 1991.

28. "V upominku Heinrich Himmler" (In Memory of Heinrich Himmler), *Respekt,* April 5, 1992.

29. "Vliv židú je neúnosny" (The Influence of the Jews Is Unbearable), *Týdenik Politika* (Weekly Politics), no. 71, June 11-17, 1992.

30. "Jsme antijudaisté, nikoli antisemite" (We Are Anti-Jewish but Not Anti-Semitic), *Týdenik Politika,* no. 70, June 4, 1992.

31. "Gojimové na prodej...." (Gojimove For Sale), *Týdenik Politika,* no. 62, April 9-14, 1992.

32. "Dopis presidentovi Federalního shromáždeni" (Letter to the President of the Federal Assembly), *Roš Chodeš,* September 1991, p. 2.

33. "Trestni oznameni" (Criminal Complaint), *Roš Chodeš,* May 1992.

34. "Kniežata zloby v Praze" (Princes of Anger in Prague), *Respekt,* April 16, 1992.

35. "Odpověd prokuratora" (Answer to the Procurator), *Roš Chodeš,* June 1992.

36. "Šefredaktor *Týdenik Politika* obviňen z hanobení naroda" (Editor-in-

Chief of *Weekly Politics* I Accused of Vilifying the Nation), *ČSTK*, July 16, 1992.

37. *Jewish Telegraph Agency*, December 15, 1992.

38. "Čekani na mrtvého" (Waiting for the Dead), *Lidové Noviny*, February 18, 1992.

39. "Stále dokola" (Always In a Circle), *Respekt*, June 13, 1990.

40. *Anti-Semitism World Report* (London: Institute of World Affairs, 1992).

41. From a speech by President Vaclav Havel on October 19, 1991 on the occasion of a visit by President Herzog of Israel in Czechoslovakia.

Anti-Semitism and the Treatment of the Holocaust in Germany

Ruth Bettina Birn

Germany is a special case when dealing with the aftereffects of Nazism. The most important reason, of course, is that Germany was *the* Nazi state. But there is also a second special reason: after the war, there were two German answers to the Nazi legacy, two separate political ways. Germany separated into an Eastern part that was under a communist regime, and a Western part. Thus we are able not only to observe the tendencies that came to the surface after the end of the communist period in all of Eastern Europe, but also to compare the communist-ruled areas and developments there to their Western counterparts.

In recent times developments have accelerated and there has been quite a change in the political atmosphere. Changes occur very rapidly, and every analysis can be rendered obsolete overnight by the next new occurrence. At present (early 1993), a well founded analysis of recent events and of the most important undercurrents in Germany's political life does not seem possible—not only because events are developing so fast, but also because so far no solid research has become available on which an explanation could be based. This, therefore, cannot be a scholarly paper, well researched and based on solid facts. What follows should be viewed as the comments of an interested observer, and my views on how, to my mind, the Nazi past has influenced present events.

When talking about the two Germanies that appeared after World War II, it seems useful to give a very brief outline of the major developments in the two countries.

In *West Germany* there was some continuity with the Nazi period throughout the 1950s which showed through in the political culture. In certain parts of society, elites remained untouched. This was especially noticeable in certain professions; for instance, in the 1950s the high-school teachers were basically the same people who had been teachers under the Nazis.

The mid-1960s saw the beginnings of the change expressed radically in the 1968 student revolt, a movement that to a large extent was an expression of a generational conflict and included the children's questioning of their Nazi parents.

From this time on, Nazism along with its political and moral consequences was a public issue, and one cannot speak of a suppression of facts or a general conspiracy of silence after that. This doesn't mean that the air had been cleared, in a manner of speaking. Scandals about pro-Nazi manifestations, including speeches by politicians, continued, but there was a continuous process of public debate which was widely noticed.

Trials relating to Nazi crimes reflect the same change in political climate. Some exceptions notwithstanding, there was low interest in such trials in the 1950s until the public became thoroughly aroused as a result of the *Einsatzgruppen* (Task Units) trial in Ulm in 1958. The Frankfurt Auschwitz trial in the early 1960s had an even stronger impact on the public. Thereafter prosecutions of Nazi crimes took place continuously; some of them ended in rather devastating verdicts, some have had better results. But even if one can't point to a glorious overall record there was at least one important positive result: the growing public awareness of the crimes the Nazis had committed. These facts could no longer be denied.

It should be mentioned that when talking about the Nazi legacy it is not useful to talk about "the Germans" in general. Right from the outset a political division was noticeable: communists, social democrats and parts of the Protestant church were opposed to it, while the conservatives were more inclined to sympathize or gloss things over. This, of course, reflects the situation in the Nazi period. Thus, when in any small town the town council discussed whether to put up a memorial for the 1938 pogrom, one could also be sure to which party the people who voted against it belonged.

Throughout the whole postwar period, a certain rather small group of neo-Nazi ideologues was active. Taking advantage of the political and social conditions at any given time, they were able to collect groups of followers who seem to have come from specific social groups. This pattern did not change much; Nazi sympathizers did not disappear, nor did their number increase alarmingly.

Another effect of the 1968 student movement should be mentioned. Nazism was identified as "fascism," following the definition given by the communist party in the 1930s. One consequence of this definition was an exaggerated use of these political labels: everything one did not agree with from a left-wing political standpoint was immediately labeled "fascist" and therefore, by extension, to be part of what went on during the Nazi period. This continued through the following years. Auschwitz was an argument that ended all other arguments, and it was frequently abused.

The *German Democratic Republic* (GDR) was a state which rested on very different foundations. From the beginning it defined itself by its anti-fascist nature. This was enforced by the GDR's close alliance with the Soviet Union, the country that had suffered the most among the Allies in World War II.

This anti-fascist tradition was displayed with pride; concentration camp memorials, for instance, were erected to which school children had to go on regular visits and where army ceremonies such as the swearing in of recruits took place. This was done to emphasize that these were the political traditions with which the East Germans wanted to see themselves linked.

The few war crimes trials we know about were conducted swiftly and ended in exemplary sentences. The East Germans regularly embarrassed the West by revelations about former Nazis who were still in leading positions in the West.

The GDR claimed to be the "better" Germany in general. To what extent this was correct is unclear because of the general lack of information about what was going on inside the GDR. It was often hinted that in East Germany also former Nazis had been incorporated into the elite, but as this information very often came from very right-wing sources there is some doubt about its trustworthiness. Nevertheless, among the public outside of Germany as well as in academic circles dealing with the Holocaust, in recent years there was a tendency to agree with the claims made by the GDR and give it credit for having overcome Nazism better than its Western counterpart.

In the West, a number of developments in recent years gave rise to concern. (In the East, because of the lack of precise information, it was not possible to identify these subtle changes.) These tendencies were:

* Chancellor Helmut Kohl and his Conservative Party showed a tendency to push towards a change in values that included an enforced "historical normalization," meaning that the past should be considered to be over: the Nazi period should be considered done with and forgotten, and Germany should be getting rid of any remnants of the past. This led to a number of impossible and embarrassing situations, of which President Reagan's and Chancellor Kohl's 1986 visit to Bitburg has received the greatest media attention. The same tendency was at work in the attempt to make historiography in the Federal Republic more neoconservative and nationalistic.

* In the political spectrum there emerged a group of protest voters, potentially about 10 percent of the total vote, consisting of people who would normally vote conservative but would vote more to the right when really aggravated about the politics of the Conservative government. It follows that

even if they were not fully convinced Nazis they had not much against Nazism, or at least not enough to prevent them from voting for the extreme right. A new party—the Republicans—was established; its head, Franz Schönhuber, had been a *Waffen-SS* man.

* On the left, a new anti-Semitism in the disguise of anti-Zionism became evident. This became an issue particularly in regard to the party of the environmentalists, the "Greens." Questions of subconscious anti-Semitism were hotly debated during the 1991 Gulf War when the left-wing peace movement demonstrated against war on principle; it was mostly only after Scud missiles were fired on Israel that people started to look in more detail at the implications of their support.

* In the 1980s, the "third generation"—the grandchildren of the Nazi generation—entered the high schools and universities. Its members did not show as much personal involvement with the Nazi past and its legacies as the second generation had. In general, the reactions of these young people fell into one of three categories: some of them are mainly indifferent; others (in my estimation, the majority) know about the historical facts but see them increasingly as history, something that is connected with the life of their grandparents; and a small number seem to react in a subtle way against the convictions of their parents and to take sides with their grandparents. One reason for this may be that their parents' generation tried so hard to influence their emotions.

* Another tendency was noted as well: the media had become so full of the Nazi period that the public seemed to be becoming satiated. A good indicator of the increase in public attention on the subject is given by the treatment of anniversaries of the major historical events. While the 30th anniversary of events from 1933 to 1945 still did not receive

much public notice, the 40th anniversary attracted much more attention, and the 50th anniversaries (which are not yet over) produced a veritable flood of media coverage and public events–publications, speeches, talks, exhibitions. One wonders whether there is not a point where the issues are being trivialized.

The years 1989 and 1990 brought major political changes. After political support by the Soviet Union was withdrawn, the GDR slowly disintegrated. Almost along with the first emergence of individual political pronouncements after the long years of rigid communist rule, the liberal or left-wing public opinion in the West started to view some trends with uneasiness. The communist regime had been shaken by demonstrations; political opponents to the totalitarian communist state called for political freedom and civil rights. Suddenly a change in political climate could be noticed, and nationalistic overtones could increasingly be heard. Demonstrators carrying German flags shouted "Germany, Germany" or "We are one people," and GDR car stickers appeared with the inscription "I am proud to be a German." It was not surprising that the Conservatives were pleased with this, in light of their increasingly nationalistic tendencies. It was noticed, however, that these nationalistic demonstrations were becoming too much of a rationale for unification, and the opponents to the communist regime on humanitarian or moral grounds were no longer heard from. (The first freely elected parliament of the GDR had come out in the spring of 1990 with a strong statement, accepting coresponsibility for the Holocaust. Due to the subsequent disappearance of the GDR it was never put to the test.)

Unification took place on October 3, 1990; it was engineered to fit in conveniently with the upcoming elections, a political move that allowed Helmut Kohl's government to remain in power. A number of serious mistakes were made whose political consequences are still haunting Germany: too many unrealistic promises were made to the people in the East about how quickly prosperity for everyone would come; the Germans in the West were never allowed to give an opinion as to whether they actually wanted unification and, in order to create a favorable climate, predictions were made about the costs of unification that were simply untrue. Finance Minister Waigel staked his reputation on the promise that there would be no costs or increase in taxes; he predicted that the market economy would pay for unification and all it involved. Little wonder, therefore, that people who had spontaneously greeted the fall of the Berlin Wall now became somewhat ambivalent, and that no general rejoicing was to be seen when unification took place. There was no national euphoria. This seems, by the way, not to have been represented correctly in the Western media, which generally exaggerated the extent of approval for unification.

Thus, for a second time in this century, Germany saw itself confronted by the political and moral problems it had had to face after 1945, and which had been so crucial to the moral fiber of its society: how should one cope with the legacy of a dictatorship, and to what extent has the Nazi past been overcome and worked through? At this point one should add, of course, that the legacy of the communist dictatorship in the East cannot be fully compared to the situation in 1945. The most fundamental difference is that the GDR did not conduct mass murder and did not start a war of aggression. The situation is comparable only with regard to the political and moral consequences that should be drawn from the experience of a totalitarian regime.

The period immediately after unification was mostly overshadowed by practical problems. However, a number of disturbing facts and tendencies were noticed indicating that the East Germans had not actually overcome the Nazi past as well as they had claimed. There was the case of Hans-Peter Just, a social democratic member of parliament in Brandenburg, who was found to have participated in the murder of six Jewish men in the Ukraine in 1941; in 1991 Just had to resign. This was, admittedly, an isolated case, but it was unsettling because of the inability not only of the politician concerned but also of the people around him to understand the seriousness of the matter.

What seemed to have been thoroughly internalized by the overwhelming majority was the idea that subsequent actions taken against him by the GDR authorities had wiped out any responsibilities for his Nazi crimes. This incident is an indication of the climate in the former GDR.

A number of scandals involved concentration camp memorials. In one instance, a private company planned to open a supermarket on the grounds of a former concentration camp and it became quite clear from the reaction of the local population that they preferred the supermarket to the memorial. This was another indication of how state sponsored anti-fascism had failed to create genuine anti-Nazi feelings.

Another problem area involved the so-called "special camps" that had been run by the Soviet occupation force on the grounds of former Nazi concentration camps. On these sites, mass graves of victims of Stalinist terror were being discovered. A bitter public debate ensued on the extent to which these special camps should be given notoriety; one argument was that the Nazi past should now fade into oblivion and only the Stalinist crimes should be considered. The same attempt to erase any memory of the Nazi past and to see it only as part of Soviet propaganda could be observed in the renaming of streets: not only were the names of former communist functionaries taken down, but also those of communist resistance fighters against the Nazis.

On the West German side, the drive toward stressing the nationalist component in public life was strengthened by unification. Nazism, it is suggested by some, should be looked at only in a comparative framework, not as something unique but rather in the context of "other totalitarian regimes." This was similar to reactions after 1945, where every mention of Nazi crimes was immediately countered with the omnipresent "but": the Soviets had done much worse things.

This redefinition of the perception of Nazism has already produced results in historiography. The Institute for Contemporary History in Munich, for instance, has just recently undergone a change in directorship, at which occasion both the new Director and the Chairman of the Board of Advisers made the new research objectives quite clear. They wanted to move out of the Nazi period, and as far as they were prepared to deal with it at all they felt it should only be done in the context of a comparison between dictatorships.

Developments in the East also do not give much hope for any contribution by the historical profession to provide insights or draw lessons from the Nazi period. More and more information has emerged on how many of the contemporary historians in East Germany used to view the past through straight communist blinders. Many facts such as, for instance, local collaboration with the Nazis in the occupied Soviet Union, were simply suppressed because they did not fit into Marxist beliefs. It was also depressing to learn how many historians, scholars with an international reputation, had no qualms about serving as informers for the secret police ("Stasi"), either abroad or at home.

Unfortunately, attempts to replace the historians on the staff of East German universities with historians who could provide a balanced perspective on the period before 1945 and study how it influenced the postwar period in the East appear to be going slowly. Many historians (in Germany and North America) appear to have great difficulties taking a stand against their former colleagues. It seems that the victims of the former system will remain forgotten, and that those whose careers have been ruined during the communist period are still excluded from making their contribution to historiography–in this respect too, surprising similarities exist with the situation after 1945. Even if they had not been pro-regime before, after unification the people in East Germany suddenly closed ranks and saw all Westerners as intruders and imperialists. The question was asked why one should be more rigid now, when the treatment of Nazis had been quite mild after 1945. It is also interesting to note that in West Germany, where polls show that in a general sense the majority of the population was staunchly anti-communist, 1992 polls show that 61 percent feel there should be an end of "mud-slinging" about the past.

The above are only isolated tendencies that surfaced after unification and caused concern to some observers. In the more recent past, especially in 1992, there was a flood of events that showed only too clearly how well-founded any uneasiness has been. These developments, which had been widely reported in the media, started out with attacks by skinheads and other right-wing gangs in East Germany on foreigners living there.

The discussions about foreigners living in Germany not only involve present political or economic problems but also have their roots in the German past. Germany, like other European countries, does not think of itself as an immigrant country. Except for personal reasons such as marriage, there are only two ways to come into the country:

First, Section 16 of the German Constitution offers asylum for everyone who is politically persecuted. This provision has been included because of a sense of responsibility for what has happened in the Nazi period. While this was not a problem at first, in recent years increasingly greater numbers of the people applying for the status of political refugees do not appear to qualify; only about five percent of them are accepted after court hearings. (This does not include fugitives from wars and catastrophes.) The problem that Germany must face is that a choice must be made between two major objectives that no longer seem compatible: to remain a country with open borders in the context of the European community, and to maintain a functioning social system in which everybody is taken care of.

Resentment has been rising over the years against people viewed as abusing the provisions relating to political asylum. (Even recent polls show, however, that over 80 percent of Germans want to maintain the principle of the right to political asylum *per se*.) What fueled the resentment in the West, and again this is something which is connected to the Nazi past, was that for a long time the left-wing or liberal spectrum of society saw it as taboo to raise the issue. I have previously mentioned the greatly increased use of Nazi-period specifics as a basis for comparisons. This became very prominent in the asylum debate. I remember, for instance, that in the small university town where I lived absolutely inappropriate comparisons were constantly used. For example, housing provided for people seeking refugee status, which admittedly left much to be desired and was rightfully criticized as inadequate, was consistently compared to Auschwitz and Majdanek. Anyone who voiced doubts about the legitimacy of some of the claims for refugee status was immediately labeled a "racist" who was still at the Nazi level of thinking. This prevented an open discussion of the existing real problems and only added to the growing silent resentment among the population. Similar resentment was created by a tendency in parts of the Western media to use double standards when dealing with Germany and to constantly discover Nazi legacies in every political issue, regardless of appropriateness.

The same line of argument was used by some of the groups who were trying to enter Germany. Another example from the same town is an incident in 1990-91 when a group of Roma (Gypsies) from Czechoslovakia squatted in the town's main church after their claim for political refugee status had been rejected by the courts, claiming that if they were sent back to Czechoslovakia they would be murdered on arrival. And this, it was publicly proclaimed, would be equal to the sending of Gypsies to Auschwitz 50 years earlier.

The second provision allowing immigration to Germany is considered by many a simple hangover from Nazism. This is Section 116 of the Constitution, which allows people of so-called ethnic-German origin–i.e., people whose ancestors emigrated as long as 200 or 300 years ago–to return to Germany. How much this is linked to the Nazi period is shown by the fact that the files on ethnic Germans compiled by the Nazi authorities during the war in Eastern Europe are used to prove these ethnicity claims. This provision also was not an issue for quite a while and was only kept up as a part of Cold War rhetoric, but became controversial when the disintegration of the Eastern bloc and the bad economic conditions there brought large numbers of newcomers into Germany.

Both questions have been hotly debated in West Germany. Generally speaking, the conservatives were against political refugees, who are often non-white and viewed as left-wing troublemakers, and the social democrats opposed the influx of ethnic Germans, who were viewed as not having any connection to present-day Germany.

The growing resentment about increasing immigration to Germany is not merely an expression of xenophobia; it must also be considered a result of substantial changes in social conditions in recent years. Chancellor Kohl's conservative government was not famous for providing for the socially weak; the welfare state has been dismantled step by step, while at the same time tax privileges had been given to the business community. This policy is presently being continued, with the costs of the unification mainly imposed on lower and middle class income earners. This partially explains the social unrest and also shows why it is so very convenient for the Kohl government to have a scapegoat ready with which to distract public notice from the real social problems, focusing it entirely on the question of illegal immigration.

In Eastern Germany the issue became explosive when, as is the practice in the West, people seeking asylum were divided up among the individual communities who have to provide housing and material care for them. Violence erupted, houses were set on fire, foreigners were attacked in the streets. There was a wave of criminal attacks against foreigners; 3,374 criminal offenses were committed up to October 25, 1992, which as of the end of November 1992 had brought about 17 deaths.

Initially, the rationale behind these violent acts was assumed to be the resentment of East Germans against people whom they considered to be taking advantage of the welfare state. The crowd reactions at the scenes of these attacks made apparent how widely these sentiments are shared. Soon, however, it became clear that this was not the only reason behind the upsurge of violence: anti-Semitic acts and manifestations of neo-Nazism followed. A rising tide of neo-Nazi terror spread over Germany: Jewish cemeteries and memorials to Nazi victims were vandalized, buildings in concentration camps were set on fire, the Hitler salute and Nazi insignia were proudly displayed, one man was murdered because he said that Hitler was a criminal, another severely wounded and beaten up because he refused to give the

Hitler salute. This cannot be viewed as a reaction against present social problems–the dead Jews in their graves certainly do not take anything away from anyone. Mainly the violence took and still takes place in the former GDR, but it also spread to the Western part of Germany. As noted earlier, developments have been extremely rapid. In mid-November 1992, violence had been confined to refugees and to anti-Semitic acts; shortly afterwards, another group of foreigners, so-called guest workers, who had lived in Germany for 20 to 30 years, have been attacked and, occasionally, even disabled persons have become targets. The most notorious crime was the fire-bombing of a house in a small town in northern Germany where a Turkish grandmother and her two grandchildren were murdered.

Other incidents show that we are dealing not only with widespread support for driving away so-called phony refugees but also with a resurrection of anti-Semitism in a broader sense. In an incident in Rostock, for example, a conservative member of the City Council, Karl Heinz Schmidt, attacked Ignaz Bubis, the Chairman of the Jewish Council in Germany.

Mr. Bubis was the target of another anti-Semitic scandal some years ago in West Germany. It is interesting to compare the two incidents to illustrate the two different forms in which anti-Semitism is manifesting itself in the two parts of the country. The verbal attack in Rostock consisted of the crudest form of anti-Semitic stock phrases, basically telling Bubis that Jews have no business in Germany; it boiled down to the Nazi slogan "Juden raus" ["Out with the Jews!"]. The other scandal took place in Frankfurt some years ago and was caused by a play by motion-picture director and playwright R. W. Fassbinder. The play showed how greedy real estate brokers cause the ruin and destruction of cities, the central figure being "the rich Jew." Bubis, who at that time was not the Chairman of the Jewish Council, was a well-known real estate broker in Frankfurt, and so, while his name was, of course, not openly mentioned, it became quite apparent at whom the attack was aimed. A big discussion ensued: was this really anti-Semitic, or only critical of social problems existing in Germany? Fassbinder was certainly a man of the left, and his supporters came from the left. No open or crude forms of anti-Semitic prejudices are to be seen in the play, but on a deeper level all the well-known anti-Semitic topics emerge and "the rich Jew" is shown as a cold, manipulating, poisonous, deadly figure.

The question on everyone's mind is, of course, how it is possible that in East Germany, which moved away so clearly from the Nazi past, which severed any links to it, violent neo-Nazism could spring up so quickly? Opinion polls taken in the summer of 1992 still showed that Eastern Germans had moved away more clearly, more distinctly, from the Nazi past than their Western counterparts. The question is, therefore: What are the motives behind the violence? At present any answer must remain, to a certain extent, speculative. We still know very little. Two facts are clear: the neo-Nazis are very young, mainly young men from 15 years of age or even younger to the early 20's, and they express a tremendous amount of violence.

A number of explanations have been suggested:

* It is the expression of a generational conflict. This can work in two ways: One is that the presently active generation–i.e., parents, teachers, politicians–in the East have lost all credibility and authority because of their former involvement and compliance with the communist regime. This is important, because present manifestations of Nazism do not exist in a void. A 16-year-old, whether in East or West Germany, has no direct magical connection to the past. Either he has accepted neo-Nazi preachings or he is reacting to and attacking taboos in society. The ostentatious anti-fascist attitude of the East is seen only as hypocrisy and, therefore, is discredited: while Nazism was depicted as evil, Stalin's crimes were glorified. This reaction is understandable in the East, where anti-fascism is seen merely as something prescribed by the state. But in the West as well as in the East showing Nazi sympathies is a violation of the greatest taboo of society, the most unconditional confrontation with the parent and teacher generation. Furthermore, Nazism has

become synonymous with terror and Nazi symbols are the ideal vehicle for violence. Another form of this explanation, leading in the opposite direction, sees these violent youngsters as a sort of "avant-garde" that expresses the emotions and views of their parents in a more open and brutal form.

* The German phenomena can be placed in the larger picture of a common trend in all Eastern European countries, where nationalism and anti-Semitism surface again after the end of the communist era. It is simply in fashion to be right-wing. In this context it should be pointed out that in 1989-90, as soon as East Germany opened up, neo-Nazi ideologues from the West went there for missionary work. At present it seems quite easy for all varieties of right-wing organizations, such as for instance the Klu Klux Klan, to gain supporters there.

* In the old GDR, young people could not learn how to solve social conflicts since no open discussions were possible. Conflicts were either swept under the carpet or the security organs reacted swiftly. Xenophobia and attacks and confrontations with foreigners seem to have a certain tradition, albeit not in such a violent form.* Thus, young men in the East are now pushing the limits, testing how far one can go. Opinion polls show that there must be a certain feeling of paranoia about foreigners among East Germans. While in reality only one percent of the population are foreigners, polls show they are viewed as comprising 10 to 15 percent.

* Foreigners are a convenient scapegoat. The young generation is disoriented and jobless, and feels it has no future. This is particularly pronounced in the East, where people are still not fully oriented in the new society; they also feel

---

* I am grateful to Harry Waibel (*Institut für Antisemitismusforschung, Berlin*), for this information.

they are treated as second-class Germans. A growing frustration with the sudden complexities of everyday life is vented in outbursts of anger and violence. An argument against this explanation is the fact that the majority of anti-foreigner offenders in the West are not jobless, as is made evident by the fact that most violent attacks take place on weekends.

* It should be mentioned that in the last ten years resentment and disillusionment with politics and politicians has also grown in West Germany. This has been caused, for instance, by a number of political scandals that have never resulted in the forced resignation of the Minister responsible. Certain social groups who at some point no longer fit well into the market economy have simply been pushed to the fringes of society. While some social groups prospered enormously, many young people and university graduates find themselves in a devastating employment situation. This leaves its scars in a society even if it does not express itself immediately in voting behavior.

  We still do not know much about the political climate in the former GDR, i.e., about what the silent majority really thinks. The number of right-wing supporters is difficult to estimate; recent polls showed that 80 to 90 percent in East and West were opposed to violence. The media present only a very small segment of the overall picture. In the summer of 1992, for instance, I visited Theresienstadt in Czechoslovakia, and the majority of visitors of the concentration camp were East Germans. I would never have expected this from reading the newspapers.

* There is an indication of a split in East German society. Some positive events are reported where people organized themselves locally to protect foreigners living among them. Interestingly enough, these seem to be the same political groups who had formed the backbone of resistance against

the old communist regime and then disappeared from the political scene for a while.

The terrifying pictures of houses set on fire by skinheads and a mob of cheering bystanders have caused thoughtful observers both in Germany and abroad to ask: Is this not like the Nazi pogrom in 1938? Subsequent events seem to show, however, that the answer is negative. There are numerous differences. The present situation cannot be compared to Weimar, because it is not the ruling elites that are corrupted and rejecting democracy, but rather a small core of right-wing radicals and a larger group of supporters. In the German army, for instance, incidents were reported where 24 soldiers were identified as having participated in neo-Nazi activities; however, this was reported by the army authorities themselves and they subsequently dealt with the persons involved. Cause for concern is given by the fact that Chancellor Kohl obviously played with fire, and was trying to keep the refugee problem unresolved in order to stampede the opposition into dumping Section 16 and thus obviating the provision of a basic human right.

What also caused uneasiness is that the police and the judiciary system initially dealt too leniently with offenders. That was seen especially in contrast to the way the state had cracked down on left-wing terrorist groups in the 1970s. It was felt that reactions had been quite different when the shooting victims had been bankers and leading business managers rather than refugees.

Another difference from the times of either Weimar or the Nazis is that a critical public opinion has developed. The media have reacted very well, not only in the way they reported the incidents but even in active intervention. That was particularly pronounced in the Rostock violence, where a TV team was instrumental in rescuing people from a burning house. From October 1992 on, a widespread reaction against neo-Nazis has appeared, which shows that the liberal public is now taking sides. Numerous demonstrations took place, the first one being organized on November 8, 1992 by the President of the Republic, Richard von Weiszäcker, in Berlin. Roughly 350,000 people were on the streets for this event. This demonstration was followed the next day, which was the anniversary of the Nazi pogrom of November 9, 1938, by others in German cities. Figures differ, but from what can be gathered from the local press the attendance rate was 5 to 10 percent of the population. In Munich, the capital of the most conservative part of Germany, another huge demonstration on December 6 brought 400,000 people into the streets, all carrying candles. Every day public announcements and newspaper advertisements appear, sponsored by all sorts of organizations ranging from theaters in Berlin to the Council of Catholic Bishops, all calling for a stand against right-wing terror. Companies and organizations of industrialists have also advertised, in one instance simply recommending that neo-Nazis be fired from their jobs. Nothing of this kind happened in the Weimar Republic. One German automobile concern offered an award for anyone who would help to identify the murderers of the three Turkish women. It also seems that the police are now putting more effort into investigating crimes; for instance, when a Federal agency investigated the murder of the Turkish family, they started to get results almost immediately. Further, sentences seem to be less lenient than they were in the beginning. (It should be pointed out, however, that the offenders are usually very young so that many of them fall under juvenile law and some are even too young to be prosecuted at all.)

While all this may give reason for hope, there is certainly no cause to relax and feel that the problem has been overcome. We have certainly not seen the end of neo-Nazi violence. The very fact that so many people now dare to say openly what before they were afraid to say, that certain inner thresholds have been passed, will leave its scars on society for a long time to come. As the writer Inge Deutschkron put it, she formerly received anti-Semitic letters that were anonymous, now she receives them signed with names in full.

We will have to come to some bitter realizations that will, perhaps, change our perception of how we can deal with the

Nazis and their legacy. It looks as though there are severe limits to what education and teaching about the Nazis and the Holocaust can achieve. For a long time one could hear at every academic gathering dealing with this subject the hopeful conviction being voiced that if only people can be made to know, if only people are taught, there will be no repetition. I think we cannot be so sanguine in the future–genuinely dealing with the Holocaust is walking on a very fine line. Recent events have shown how terribly any attempt to exploit the Nazi past and its legacy, politically or emotionally, comes back to haunt us.

We must also prepare ourselves to acknowledge that it does not seem possible to really cope with the legacy of a dictatorship, in the sense of clearing the ground of rubble and starting afresh. It will take yet another generation before the German social climate has changed.

Anti-Semitism and the Treatment of
the Holocaust in Hungary

István Deák

Hungarians, like all other nations with a traditionally significant Jewish presence, have had a long history of anti-Semitism,
one which culminated in the mass deportations to Auschwitz in
1944. Yet unlike many other European nations with a large
Jewish minority, Hungarians have also had a remarkably long
history of what, for lack of a better term, might be termed philo-
Semitism. Perhaps nowhere else in Europe were Jews more
enthusiastically encouraged, at least in certain periods, to become members of the dominant national group, and probably
nowhere else were Jews more willing to become patriotic citizens.

The result of this rapid assimilation, which took place mainly
in the late nineteenth century, was a unique Jewish contribution
to Hungarian culture, society, and the economy. These two
phenomena–anti-Semitism ranging all the way from traditional-
ist to racist, and pro-Jewish sympathies ranging all the way from
willing toleration to a complete lack of prejudice–often appeared
at the same time. Moreover, rather than dividing the nation into
two distinct and hostile camps, such conflicting sentiments often
manifested themselves in the same group, or even in the same
individuals. It might well be that the majority of Gentile Hungarians were both anti-Semitic and philo-Semitic, some in
different periods of their lives, others simultaneously. To embrace a Jew in a drunken moment and say: "I love you, yet I hate

you" was not an uncommon event, and it expressed the ambivalence of the public toward the Jewish phenomenon.

In the presentation that follows I shall first try to outline the historic Jewish presence and Jewish achievements in Hungary, as well as attempt a very brief overview of Jewish-Gentile relations. I will subsequently say a few words about the Hungarian Holocaust and the factors that influenced Jewish-Gentile relations under communist rule, and conclude with a discussion of the situation during the postcommunist era.

History and Achievements

Although far from numerous at that time, Jews lived in Hungary even in the Middle Ages. They were, however, only one group of foreigners among many engaged in the business of buying and selling in the medieval Magyar kingdom. Alongside them were Muslims (or as the Hungarians called them, Ismaelites), Italians, and other Europeans. The fabulous cultural and economic upsurge around the Renaissance court of King Mathias Corvinus in the late fifteenth century also allowed for some Jewish successes. Foremost among them was Imre Fortunatus, a Jewish convert of Spanish origin, who became royal treasurer early in the sixteenth century. Not long after, however, the nation faced its most profound crisis: in 1526 the Ottoman Turks invaded the country, inflicting a crushing defeat on its armies at the Battle of Mohács. The invasion and subsequent partition of Hungary deeply affected Christian-Jewish relations. In the sixteenth and seventeenth centuries Hungarians lived under three different rulers: the Catholic Habsburgs in the west and the north, the Muslim Ottomans in the center and the south, and the confessionally mixed princes of Transylvania in the east. The Sublime Porte was generally tolerant of the Jews, and even favored them, in part because of their business acumen and in part simply because the Jews were not the Christian enemy. In Transylvania, the situation varied, depending on whether the Hungarian princes of that semi-independent vassal principality under the Turks practiced general toleration, as they most often did, or pursued a more militant confessional policy. Finally, in Habsburg Hungary, Jews were not infrequently the target of counter-Reformation zealots.

A major tragedy visited Hungarian Jewry during Europe's last crusade, in the final decades of the seventeenth century, when large Christian armies recruited in Western Europe liberated the country and, in the process, massacred Muslims and those whom they viewed as Muslim hirelings, namely the Jews. In the city of Buda, for example, which was liberated in 1686 in one of the greatest military triumphs of Christian Europe, all but a single Jewish inhabitant were killed.

The end of the great Turkish war meant a new beginning for both Gentiles and Jews. There was massive immigration from the west and the south into the vast empty spaces of war-torn Hungary; among the immigrants were Jews, who at first came mainly from Bohemia and Moravia but later increasingly from Galicia as well. The latter province had been acquired by Maria Theresa in 1772, and the massive presence of Jews there forever changed Jewish-Gentile relations in the Habsburg monarchy. The immigrant *Ostjuden,* strangers in dress and language, often illiterate and generally poor, became a permanent feature of life in Budapest and Vienna. They proved themselves an inexhaustible source of dynamism and entrepreneurship, but they also embarrassed their more sophisticated coreligionists from the West.

In the late eighteenth and early nineteenth century, Jews in general found shelter and employment as artisans and innkeepers on the estates of large landowners. Their elite functioned as sellers of the landowners' flour and wine. Jews were much less welcome in the cities, from which such unwanted competition was carefully excluded by a mostly German artisanry and merchantry. Indeed, it was one of the cherished privileges of free royal towns "not to receive Jews."

A Silent Pact

The late eighteenth century inaugurated an age of reform, instituted from above mainly by Emperor Joseph II, who wanted the Jews, and everyone else in his realm, to become useful and productive citizens. This reforming drive was later adopted, often in defiance of the Vienna court, by the so-called Hungarian Reform Generation. The educated young noblemen who formed the bulk of the Reform Generation in the first half of the nineteenth century were anxious to modernize backward Hungary, and in this effort welcomed the Jews as allies. After all, the Jews, especially the small enlightened elite among them, were neither centralizing Imperial bureaucrats, nor landed gentry tied to anachronistic customs and ideas, nor obscurantist priests, nor German burghers anxious to protect their ancient privileges; nor finally were these Jews illiterate and dangerous peasants. On the contrary, the upcoming Jewish elite was dynamic and keen to embrace liberalism and Hungarian patriotism in exchange for their emancipation. It was understood, of course, that the Jews, like the rest of the nation, would reform their community and religious practices in accordance with enlightened, liberal philosophy.

Thus was born an unacknowledged pact between the liberal and nationalist Gentile elite and the educated Jews. Together the two groups constituted a common front against the autocratic Habsburgs, conservative Hungarian noblemen, and troublesome ethnic minorities. (The latter, incidentally, formed an absolute majority of the country's population.) There was also a tacitly agreed-upon division of labor between the two groups, with the Gentile elite shouldering the burden of politics and administration, and the Jews developing commerce and industry. In the revolutions of 1848 both sides lived up to the pact: the government of Louis Kossuth emancipated the Jews (if not in practice then in theory, for the revolution was defeated in 1849), and the majority of Jews sided with Kossuth. The foremost symbols of this alliance were the many Jewish soldiers and officers in Hungarian uniform during that struggle. In fact, as long as the 1848 generation and its spiritual heirs remained on the scene, that is, until late in World War I, the two sides respected the original agreement, the Hungarian leaders according the Jews complete equality and unlimited business opportunities and the Jews offering unconditional devotion to the Hungarian cause and its economic prosperity.

Emancipation had become a reality even before its formal adoption as Law XVII of 1867, opening the road to Jewish immigration and urbanization. In 1787 there were only 83,000 Jews in Hungary, constituting one percent of the total population. By 1848 the number of Hungarian Jews had increased to 336,000, or two percent of the population, and by 1910 the number had risen to 909,000, or five percent. Even more striking was the level of Jewish urbanization. Whereas in 1848 there had been only a few hundred legally admitted Jewish families in Budapest, by 1910 Jews in the capital numbered 200,000, representing nearly one-fourth of the city's population. Given the restrictive character of the Hungarian franchise, the Jews of Budapest, being generally more prosperous and better educated than the rest of the population, accounted for nearly half of those entitled to vote in that city. Not too astonishingly, however, they consciously refrained from forming Jewish political parties, and there thus was never such a thing as a clearly defined Jewish political force in the country.

The heyday of Jewish emancipation came in the early 1890s, when parliament made the Jewish confession equal to all others by declaring it not only an accepted but an "integrated" confession. This meant that the state would now collect church taxes on behalf of the three main Jewish communities, the Orthodox, the Neolog, and the Conservative or Status Quo. The new laws also brought seats in the upper house of parliament for the heads of the three Jewish communities; they allowed for the conversion of Catholics to Judaism, and they enabled those living in a mixed marriage to decide whether their children should grow up as Jews or as Christians. These measures created a storm of indignation in Catholic circles and poisoned relations between the Vatican and the free-thinking Hungarian government. The measures also caused the leaders of the Slovak, Romanian, and other ethnic minorities to charge that the Hungarian government was favoring the Jews to the detriment of all other minorities. To this the government and the Jewish leaders replied that the Hungarian Jews were not an ethnic but only a confessional minority.

Anti-Semitism, in both its traditional religious and more modern racist form, predated the abovementioned legislation. In fact, the high point of organized political anti-Semitism was reached in the early 1880s at the time of the Tiszaeszlár blood libel affair and the creation of Hungary's first and only official "Anti-Semitic Party." The Tiszaeszlár affair revealed astonishing prejudices and bigotry in virtually every social stratum, but the government and the judiciary did not fail to stand up for human rights and civilized procedures. Those accused of having taken the blood of a Christian maiden were acquitted, and the Anti-Semitic Party soon collapsed, which did not, of course, mean the end of political anti-Semitism.

The contrast between the situation in Budapest and that in Prague or Vienna could not have been more conspicuous. In Prague Czech politicians routinely identified the German-speaking Jews of the city as belonging to the enemy camp, although this did nothing to endear the Jews to the German nationalist parties in Bohemia, while Vienna's role as not only a great center of Jewish culture but also the home of an open and public anti-Semitism is such a historical truism as to require no further comment. Budapest, on the other hand, was "Judapest," as Karl Lueger, the anti-Semitic mayor of Vienna, put it. In truth, Jews owned and managed the overwhelming majority of Hungary's investment capital, its banks, and its mines and heavy industry. Jews owned most of Hungary's theaters, nightclubs, newspapers, and art galleries; they formed the majority of Hungary's journalists, medical doctors, and lawyers, and they played a most important role in cultural life as artists, writers, poets, philosophers, editors, and scientists. Significantly, however, the vast majority of these creative intellectuals were not practicing Jews; nor did they publicly acknowledge their Jewish origin.

Finally, in the natural course of events, Jews began to enter public service as high-school teachers, university professors, judges, civil servants, and army officers. In 1910, six percent of Hungary's civil servants were Jews, slightly exceeding their proportion in the general population. In the so-called Common Army of the Austro-Hungarian Monarchy, Jews made up nearly twenty percent, and in the Hungarian National Guard, or *honvéd,* nearly thirty percent of the reserve officer corps.

Political Crisis, War, and Revolutions

By the first decade of the twentieth century signs of danger to the entire political system had begun to accumulate. The ethnic situation in Hungary went from bad to worse, with the Slovaks, Romanians, and Serbs demanding self-government while Croatia, a self-governing kingdom subordinated to Hungary, threatened outright secession. Meanwhile, many Hungarian leaders and parts of the public clamored for complete separation from the other half of the Austro-Hungarian Monarchy. In attempting to struggle against the ethnic minorities and the emperor-king in Vienna at the same time, the Hungarians managed to contrive their own destruction, particularly given the mood of growing impatience and exasperation with which that struggle was conducted. There was more and more talk in the highest political circles about a struggle for survival, about the inevitable and necessary clash between the strong and the weak, from which Hungary, the stronger, must emerge triumphant. This new Social Darwinistic outlook on life, combined with a very pragmatic quest for good jobs on the part of the rising Gentile urban middle class, began to envenom Christian-Jewish relations and made some people doubt whether a continued symbiosis was possible.

The fatal turning point came with World War I, when relations between Hungarians and the ethnic minorities deteriorated completely, making the country's partition inevitable if the Central Powers were to lose the war, and perhaps even if they were to win it. The Jews were not an ethnic minority in the eyes of the law, themselves, or the public, but as general suffering increased they nonetheless became an easy target. Critics pointed out that Jews were somewhat underrepresented among combat soldiers, which was true, but it should have been added that, in general, there were relatively few urban workers, artisans, clerks, and businessmen in the front lines. Urban and educated people were particularly rare, except as officers, in the infantry, which suffered proportionally the greatest losses. As anti-Semites pointed out, Jews were overrepresented among the war profiteers and black marketeers, which again should have been perfectly understandable in view of the very large Jewish presence among entrepreneurs and traders. In fact, the overwhelmingly Christian large landowners profited as much from the war economy as the owners of heavy industry.

By 1917 the sufferings of the war had brought about a radicalization of politics, which, following the military defeat of the Central Powers in October 1918, led at first to the outbreak of a democratic revolution and then, in March 1919, to the creation of a Republic of Soviets. In both of these events, and in the democratic Károlyi government and especially in the equally short-lived communist Béla Kun regime, Jews played a conspicuous, nay, overwhelming role. Practically all the important People's Commissars in the Republic of Soviets were Jews. Patriotic Jews later tried to excuse this by saying that the Bolsheviks had been unassimilated *Ostjuden;* some historians today attempt to explain the phenomenon by arguing that these young men had turned to Bolshevism out of despair over the failure of their assimilation. Neither of these explanations seems to be correct, however, for the Bolshevik commissars generally came from well assimilated, patriotic, and successful families; nor did they themselves ever complain of feeling rejected by the society of Gentiles. In fact, no Jewish communist ever even admitted to being a Jew, and none ever confessed to having been inconvenienced by anti-Semitism. They attributed anti-Semitism to the sins of capitalism and imperialism, and they easily dismissed the whole issue by saying that the Jewish problem would solve itself automatically under socialism. Not so Christian middle-class society, which now tended to lay all the blame for the lost war, the loss of two-thirds of Hungary to its neighbors, and the enormous suffering, hunger, inflation, unemployment, and mad social experimentation of the Republic of Soviets at the feet of the Jewish Bolsheviks, and, by extension, the Jews in general. Anti-Semitic resentment was systematically whipped up by the White counterrevolutionary movement of Admiral Miklós Horthy. White officers' detachments organized pogroms, using the opportunity of post-revolutionary chaos to murder Jewish Bolsheviks, Jewish bankers, trade-union leaders, and rebellious peasants.

What really had motivated the Jewish revolutionaries is too complex an issue to discuss here, but in my opinion the explanation must be sought in the tradition of Jewish messianism, and even more in the fact that the Jews, being overrepresented at the universities and in the free professions, were more likely than other groups to be open to current Western ideologies. These intellectuals were also especially sensitive to social injustice. In any case, the great majority of Hungarian Jews wanted to have nothing to do with proletarian dictatorship.

Counterrevolution and the Holocaust

The new regime, led by Admiral, now Regent Horthy, heralded an essentially negative counterrevolutionary ideology which repudiated not only democracy and Bolshevism but also the pre-war liberal-conservative system. This also implicitly meant the repudiation of the silent pact once concluded between the Jews and the liberal gentry. It is true that dire economic necessity soon drove the Horthy regime to make concessions to both Western and domestic Jewish capital: between 1921 and 1932, under the conservative leadership of Count István Bethlen and his immediate successor, Jewish great capital was restored to its previously dominant position, and overt anti-Semitism was no longer tolerated. But the old liberal alliance between Jews and nobles had ceased to exist, being replaced by a merely temporary and pragmatic alliance between the government and Jewish business leaders. The Jews were about to become a tolerated minority in Hungary.

All the new intellectual-political currents were hostile to Jewry: the Catholic "neo-Baroque" renaissance, which repudiated the entire heritage of the Enlightenment and the French Revolution; the aggressively anti-urban and anti-Western peasant-populist movement: and, of course, the radical far-right parties which directed their wrath both against Horthy's "reactionary" regime and against the Jews. The 1930s saw Hungary entering the German Nazi orbit in the hope of recovering the territories it had lost at the end of World War I. Also, late in the 1930s, a series of official anti-Jewish measures were adopted. After Hungary had actually recovered some of the lost lands, and after it had joined the German military drive against the Soviet Union, the Hungarian army committed a series of anti-Jewish atrocities in the occupied territories. In addition, about 40,000 Jewish forced laborers perished on the Eastern front alongside more than 100,000 Hungarian soldiers. At home, however, the bulk of the Jewish population enjoyed the protection of the government. Why this protection at a time when most other East European Jews had long been gassed? Because of conservative, aristocratic humanitarian impulses that caused even the old anti-Semite Horthy to resist Hitler's insistent demand for a "final solution" of the Jewish question; because without Jewish expertise the Hungarian war industry would have ground to a halt; and because, by 1943, the Hungarian leadership was desperate to leave the German alliance. In a mistaken analysis of world-wide Jewish power, the government saw a nearly intact Jewish community as Hungary's entry ticket into the Allied camp.

The government's daring scheme collapsed in March 1944 when the German army occupied Hungary, arrested the liberal and conservative leaders, installed a pro-Nazi government under the nominal authority of Regent Horthy, and proceeded to "solve," at last, the Jewish question. The new anti-Jewish measures affected about 800,000 persons; typically for Hungary, at least ten percent of them were Christian by religion and many even by persuasion. More than half of these Jews and ex-Jews were deported to Auschwitz with the active assistance of collaborationist elements in the Hungarian civil service and the particularly brutal gendarmes. According to Randolph Braham, total Jewish losses in "Enlarged Hungary" accounted to 560,000 persons; in so-called smaller Hungary, as it had existed between 1919 and 1938, about one-half of the Jews were lost, but in Budapest itself, from which Jews had not been massively deported, the survival rate was much, much higher. Jewish survival in Budapest was due mainly to Regent Horthy and such of his advisors as Count Bethlen who in July 1944 finally succeeded in reasserting themselves by forcefully intervening to stop further deportations. Considering that the wealthy, educated, and well assimilated Jews lived mainly in Budapest, and that such individuals were more successful in general in disguising their identity, to hide with Christian friends, or to find shelter in buildings protected by the legations of neutral countries, it is clear that in Hungary, as elsewhere, the poor were the Holocaust's principal victims.

Did the Holocaust spell an end to the Jewish-Christian symbiosis? Yes, if we consider the extent of the cataclysm and the postwar flight or departure of the majority of survivors. No, if we take into consideration that many survivors, even among those who chose to go to Israel or the United States, continued to think of themselves as Hungarians.

The question became: what type of government could be more trusted with the job of expiation and restitution, and what kind of government would offer the best guarantee against the return of fascism? According to the Hungarian historian Miklós Szabó, Jewish survivors reacted in three different ways to the Holocaust and the end of Nazism. Those who felt that non-Jewish Hungarians could no longer be trusted chose emigration. Those who believed that Hungary hadn't been democratic enough opted for the democratic coalition government which had been installed by the victorious Red Army, and in which the communists were only one of several partners. Finally, those who considered Hungarian nationalism the greatest menace immediately embraced the once minuscule but now rapidly growing internationalist Communist Party that promised to bring about a totally different and putatively better society. The dilemma of choice between the latter two solutions was, however, soon solved by Stalin, who caused a totalitarian communist regime to be installed in Hungary between 1947 and 1949. The consequences of this event were momentous, distinctly so in terms of Jewish-Gentile relations.

Jews and Christians Under Communism

The top leaders of Stalinist Hungary were, almost without exception, communists of Jewish origin who, of course, carefully concealed this fact, often even from their own children. Moreover, the four or five persons who constituted the supreme leadership of the Party had been in Soviet exile during the war; they had not personally experienced the Holocaust and, like many other outsiders, were inclined to generalize about the World War II behavior of entire ruling elites and entire nations. While publicly courting Hungarian national sentiments and heaping honors on nationalist peasant-populist writers, these Stalinists are known to have referred to the Hungarian people in private as "a bunch of fascists." Finally, some of these leaders had spent many years in Hungarian prisons. Mátyás Rákosi, for instance, who was to become Hungary's Stalin, spent 15 years behind bars. He was freed only in 1940 and departed immediately for the Soviet Union. Hence, he and others like him were familiar only with the Hungary of the immediate post-World War I White Terror. They now took their revenge upon all whom they had perceived as the enemy back in 1919: aristocratic landowners, old-regime politicians, army officers, civil servants, wealthy bourgeois, Catholic clergy, well-to-do "counterrevolutionary" peasants, and social democratic "traitors." This transplanting of the 1919 civil war into the late 1940s soon added thousands of former victims of Nazism to the population of the communist prisons and concentration camps. It was not at all unusual to find a former gendarmerie officer sharing a cell with his former social democratic victim, or to have a Jewish intellectual breaking stones at the Recsk concentration camp alongside a former prince. Both were watched over and tortured by camp guards who were often former fascist Arrow Cross militiamen.

The persecution of the real or putative enemies of the communist dictatorship was soon followed by monster purges within the Party itself, which landed hundreds of communist leaders in the camps and prisons. Not a few of these new-fangled victims, such as former communist minister of the interior László Rajk and his successor János Kádár, had been among the most cruel persecutors of non-communists and of each other. This complete mixing of common and political criminals, of persecutors and persecuted, made a mockery of the idea of punishing those guilty of fascist crimes. Instead of honestly dealing with the tragedy of the Holocaust, the communists perverted and falsified its memory. World War II was officially remembered as the era when "communists and other progressive elements" had struggled heroically against, or become victims of, "Hitlerite and Horthyite fascism." Somehow there seemed to have been no Jews among these heroes and victims; instead, all were "anti-fascist Hungarians." Even when the persecution of the Jews was mentioned (always in the vaguest terms), responsibility was thrust on the shoulders of the Hitler fascists and their Hungarian helpers, never on the Hungarian people itself. In any case, the American and British imperialists as well as their running dog, Marshal Tito, had by then become a worse enemy than the Nazis had ever been.

All this had a grave effect on the views of an undetermined minority among the Hungarian Gentiles regarding the Jewish tragedy. Those who had felt shame after World War II–and many did–for having been silent during the deportations, were now offered the spectacle of Jewish dictators and Jewish political policemen persecuting fellow Hungarians. That there were many Jews among the victims, too, could be easily overlooked, if for no other reason than because no one in Hungary, whether executioner or victim, was publicly identified as a Jew. For the unthinking part of the public, recent Hungarian history began to look increasingly as a long-drawn out struggle for power between Jews and non-Jews, in which at one time one side had the upper hand and at another time the other side. To yearn for an end to communist rule became equivalent for these people to yearning for an end to Jewish rule. Such views ignored the fact, of course, that most Jewish survivors had voted against communism by leaving the country after 1945, and that even among those who had stayed behind, the communists were only a minority. Moreover, a great many of the young Stalinist intellectuals who began rethinking communism after Stalin's death in 1953 and ended by repudiating it altogether were also Jews.

Remarkably, however, the above opinions were characteristic of only a minority among non-Jewish Hungarians. As the events of October-November 1956 proved, when there were only a handful of absolutely minor anti-Semitic incidents in the heat of a violent revolution, or as sociological and public opinion research has amply proven in the last twenty odd years, the majority of the Gentile public refuses to engage in anti-Semitic actions. In fact, the majority of the public is simply not anti-Semitic.

How did the Jews themselves feel about the great crisis and the new possibilities of a Jewish-Gentile symbiosis? I have already mentioned that the majority of survivors left either between 1945 and 1948 or after the revolution in 1956. But this did not necessarily mean the repudiation of the Hungarian nation; on the contrary, many left only because Hungary had become communist and because they, unlike many Gentiles, had family ties in the West and could therefore more easily settle elsewhere. Among those who remained at home, many chose complete assimilation by marrying Christian men or women and by bringing up their children without the slightest reference to their Jewish heritage. How many did so remains anybody's guess; we know only that among those of Jewish descent in

Hungary today (a group estimated at between 80,000 and over 100,000), only about 15,000 publicly practice their religion. Between 1953 and 1956 young communist Jewish intellectuals spearheaded the movement for the liberalization of communist rule. Some, like Miklós Gimes, István Angyal, and Gábor Földes, later paid with their life for this activity. In the 1970s and 1980s, it was again young Jewish intellectuals, themselves often the children of high-ranking Stalinists, who spearheaded the movement for a free market economy and political democracy. Without such people as the philosopher János Kis, Hungary's peaceful democratic transformation in the late 1980s would have been much more difficult.

The End of Symbiosis or the End of Hungarian Jewry?

Gradual transition to democracy in the 1980s meant the ever freer airing of all problems, including the problem of continuing Jewish-Gentile symbiosis. Following the official establishment of a non-communist regime in 1990, debate on the subject has assumed a more disturbing character. One affair in particular has served to split Hungary's intellectual community, and may even be considered a kind of watershed in Hungary's postcommunist development. It concerns an article written late in the summer of 1990 by Sándor Csoóri, a poet and essayist fascinated by rural life and Hungary's foremost populist writer. Many regard him as the rightful successor to Gyula Illyés, the country's literary king. The populists are, as stated before, a special breed of literati who have agitated public life for at least seven decades by reporting on the misery of village life but also by advocating a peculiar approach to politics often called "The Third Road," neither West nor East, neither capitalist nor communist. Yet Csoóri, like nearly all other members of the Hungarian intelligentsia, is also very much an urban intellectual. He lives in Budapest and is at home in liberal circles, which in Hungary has always meant having a number of Jewish friends.

In the communist era, Csoóri was associated with the opposition, but he was also repeatedly rewarded by the authorities for his literary activities. In fact, like other populist writers of peasant background, he enjoyed the special protection of the Jewish György Aczél, unofficial communist dictator of Hungarian literature under János Kádár from the late 1950s to the 1980s. In the early 1980s, however, Csoóri was placed under a temporary interdict on account of having published, in the West, an essay critical of the communist regime. The target of Csoóri's criticism was not domestic policy but the government's indifference toward the plight of the Hungarian minority in Czechoslovakia. Later Csoóri emerged as one of the intellectual lights of the center-right Hungarian Democratic Forum.

Sándor Csoóri's controversial and rather rambling essay appeared in *Hitel,* the cultural mouthpiece of the Democratic Forum.[1] In it, he discussed what he saw as present-day Hungary's main problems: the moral devastation of society after forty years of communist rule, uncertainty about what it means to be a Hungarian, and the country's headlong rush into Western materialism. His conclusion was that Hungary is facing a dire future.

So far, there was nothing unusual about Csoóri's argumentation, for pessimistic predictions and prophetic scoldings of the public have been a stock in trade of Hungary's intellectuals since time immemorial. In the second half of his essay, however, Csoóri came up with a more serious thesis. He declared that only those people capable of experiencing the pain of being Hungarian could be called true members of the nation. In the past, especially before World War I, he continued, such immigrant groups as the German *Schwaben* or the Jews had been able to empathize with Hungary's tragic fate. But no longer! The combined experiences of the Hungarian Republic of Soviets in 1919, the interwar Horthy regime, and especially the "Age of Disaster," by which he meant the Holocaust, had put an end to the Hungarian-Jewish symbiosis.

"Today," Csoóri wrote, "we are experiencing a reverse assimilationist trend. It is no longer the Hungarian nation that wishes to assimilate the Jews, but liberal Jewry who wishes to assimilate the Hungarian nation. For that purpose it possesses a more powerful weapon than it has ever possessed, namely, the parliamentary system." In an unmistakable reference to the oppositionary Free Democrats, whose leadership then included several Jewish intellectuals, Csoóri accused that party of being in the forefront of the Jewish assimilationist drive. He asserted that the Jewish liberals, and by extension Jews in general, could never understand Hungarian pain, for while they, the Jews, think in practical, pragmatic terms and would be perfectly happy to bring today's truncated Hungary into the European Community, true Hungarians are idealists, whose activity is determined by the plight of the Hungarian minorities in neighboring countries. Compared to the magnitude of the latter problem, Csoóri concluded, Hungary's entering the House of Europe or not was a matter of little significance.

Needless to say, Csoóri was not the first to deal with the problem of national identity and the place of Jews in the nation: these questions have long been favorite topics among Hungarian intellectuals. Nor has Csoóri been the first to argue–since the collapse of communist rule–that the Jewish-Hungarian symbiosis is no longer possible. Alleged Jewish attempts to assimilate the Hungarians have figured in the new Hungarian right-wing press. Such a well-known writer as István Csurka claimed, well before Csoóri, that "the [Jewish] Béla Kuns are about to return to power in a liberal disguise." Yet Csoóri's article created a sensation, precisely because of his reputation as a political moderate and a friend of Jewish writers.

In a series of indignant articles, Jewish and non-Jewish writers protested against the exclusion of Jews from the body of the nation. Among them was a Jewish friend of Csoóri, the well-known historian Péter Hanák. What made Hanák's published protestation all the more significant was the fact that he has been, for the last twenty odd years, one of the major advocates of Hungary's national renaissance. Hanák's many essays on the subject, published under the Kádár regime, were considered milestones in the renewed search for a Hungarian national identity and were seen as important events in the drive against the Marxist-Leninist regime. Indeed, some of Hanák's liberal friends accused him of going too far in catering to nationalist sentiments.

In his rebuttal–forceful but friendly–Hanák pointed out the irony of the Jews being made responsible for their own decimation; he emphasized that the 80,000 Jews still remaining in Hungary were politically divided and that, since most of them were indifferent to Judaism, one could not possibly accuse them of wanting to assimilate anyone. Rather, they want quickly to assimilate into the Hungarian nation, he affirmed. It was extremely dangerous for Hungary's future, Hanák concluded, to make a minority responsible for the catastrophes which have befallen the country since World War I.

While the debate was raging, Csoóri published another essay in *Hitel,* explaining at great length that, despite his name and looks, he, Csoóri, was a true Hungarian and not, as many assumed, a Gypsy. Going further, Csoóri claimed to be a Petcheneg, that is, a descendant of a nomadic Turkic tribe which moved into Hungary from the East in the twelfth century, apparently a more illustrious ancestry than a Gypsy one.

What are we to make of this incident?

Like other intellectuals of the so-called populist tradition, Csoóri must surely feel embarrassed about having displayed very little stamina during the communist period and having left the task of anti-communist, samizdat activity to such radical "urbanist" intellectuals as György Konrád, János Kis, György Bence, Gábor Demszky, László Rajk, Jr., and Miklós Haraszti, most of whom are Jews. In particular, what must embarrass Csoóri and other nationalist writers is the fact that they accepted repeated favors from György Aczél, who was always much harsher on cosmopolitan writers than on the populists. Thus, thanks to the activities of Aczél and the communists in general, the time-honored enmity between the so-called urbanist intellectuals and the populist writers is experiencing a resurgence today, with the urbanists accusing the populists of having–just as in fascist times–given in to a totalitarian regime, and the populists accusing the urbanist intellectuals of being ex-Marxists or the children of former communist leaders.

Undoubtedly, envy also motivates Csoóri and other populist writers. The fact that the urbanist oppositionary writers are often invited to the West and have excellent Western contacts, whereas the populists neither speak a foreign language nor are consulted by visiting Western journalists, is a major cause for their dislike of the urbanists and, by extension, of Western democracies.

There are other, more general conclusions to be drawn from this incident. The renewed populist attacks on the urbanist intellectuals and their party, the Free Democrats, reflect the traditional hostility of the countryside to Budapest, the monster capital of over two million people in a country of just ten million. In Budapest are located all the government offices and all the major educational and cultural institutions as well as much of the national wealth. Indeed, the interwar Horthy regime's main popular appeal derived from its evocation of rural values, its extolling of the Hungarianness of peasants, and its contrasting of the pure and healthy lifestyle of farmers with the Judeo-Bolshevik-liberal lifestyle of the capital. Never mind that the Horthy regime was itself firmly installed in Budapest, or that its main political support came from the Christian middle class in the capital and the country's other urban centers! But then, the populist writers of the interwar period, too, lived in Budapest and derived their livelihood in great part from urban Jewish patrons and readers.

There is, furthermore, the uncertainty of many Hungarians concerning their ethnic identity. Few nations have been more mixed in origin than the Hungarians. Khazars, Avars, Cumans, Petchenegs, Tatars, Turks, Germans, Slovaks, Croats, Serbs, Romanians, Armenians, Jews, and Gypsies are included among the ancestors of today's Hungarians and, as a consequence, no one can be sure who is of "pure Hungarian blood" or, for that matter, just what it means to be a Hungarian. Hence Csoóri's protestations that he is not a Gypsy, and hence the Jewish intellectuals' indignant protestations that they, too, are good Hungarians.

There is a great difference, of course, between what a Gentile Hungarian thinks of his German or Slavic or Turkish ancestry, and how he regards his Jewish neighbors, or how he deals with the possibility of having some Jewish blood himself.

The Holocaust in Textbooks and Literature*

Keen to show the uniqueness of communists as anti-fascist fighters and simultaneously to present class struggle as the main if not only factor determining historical progress, orthodox Stalinist communists acted as if the Holocaust had never happened. Clearly, an ideology that regards ethnic and religious problems as mere cover-ups for class conflict cannot deal adequately with a historical process that had as its goal the extermination of all members of a particular group, whether progressive or reactionary, whether exploiters or part of the exploited. Hence the 1953 official Hungarian history textbook for high school students, which did not contain the word "Jew" in its section on World War II. Hence also the general Stalinist practice to treat such Jewish victims of the Holocaust who happened to be communists or social democrats as "martyrs of the international working class movement" while relegating all other Jewish dead to the general category of "victims of fascism."

It is true, however, that in Hungary, much earlier than in any other communist country, efforts were made to face up to the dilemma of anti-Semitism and Hungarian participation in the Final Solution. While official Hungary still parroted the anti-Zionist/anti-Semitic propaganda line of the Brezhnev period, the same party leadership quietly encouraged an increasingly objective evaluation of the persecution of Jews in World War II. When in the Soviet Union some writers engaged in wild anti-Semitic agitation and made the Zionists, more than the Nazis, responsible for the massacre of the Jews, Hungarian textbooks, although full of omissions, went into great details on Europe's collective guilt about the Holocaust. Simultaneously, such well known writers and poets as György Száraz, János Pilinszky, Tibor Cseres, as well as such filmmakers as András Kovács and Gyula Gazdag, tried to comprehend and to make understandable the incomprehensible tragedy of the Holocaust. In Gyula Gazdag's

---

* I am indebted to Professors Randolph Braham and László Karsai for their ideas and suggestions concerning this section.

"Return to Auschwitz," for instance, the camera follows for two hours a group of elderly Jewish survivors from the Hungarian countryside as they walk through a reconstituted terrain that is both terribly familiar and quite unfamiliar.

As official preoccupation with communist ideology gradually declined, until not even the highest party leaders pretended to be true believers, it became possible to face the truth. By the time communism officially ended, in 1989, no educated person in Hungary could pretend not to have had access to some fairly detailed accounts of the Holocaust, or not to have heard of Hungarian responsibility in the deportation of half a million Jews.

Postcommunist Hungary is governed today by a coalition of center-right parties, which—as has been demonstrated earlier—harbor some radical right-wing elements. Inevitably, the official view of the Holocaust is a mixture of disparate desires and ideologies. Prime Minister József Antall, who died in December 1993, was keen on having both government and nation accepted as parts of the liberal West. Like other political leaders in the industrialized world, Hungary's leaders dutifully participate in official commemorations of the Holocaust, and they unhesitatingly condemn the Nazi atrocities. Prime Minister Antall's father, an official under Regent Horthy, was honored by Yad Vashem as a Righteous Among the Nations; there was no evidence whatsoever of the prime minister himself being an anti-Semite. As for President Árpád Göncz, who is from the left-liberal opposition, he had fought both the Nazis and the communists. Thus genuine humanitarian sentiments, too, must motivate many of these politicians.

There is, however, another side to the coin: a conviction shared by the entire political center-right, that Hungarian participation in and responsibility for the Holocaust has been exaggerated by the country's hostile neighbors, especially Romania, and by the Hungarian left. They feel that much more ought to be done to propagate the fact that, during the war, Admiral Horthy's Hungary harbored 70,000 foreign Jewish refugees as well as the Hungarian Jews. Members of the governing coalition are convinced that both the communist regime of the past and the left-wing opposition of today have deliberately ignored the fact that not only Jews, communists, and liberals, but also other Hungarians suffered during and after the war. Hence this government's insistence to commemorate the hundreds of thousands of Hungarian soldiers and non-Jewish civilians who were killed in the war as well as the hundreds of thousands of Hungarians who languished in the communist prisons and concentration camps. Hence also the governing coalition's attempt to pass in silence over the instances of anti-Jewish atrocities committed by Horthy Hungary and its army well before the German invasion of the country in March 1944.

No doubt, the sufferings of non-Jewish and non-communist Hungarians, for instance that of the Hungarian POW's in Soviet camps, were criminally ignored in the past and the revival of their memory has been long overdue. But things take an ugly turn when radical right-wing elements in the governing coalition claim that the Hungarian soldiers who perished at the Don River in 1942-1943 were more than victims: they were heroes who had given their lives voluntarily in Europe's anti-Bolshevik crusade. Or that Hungary bears no responsibility for the Holocaust because the latter had been perpetrated by the Germans and a handful of their Hungarian hirelings. Or that the sufferings inflicted on the Jews by the Nazis were matched or even surpassed by the sufferings inflicted on Christian Hungarians by Jewish communists. Finally, there exist some "historical revisionists" in Hungary who claim that there never was a Holocaust; that all we have is a historical myth perpetrated by Jews to legitimize their world rule.

In all this, the Hungarian center-right government acts no differently from, let us say, the French conservatives, and it acts certainly better than the Romanian or the Croatian regime. After all, the Romanians still present themselves as total innocents, and the president of Croatia is himself a "historical revisionist." Nor does the Hungarian far-right differ in any way from, let us say, the French or the American far right. In fact, there are proportionally fewer historical revisionists in Hungary than in France or the United States.

Conclusion

How strong is today's anti-Semitism and what are its prospects? The question is nearly impossible to answer, yet I tend to be optimistic. Consider that all polticial parties in the new Hungary have officially denounced anti-Semitism, even the Democratic Forum which, incidentally, expelled the vociferously anti-Semitic writer István Csurka. It is true that Csurka continues to have a large following in his former party, and that his newspaper, the *Magyar Fórum,* is thriving. But other openly anti-Semitic papers have folded. Even more importantly, every public opinion poll shows that Csurka and other extreme rightists are far from being the most popular politicians in Hungary. For instance, the popular approval rating of the main targets of their attack, the very liberal, non-Jewish President of the Republic, Árpád Göncz, and the President of the Free Democrats Iván Pető, who is of Jewish origin, ranges in the 70 and 80 percentiles; those of Csurka and other far-rightists are at the bottom, in the teens. It might well be that Csoóri, Csurka, and others are misjudging the mood of the public. They fail to realize that most Hungarians are preoccupied with other things and are rather in-different to the Jewish issue. Nor do most people care about the rightist slogan that "the media are under the control of the enemy." It might also well be that the intellectuals, once considered the unofficial leaders of the nation, will soon see their concerns increasingly ignored by a consumption-oriented public.

Hungarians as a whole feel a strong desire to join the democratic and free market-oriented West. This might mean that openly voiced anti-Semitism will remain the pastime of a few intellectuals and skinheads, and that political anti-Semitism has no future in Hungary. There is the danger, however, of a growing conflict with neighboring Romania, Slovakia, and Serbia over the vast Hungarian minorities in those countries. If the Serbian, Romanian, and Slovak authorities continue to harass the Hungarians, or turn harassment into genuine oppression, then it is just conceivable that the populist-nationalist faction could make more headway. Xenophobia and anti-Westernism could then become truly acute problems.

Jews form a smaller minority than Gypsies and Germans in today's Hungary, and their number is steadily diminishing because of intermarriage and emigration. Their problem is, therefore, not–or not only–anti-Semitism, but how to preserve the legacy of the historic Hungarian Jewish community. The answer to the dilemma on the part of a handful of Jewish intellectuals has been to form a Jewish nationalist party and to request the recognition of Jews as a separate nationality. This attempt was, however, rejected by most other Hungarian Jews. To complicate matters further, a number of young Hungarian Jews are showing signs of pride and interest in their identity; this, without being Jewish nationalists.

In all likelihood more Jews will leave Hungary in the near future, in large part for economic reasons. Those who stay behind, and thousands will stay, will continue the process of integration. Barring an unlikely catastrophe such as the collapse of the Hungarian economy or armed conflict with a neighboring country, this integration will be successful. The end result will be the disappearance of the Jewish minority from Hungary, just as Jews have disappeared from most other East European countries.

A hundred years ago, Eastern Europe was a colorful mosaic of many cultures. This great age has now come to an end through decades of war, expulsion, deportation, mass murder, and forced assimilation. It is a great tragedy, but just as the rain forests, once annihilated, can never be replanted, so the multiethnic and multicultural existence of Eastern Europe cannot be reconstituted. It is a sad reality that must be faced.

NOTES

1. "Nappali hold" (Daytime Noon), *Hitel* (Credit) Budapest, no. 18 (September 5, 1990), pp. 4-7.

Anti-Semitism and Jewish Identity in Postcommunist Hungary

András Kovács

Nearly all over the world, public opinion at first received the news about the downfall of the communist systems in Eastern Europe with a happiness verging on euphoria. Many seemed to have forgotten the German example: a long time has to pass after the introduction of the institutions of parliamentary democracy before the political culture of a society can rise to the requirements of the new democratic system of political institutions. The question in Eastern Europe today is whether there will be enough time to follow through with this development process. "The wounds inflicted by World War II were bandaged with the dirty rags of communism after the war," Gabriel Becker, a commentator of the most recent developments in Eastern Europe has said recently, and today, after pulling off the rags, the suppurating wounds are bursting open one after another as septic national conflicts, social animosities, and ethnic hatred erupt in almost every country of the fallen communist camp.

Although Hungary belongs to the quieter regions of the one-time empire, since the abolition of the old system some alarming phenomena, such as anti-Semitic manifestations, occurred more and more frequently. It is difficult to decide whether anti-Semitism has become stronger in Hungary since the abolition of the old system or whether emotions, attitudes, and opinions that already existed earlier are now being expressed more openly. Whichever may be the case, we must raise a question of special

125

importance for Hungary, the country of Central-Eastern Europe where the greatest number of Jews, and the Jews who–even in their own judgment–are the most integrated, live: there is a danger of a turn of events similar to what Hungarian Jewry had to experience once before, after World War I. As Ezra Mendelsohn put it, Hungary was a singular example of "how a country previously 'good for Jews' is transformed almost overnight into a country wrecked with pogroms and permeated with anti-Semitic hysteria."[1]

Some of the manifestations of anti-Semitism in Hungary today are no different from the phenomena which have become more frequent in the past years even in the Western world. Impoverishment, unemployment menacingly growing among young people, and the disappearance of certain prohibitions and taboos in society have brought to the surface unarticulated forms of racism, and within it anti-Semitism, that exist on football grounds and in subways, and the function of which is an aggressive compensation for social frustrations. Yet another variant of anti-Semitism has also been manifested openly recently. This anti-Semitism serves as a tool enabling certain professional groups to differentiate their identity from that of other competing groups. While earlier in certain professions career lobbies in competition with one another used to legitimize their informal organization by declaring that it was all merely a defense against "the Jews loyal to one another," today the organizations of such professional career groups are beginning to become formal and institutional. The first manifestation of this was the establishment of a separate corporation of Christian doctors, which caused a great upheaval, and the efforts to form an association of Christian teachers.

The manifestation of various forms of anti-Semitism in Hungary after the fall of communism bears witness to the unquestionable existence of an anti-Semitic potential. However, what happened after World War I could only happen again in Hungary if this anti-Semitic potential were combined with a political ideology elevating anti-Semitism to a political program. Anti-Semitism has indeed appeared in Hungary after the abolition of communism, and it has appeared in the well-known disguise of the self-protection of the nation. So far, however, this anti-Semitism has only functioned among the cultural and political elite as a symbolic tool for establishing a political identity, and not as an ideology directing political action. Nevertheless the fact that it has surfaced openly has brought along remarkable changes, among other things, in the self-image of their social status held by the assimilated Jews represented in significant numbers among the country's intellectuals.

The national ideology that provides a conceptual framework for anti-Semitism, which also appears in a political context in Hungary today, dates back to the nineteenth century. In the second half of the nineteenth century the relationship between the liberal Hungarian nobility and the Jewish middle class had reached the stage of what may be called a social contract of assimilation.[2] This unwritten contract meant that the liberal nobility supported the Jewish middle class in carrying out the modernization of Hungary, which the nobles themselves were unable to achieve. The nobility protected the Jews from the anti-Semitic efforts directed against emancipation, but at the same time considered political power its own monopoly. The more the economic positions of the Jewish middle classes improved, the faster their social mobility and assimilation process became, the greater importance was given to the concept of nation, one of the functions of which was to guarantee that even if the economic power of the middle classes of Jewish origin grew they could not demand a greater political role.

In the age of nationalism, only a person who was considered the legitimate representative of the nation had any chance of becoming part of the political elite. Thus the guarantee for the political hegemony of the Hungarian historical classes was that, in spite of their best efforts and actually achieved assimilation, the middle classes of Jewish origin could never be considered Hungarian but would always remain aliens.[3] One of the means of accomplishing this objective was the anti-modernist ideology which declared capitalism, Western-type liberal political structures, and the social and cultural consequences of modernization such as urbanization or the formation of an urban mass culture, alien to the Hungarian tradition, mentality, and mind. According to this ideology modernization, which began in the nineteenth century in Hungary, is not the integral result of Hungarian development but has been imported by aliens, first of all Jews, and in the long run serves their interests exclusively. Assimilation, on the other hand, is considered to be merely superficial and/or pretended, with the Jews putting on a Hungarian disguise simply in order to gain more opportunities to force back the Hungarian historical classes. Real assimilation is held to be actually impossible as it could only happen if Jews could take on the Hungarian national character, "Hungarian mentality," which "aliens" are unable to do. After World War I, this anti-Semitism based on the ethnic concept of nation was no longer directed against Galician immigrants wearing caftans and being reluctant to become assimilated–the focus of the assimilational and cultural nationalistic rhetoric during the Dualist Era (1867-1918)–but against the middle-class "cosmopolitan" Jewish citizens who appeared to have become assimilated and found their place in society. With their pretense to have been assimilated, went the anti-Semitic rhetoric after World War I, they diluted and, unnoticed by others, damaged the once unified national character from the inside, and by emaciating the deep roots of the nation brought about its slow devastation. The anti-Semitism that has appeared as an articulated ideology after the downfall of communism revives this anti-modernist tradition based on an ethnocentric concept of nation.

After the fall of the communist system and the first elections some of the leading ideologists of the Magyar Demokrata Fórum (Hungarian Democratic Forum), the largest government party, first rejected the concept of Western-type capitalism on principle because, they claimed, it was inconsistent with Hungarian historical traditions and unsuitable for providing answers to the Hungarians' "vital questions." Therefore they suggested that Hungary should choose a "third way" somewhere between capitalism and communism. Later a somewhat modified version of the anti-liberal argument appeared, in which it is usually referred to as national liberalism–the obvious adjective being added to imply a difference from "anti-national" liberalism. According to this theory Hungarian society is not mature enough to successfully adapt to the conditions of well-developed capitalism, so that adopting the economic, social, and political institutions of the West would only serve the interests of a minority, specifically of the minority which can best advance its own interests under conditions alien to the natural Hungarian development. Which minority is being referred to its made crystal clear by the train of thought described above. The argument has been concluded in various ways. Some, recalling the visions of László Németh, a writer and a prominent representative of cultural anti-Semitism between the two world wars, say that Hungarians will become "natives" in their own country; others, for example, Sándor Csoóri, the leading ideologist of today's populists, are already raving about a danger threatening the "substance" of Hungarianness. "The intellectual and spiritual amalgamation [of Jews and Hungarians] has ceased to exist after the communist revolution of 1919, the Horthy period and especially after the Holocaust....What we are facing today is an attempt by Jewry at a kind of reverse assimilation: we observe an effort by liberal Hungarian Jews to 'assimilate' Magyardom to its own tastes, both in style and in mentality. For this very purpose, Jews have now become free to scaffold a parliamentary springboard of a kind they never had been able to scaffold in the past."[4]

The revival of an anti-modernist ethnocentric national ideology accompanying open or hidden anti-Semitism, as well as the looming of political anti-Semitism, have brought about some changes in the thinking of some of the Jews in Hungary who are traditionally pro-assimilation. This is because this ideology is directed specifically against assimilated Jews since, considering it to be in fact impossible, it questions assimilation as a social achievement, and also disputes the status acquired by assimilated Jews during the process of assimilation, their self-qualification as Hungarian entrepreneurs or members of the Hungarian middle class or Hungarian intellectuals. In the few decades after World War II the majority of the Jews who had already walked down the road toward assimilation suddenly realized that their stigmatization was not the result of a perceived lack of assimilation. For the people affected, the stigma was the basis of a "negative" identity: they believed that it was only anti-Semitism that made them Jewish. And they realized, too, that, they could only have very little influence on shaping the ideology defining the norms of assimilation. Therefore, in order to avoid social discrimination, they chose a form of behavior (partly inherited from their parents) which Erving Goffman calls stigma management.[5] After the fall of communism, a new change occurred with the more open manifestation of anti-Semitism. Since then the forming of a positive identity has become a stronger process even in the assimilated layers of Hungarian Jewry, as I shall analyze below.

Stigma management is a general phenomenon in society. There are two basic types of this behavior. If the stigmatizing feature is (so far) unknown to the community, the individual may try to conceal his stigma by manipulating the information carrying this feature. If the stigmatizing feature is known, he may use means during the formation of interaction situations that could minimalize the unpleasant consequences of his stigmatized situation. Both forms of behavior are completely characteristic of the group of Hungarian Jews we have examined.

One of the well-known techniques of information control is "passing." Its two basic forms are the manipulation of the symbols that make it easy to identify the person as a Jew, and the concealment of the "discrediting " facts in the family and life history. In the families of the 117 persons we interviewed, both techniques were widely used. Only 43 of our interviewees found it natural to display their Jewishness naturally, completely independent of the circumstances. Another 20 were experimenting with the technique of total passing, while 46 carefully evaluated the situation first and then, depending on the circumstances, decided whether they would reveal their Jewishness. In the generation of the parents, 63 families tried to cover up their Jewishness as much as possible, and they also tried to convince their children to follow their example. In the complete sample, 40 families were found who refrained from following any such strategies after 1945, while 19 families chose an extremely dissimulant behavior.

A well-documented manifestation of the strategy of passing and information control is the attempt to get rid of the symbols suitable for the person's identification as a Jew. Only 36 of the interviewed families did not change their Jewish-sounding family names and replace it with a Hungarian one. In 25 families the changing of the family name occurred after World War II, while in four families the interviewee himself "Hungarianized" his family name.

Information control through identification symbols is well illustrated by the next example: "...I always wear this necklace with the Star of David around my neck. It is very important for me, a very good feeling. When I go swimming, I take it off in the swimming pool, but as soon as I've come out and have taken a shower I put it back on...I don't really feel like showing it off at the place where I work because one must not display it ostentatiously...I keep telling my child that it is not a shame but one needn't show it off. It is not something one should brag about. It's a fact."[6]

Since our interviews concentrated on family histories, it is obvious that we were able to pinpoint the ambition for conscious information control most often in the accounts about family and personal histories. Thirty-one interviewees found out from strangers and not their relatives or members of their families that they were Jews or deduced the fact from certain indications. It is not surprising that 56 interviewees had no information whatsoever about the pre-war history of their families; another 42 know only very little about the previous generation. The first confrontation with Jewishness was a stigmatizing experience for 47 interviewees; the content of the identity of 54 subjects is innately stigmatic, full of feelings of persecution, defenselessness, and fear. Considering all this it may sound strange that 40 of our interviewees wished to follow their parents' strategies, nine did not wish to tell their children that they were of Jewish origin, and 31 would only do so if the situation made it unavoidable or necessary.

One can observe two main types of information control related to family and individual life histories in our interviews. In the first case, the parents followed a strategy of complete passing; after the secret was revealed, the interviewee himself or herself set up the rules for stigma management. In the second case, the parents made the child conscious of his stigmatized situation, and at the same time they passed on to him/her various forms of stigma management behavior. In the latter case, passing behavior was pursued consciously from the very beginning and parents did not have to use the same strategies with their children as with the outside world. In the former case, however, they were forced to do so and thus the revelation of the secret was a great shock for the children, and often led to the disintegration of the parental family. One of our interviewees described this case as follows: "...there was a Jewish church close to our place....We never went in there. Once I wanted to go in that particular place because I was told it was a Jewish church, but my mother was very reluctant to come in with me. I thought she was ashamed, or she was afraid she would get into trouble...that was the first time I sensed something strange. First I thought it was because she was a party member...but it was much easier to get into any other church. We could go into another church not far from this Jewish one without any problems and she showed me around....When I was ten...I asked my parents what religion I was....My father gave me an impossible answer, which he thought was very witty, that I should say I did not belong to any denomination. That was the time when I first had this hunch that something fishy was going on, but I didn't know, I didn't understand what it was."[7] The conscious instruction to children about passing can be well illustrated by two other stories: "...When I found out I was Jewish, I felt that the word was not very nice but since they informed me about it in such a normal way when I was six years old, I accepted it. And I did spread the news, or rather told other people about it, until about the age of

10. When my parents learned about it, my mother scolded me terribly, saying that I shouldn't dare to tell this to anyone. Did I want to be called "a stinking Jew?" And that was the time, I was about ten when I realized that it was something wrong, that it meant trouble. That was when I first heard that if I talked about it I would lay my family open to attacks."[8] Although learning the technique of passing is a stigmatic experience, as this interview reveals, another interviewee who is still more or less attached to tradition, i.e., celebrates only Jewish holidays, said the following: "...my daughter came home and said, 'Daddy, I'm in trouble.' She was supposed to write an essay on Christmas. Well, I said, it's a problem, because we hadn't discussed it. One is forced to tell lies....I said: 'Wait, I'll help you.' And I said this and that. And then I said: Why don't you say at the end that we lit the candles and the whole tree burnt down. It did happen to one of my colleagues....' So my daughter told a true story. We did not lie so terribly....So if it is not absolutely necessary one should not talk about it."[9]

In establishing their own information control strategy, the people we interviewed were helped by the division of social and individual spheres into different "areas." According to relevant sociological investigations, the social world can be divided into "forbidden," "civil," and "back" places. The first one is closed to the stigmatized individual. His stigma stops him completely from fulfilling the norms prevalent in such an environment, and if his secret is revealed he will face expulsion. In the second sphere he encounters the same requirements and reception as anybody else, while in the third sphere he will be among people of his own kind. The behavior of the individual will obviously be determined by the information available about him in the various social spheres. He will behave differently if people know him, if he might be recognized, or if he has a chance to retain his anonymity. The amount of knowledge involved and the chance of being identified will decide what kind of information he will reveal and what he will keep a secret about himself.

Interaction in the forbidden social spheres is risky for the individual even if his stigma is hidden for the moment. It might get revealed–and thus his behavior will mostly be determined by this risk. "I met a woman I found very pretty. She worked at the university as a laboratory assistant....Then I began courting her as usual....The whole thing was very sedate. She wanted to get married, it was fair enough....So let's go visit her father, and she would introduce me....But I suddenly felt there was something wrong and I would end up in a clergyman's home. She never said a word about her parents' profession...but somehow I had an overall picture....Her whole behavior indicated that she grew up in a seriously religious environment....And so it was....We arrived in a vicarage in a village in the middle of nowhere....I immediately broke up with her after that....How shall I put it, they didn't know that I was Jewish, we never talked about it....But I presume...that if they had found out later, they would have broken up with me....I wanted to prevent that....I wouldn't think that a Calvinist minister would have her daughter marry a Jew....I think I did the right thing."[10] If, however, the danger of getting exposed is completely nonexistent, appearing in the forbidden social sphere is the most effective form of passing. 'Until the age of 22 I was always convinced that nobody must find out about my Jewishness and did my best to keep it a secret....I did things, for example...when we were coming home from secondary school, I was in the first year, with two of my friends. We went to Pasaréti Square by bus and got off....There is a Catholic Church in Pasaréti Square and I just walked in for them to see what a serious Catholic I was."[11]

In civil places, as in the work place, the main method of information control is to check the given situation and adapt to it. "I have never had any problems [concerning the fact that I am Jewish] at the place where I work. The truth is that it is very difficult to talk about such topics with me because I cut them off immediately....If I happened to hear sentences I didn't like I immediately left, I didn't get into the ring....And when I heard sentences beginning with 'We Jews'..., I also walked away because it wasn't a topic I could go on and on about....[Whenever I met with anti-Semitic feelings] if I thought the person had common sense and it was worth talking to him I waited until the end of his speech and act and then I said: 'I'm a Jew, you see...,' and then I walked out on him."[12] This behavior, the preventive declaration of one's Jewish origin, is a widespread form of situation control. It is used regularly in civil places by 18 of our interviewees.

The creation of sheltered or back areas, as well as the acquisition of behavioral regulations required at certain places, have been part of the socialization process in the families we have examined. "Friday evenings we wear our caps. Both my father and I....The doorbell rang while we were having dinner. The co-tenant or neighbor came in. She was not Jewish but she knew that we were. We immediately snatched the cap off. My father shouted: 'Ila?' – 'Yes,'...so we took them off. I took it off and my father took off his hat....We are Jewish but we don't show it. We don't deny it but we don't talk about it."[13] The most common examples of this duality of behavior depending on the social sphere are the strategies followed at the time of Christian holidays, especially at Christmas. Among our interviewees, 50 reported that their families celebrated Christmas in the interviewee's childhood, while 40 families did not. One quarter of the interviewees who grew up in the latter families stated that this caused a serious conflict for them. In reply to the question of why Christmas was not celebrated, only a few were given an atheist explanation in compliance with the spirit of the 1950s since, strange as it may seem, most communist families did celebrate it. This casts a new light on the well-known connection between communist conviction and assimilation. The majority, as in the case described above, was either given help by their parents in establishing passing behavior to lessen the conflict, or formed behavioral rules themselves. "...I was also ashamed of the fact that we did not celebrate Christmas....They found out about it soon enough at school because in the first grade children are usually asked after the winter holidays what presents they got from Father Christmas...I too had to stand up and was asked what I had got; then on the spot I made up a story about how my birthday was in January so I always received my Christmas presents in January together with my birthday presents. Everybody stared at me thinking what a fool I was, how I could say such a thing, so the following year I made up an even greater lie about all the presents I had received."[14] One of our interviewees related a strange way of relieving the tension created by regular lying within the family: "Someone brought an air gun for us at Christmas time and then we hung all the Christmas decorations in front of a large cardboard box and shot at them one by one. It was strange because we had never been given any toy weapons before, so such a gift was quite unusual. Neither did I understand why my father allowed us to shoot at Christmas decorations. It was also very strange because Christmas for me had been an important sacred holiday, and then suddenly it was completely denounced or shot into pieces, and from the following year on we never had a Christmas tree any more....The ideology was that we wouldn't spend so much money on such ugly Christmas decorations....And three days later they took the gun away from us saying that we didn't need such a stupid present. It was at that time that I first heard about being a Jew."[15]

We could enumerate a great number of other examples of the various forms of passing behavior. In general, we can say that in the context we have examined stigmatized behavior has become part of the socialization process. First the stigmatized person learns the "normal" point of view; he accepts and becomes conscious of his being different. Then he acquires the technique of tackling the way the environment treats the people belonging to his group. During this process, he masters the various forms of passing behavior, that is he arrives at the realization that not everybody knows what he knows about himself and that therefore he has the opportunity to change or adjust his social identity. For this the identification of social spheres, the estimation of the information available for others about him, and the establishment of various forms of information control and situation management behavior are necessary.

An important consequence of the socialization of stigma-managing behavior is the fact that during interaction this behavior may become the means of external identification of the group as well as the internal identification of the individual within the group. This applies to the group of Hungarian Jews we have examined. "When I was a child I did not have a so called 'Jewish problem'. Even when I went out to work...but sooner or later I was made to feel that they knew I was Jewish. It is very interesting because you cannot tell by the look of me....Still, somehow they had found out....I can't image how."[16] But similar identification mechanisms function on the other side as well. Several of our interviewees told us how, at school, they spontaneously chose their friends from among the Jews even though they never talked about Jewishness or many times didn't even know that they were Jews themselves. One of the individuals interviewed explained the way the members of the group could identify one another, saying that "there are certain internal, emotional matters which, I do not want to say that a Jew can understand better than a non-Jew, but generally some of the Jews have a possibly more sophisticated and more sensitive receiver...maybe they have a metacommunicational ability so that they do not need to actually say all the things....According to my experiences more Jews have sensors for this than non-Jews. [These things are independent of common experiences and topics], these are emotional things, like what I feel and what I don't feel, how I react, or whether my partner can guess how I will react, such things."[17]

Passing behavior has a high psychological price. Social identity built on information control can collapse at any moment, double loyalty may generate problems, and the conscious formation and execution of spontaneous, algorythmical behavioral patterns characteristic of the "normal" group may absorb great quantities of psychic energy. Of course the individual does not have to carry these burdens in back places. Such areas, however, do not in themselves create a positive identity. The groups bound together by a common stigma are always burdened by tension. An example: "I have begun going to Purim and Chanuka recently. [Because your friends go too?] Yes, but they are not real friends....I considered it important to be there but I never felt really comfortable....[I thought it important] that I should, after all, belong somewhere. But I never felt that I belonged there. I do feel something pleasant, because I don't feel like an outsider the way I feel at a Christian holiday. In this respect it is very reassuring. Well, perhaps the fact that I have nothing to fear when I enter since I am Jewish myself. That I don't have to worry because I'm not a Jew, because I am. So I don't worry but I feel bored. Or I don't take it really seriously."[18]

This "negative identity" also involves anxiety or, at times, even a stigmatizing alienation from a tolerant environment. "Not long ago we sent our child to France on an exchange visit. We received some news about how everybody prayed there and went to church and that it was very embarrassing for our son. It was only there that he realized that it was a Catholic Boy Scout camp. There he did his utmost to be assimilated but, for example, he was warned not to eat the wafer because he was Jewish. Not in an anti-Semitic way but in his own interest. It was even explained to him that he couldn't do so because of his own religion, not because of the others. It was an incredible trauma, more so for me perhaps than for him....So it is not enough that we are Jewish, we don't even know who we are. That is the greatest problem...because we want to belong without taking on the belief. We do not want to practice religion itself but we still want to belong....A Catholic religious person goes to church, if he is not religious he doesn't belong there....He does not have any problems with that....[In our case] it is incredibly difficult, we are Negroes without the color."[19]

At the time when the system was changed in Hungary, efforts for establishing a positive Jewish identity grew more intensive. In the middle of the 1980s only seven of the 117 people we had interviewed maintained Jewish traditions and 22 were "looking for their roots" and had begun to deal with Jewish history, culture, and religious history in one form or another. To all appearances, many of the members of the "second generation" we have interviewed and especially their children, the representatives of the "third generation," are about to break free of the vise of an identity created by a stigma. Obviously an important role is played in all this by the fact that, under the new circumstances, political obstacles hindering the manifestation of various specific identities have disappeared. But, on the other hand, the main reason for the change is the reappearance of anti-Semitism in political and cultural discourse. Today people who conceive their Jewish identity only through the challenges of the outside world are more frequently obliged to feel Jewish. Thus today stigma management and information control requires much more effort and constitutes a heavier burden than before; at the same time, the desire for the establishment of other, positive identities has grown accordingly.

But what is the content of this new identity? Some people consider returning to Jewish religious tradition the only possible solution, while others strive to form a national or minority identity. A substantial group of the majority looking for a positive identity, however, define ethnicity as the positive content of their identity.

Indeed, interpreting ethnicity as a modern phenomenon is based on the observation of situations like that in which the Jews in Hungary found themselves during the last century. If a historical situation in which different ethnic groups occupy competitive positions is established, it is in the interest of a dominant ethnic group to define the value system describing "normalcy" in such a way that the rivaling group should end up in an inferior status. This is what happened in Hungary when the Jews would have been accepted as Hungarians only on ideologically defined conditions that were impossible to meet. In their turn, the people who are discriminated against must try to achieve a new definition of norms if they do not want to get stuck in a stigmatized role. Their greatest chance to accomplish this comes if they act as a group. This is what makes ethnicity an effective organizational principle. Thus the ethnic group is the political organization of a special-interest group in the society, the cohesion of which is provided by the emotions based on the ethnic identity of the group members.[20]

Establishing an ethnic identity in the case of assimilated groups is not an easy task. In many cases, if the group is no longer separated from other groups in its environment by tradition, new, clearly distinguishing identificational markers need to be found to create ethnic identity. This is true because ethnic identity is not an automatic product of the existing differences between groups but the result of a mobilization of the differences or, if the original group markers have already faded, their replacement by symbols. Consequently, a group with a specific ethnic identity is separated from other groups by the boundary between them and not necessarily by what the boundary encloses. Differentiation between the boundary and what it encloses is essential. The gradual diminution over time of (ethnic) habits, preferences, and practices is likely, but the sense of ethnic identity or ethnic self-definition may be determined or reawakened by a totally different set of factors.[21]

There is no telling today what elements the group of Hungarian Jews trying to establish an ethnic identity will use to create the boundaries establishing identity. There are many possibilities for drawing the boundary lines: the peculiar history of the Hungarian Jews, the awareness of a common fate, the memory of persecution, the special socializing mechanisms observed in Jewish families, typical life strategies or cultural preferences, the emphatically symbolical manifestation of the Jews' particular relationship with the Jewish state, or perhaps the creation of brand-new identity symbols.

Serious sociological research will be necessary to find an answer to the question of how the establishment of a Jewish identity will influence the tendency of the "social distance" between the Jews and other groups of society. However, it is quite probable that it will no longer be possible to apply the historical notion of assimilation in the course of this research. The demand for the establishment of ethnic identity was created by problems that could no longer be dealt with within the existing conceptual system of assimilation-dissimilation. The function of ethnic identity is not the changing of the status acquired during the assimilation process or the initiation or reinforcement of new stratification processes, but rather the establishment of a new norm consensus, a new type of integration. It is beyond any doubt that the establishment of various types of identities can have a modernizing effect on Hungarian society, provided one can make society accept an inclusive national consciousness having the acceptance of cultural diversity as an integral part.

NOTES

1. E. Mendelsohn, *The Jews of East Central Europe Between the World Wars* (Bloomington, IN: Indiana University Press, 1983), p. 98.

2. Viktor Karády, "A zsidóság polgárosodásának és modernizációjának főbb tényezői a magyar társadalomtörténetben" (The Main Factors of Jewry's Bourgeois Development and Modernization in Hungarian Social History) in *A zsidókérdésről* (About the Jewish Question), eds. Balázs Füzfa and Gábor Szabó (Szombathely: Németh László Szakkollégium, 1989), pp. 95-137.

3. Miklós Szabó, *A nemzetfogalom változása és a magyar társadalom modernizációja* (The Changing of the Concept of Nation and the Modernization of Hungarian Society) (Budapest, 1987), pp. 21-22. Manuscript.

4. Sándor Csoóri, "Nappali hold" (Daytime Moon). *Hitel* (Credit), Budapest, no. 18, 1990, p. 6.

5. E. Goffmann, *Stigma* (New York: Penguin Books, 1968).

6. Interview 69, 29.

7. Interview 25, 18-19.

8. Interview 29, 47.

9. Interview 82, 33.

10. Interview 47, 90.

11. Interview 43, 123.

12. Interview 68, 82.

13. Interview 60, 68-69.

14. Interview 31.

15. Interview 25, 54.

16. Interview 69, 24.

17. Interview 75, 99-100.

18. Interview 29, 106.

19. Interview 93, 27.

20. N. Glazer and D. P. Moynihan, eds. *Ethnicity* (Cambridge, MA: Harvard University Press, 1975), pp. 1-29.

21. Chun Ki-Taek, "Ethnicity and Ethnic Identity: Taming the Untamed" in *Studies in Social Identity*, eds. Th. R. Sarbin and E. Scheibe (New York: Praeger, 1983), pp. 184-204.

Anti-Semitism and the Treatment of the Holocaust in Postcommunist Poland

Abraham Brumberg

Polish anti-Semitism, or perhaps more accurately anti-Semitism in Poland, is contentious, and arouses different reactions from different people. For most Jews, anti-Semitism is an illness that has afflicted Poland for generations–an illness at once tenacious, impervious to change, and unrelated to the actual presence of Jews in the country (hence the term "anti-Semitism without Jews"). For many if not most Poles, the term "Polish anti-Semitism" is like a call to arms, at worst a vile slur on the Polish people, or at best an absurd exaggeration. Many Americans with no Polish, Jewish, or generally East European backgrounds are simply baffled by the attention paid to anti-Semitism in a country which, whatever its past treatment of Jews, can hardly be expected to be rife with prejudice against a people that has virtually disappeared from its midst–I am referring again, of course, to the notion of "anti-Semitism without Jews."

Anyway, why single out Poland? What about the resurgence of anti-Jewish violence in Germany, the openly anti-Semitic articles in the Hungarian press, the defacement of Jewish cemeteries in France or for that matter the persistent anti-Jewish sentiments in segments of the black community in the United States?

It would clearly be impossible, in a brief essay, to do justice to so complex a subject, and so I propose to do something more simple–namely, to list a few of the most troubling questions or persistent notions about Jews and anti-Semitism in Poland, and to examine to what extent they are valid, or not–and why.

My questions fall into two categories: first, the general perception of anti-Semitism in Poland, and second, what actually is the character of anti-Jewish views and feelings in that country and what explains it.

Question one: Has Poland been a country in which hatred and persecution of Jews have reigned since time immemorial, or perhaps more concretely since Jews first came to that country ten centuries ago? This charge is voiced most prominently by Jews who themselves hail from Poland or by their descendants in Europe and America who have been brought up on painful memories of anti-Semitic hatreds in that part of the world.

The answer to this question is "no." It may perhaps come as a surprise to some to learn that by the late fifteenth century, and certainly during most of the two subsequent centuries, the so-called Polish Commonwealth or Polish-Lithuanian Commonwealth was a land of remarkable religious tolerance, and that Jews benefited from this tolerance by setting up their own autonomous administrative, cultural, religious, and legal institutions and indeed frequently siding with the Poles in their wars against predatory neighbors to the east and the south.

To be sure, many Poles, in indignantly rejecting *any* imputation of anti-Semitism, point to the Polish tradition of tolerance and freedom as if that tradition continued uninterrupted over the centuries. It did not. Anti-Jewish persecution was already rife by the middle of the seventeenth century, during the time of the Polish counter-reformation, stoked and spread principally by the Jesuits. By the eighteenth century it became, as it were, a firm part of the Polish political and cultural landscape, in the form of economic discrimination and religious hatred. At the end of the eighteenth century, after Poland ceased to exist as an independent state (it was partitioned three times in succession by its powerful neighbors–Russia, Prussia, and Austria), the rise of nationalism among Poles, the sense that Poland has been victimized by History, often took on a venomous anti-Jewish and generally xenophobic character.

Scapegoats are necessary in such turbulent times, and the Jews, with the mark of "Christ-killer" on their faces, and their suspicious religious rites, their incomprehensible language and bizarre ways, fitted this role admirably. It is also true that even under optimal conditions Jews had to cope with hatred and bigotry, with economic envy and dark insinuations about their religious practices. Still and all, the sweeping generalization that Poland has been a land of unremitting anti-Semitism simply does not stand up to scrutiny.

Second question: Has Poland had a worse record in dealing with its national and/or religious minorities than other countries in that part of the world? This is a relevant query given the fact that Poland has always been a multi-ethnic country, in which non-Polish minorities–Ukrainians, Belorussians, Germans, Czechs, Slovaks, Lithuanians and Jews–often constituted about a third of the total population, as they did after World War II. During the interwar period, the Jews alone comprised about 10 percent of the country's population. During the days of the Commonwealth in the sixteenth and seventeenth centuries, non-Polish groups amounted to more than half of the population.

Other countries in Eastern Europe–one need only mention the Austro-Hungarian Empire–have also been multinational rather than what is called nation states. Some have given their minorities extensive rights, some hardly any; in some countries the attitude of the dominant group toward the smaller ones was one of unbridled hostility, in others far less so. How did the Poles fit into this picture?

This question has recently come to preoccupy–oddly or perhaps not so oddly enough–many people in Poland. Polish writers, sociologists, and historians, aware of the history of ethnic and religious animosities in their country, have asked themselves whether the Poles have had a particularly baneful record in this area, or whether there is a distinctive Polish tradition of intolerance and xenophobia. And some have concluded that Poles have indeed excelled in their hatred for other peoples, many of them neighbors for over hundreds of years.

There is no basis in fact for such a conclusion. The slaughter of nearly six million Jews during the Second World War, in which to be sure people from several nationalities took part but which was beyond and above all conceived, put into action, and pursued by the Nazi Germans with near-maniacal passion, should be enough to disabuse us of the idea that Poles are more guilty than others. The carnage of the 1990s in former Yugoslavia, where thousands of Serbs, Croats, and Bosnian Muslims have been slaughtered, is surely infinitely worse than anything Poles have ever committed against the Jews or any other minorities.

But even if Poles have been by no means the worst offenders–and this is the next question–haven't they been more brutal in dealing with the Jews than with other minorities within their midst? This question is a bit more difficult to answer. It can justifiably be argued, for instance–and this is something that many Jews seem to be unaware of or tend to dismiss–that the four million Ukrainians in post-World War I Poland were treated far more shabbily than the Jews. The Polish government's pledge to the Western Allies in 1923 to grant the Ukrainians political and cultural autonomy was violated as soon as it was formally proffered and accepted. Within a year the Polish government banned the use of Ukrainian from government offices, barred Ukrainians from attending the University of Lvov, refused to make good on its promise to erect a special Ukrainian university, and closed down hundreds of Ukrainian schools. In addition, Ukrainians were excluded from most government jobs.

The result was as could be expected: Ukrainians, i.e., Galician Ukrainians, who had enjoyed considerable freedoms under the Austro-Hungarian regime, turned more fiercely against the Poles: some joined legal Ukrainian parties, and some flocked to underground guerilla movements. The government's response was to launch the so-called "pacification" drive, which resulted in the burning down of whole Ukrainian villages, wholesale arrests, and deportations.

During the interwar years relations between the two peoples were strained, with the bulk of Polish public opinion even refusing to acknowledge that Ukrainians were a separate nation. For about two years after the end of the war pitched battles continued to be waged between the Polish army and the Ukrainian guerrillas, the latter still bent on achieving full independence. And so the Poles once again applied the policy of collective guilt and punishment: hundreds of thousands of Ukrainians were deported from their towns and villages, some of them to the Soviet Union, some to the newly occupied "Western territories" in Poland that had previously been part of Germany–Silesia, Pomerania, East Prussia.

Under communist rule the Warsaw government curtailed Ukrainian cultural activities, and placed the few extant Ukrainian organizations under the control of the security police, thus in effect continuing the old pre-war Polish policy of "polonization." There are still about four to five hundred thousand Ukrainians in Poland, and all have been subjected to abuse and discrimination until the downfall of the communist government.

The situation with the German minority has not been much different. With all the territorial changes, about 400,000 Germans remained in postwar Poland. Most of them were not only denied any cultural facilities, such as schools: the Polish government simply maintained, much as in the case of the Ukrainians, that they were not Germans, but "Germanized Poles." And for anyone with a knowledge of the virulence of Catholic anti-Semitism in Poland, it is instructive to know that the Church until recently and under the leadership of Primate Joseph Glemp, also firmly maintained that there were no Germans in Poland, and would not allow them to celebrate mass in their own language.

Finally the last in this cluster of questions: Has Polish anti-Semitism been worse than anti-Semitism in other countries? I have already dealt with this matter under the rubric of whether the Poles have been more vicious toward the Jews than toward other groups by calling attention to the role of Nazi Germany in the Holocaust. I must confess that in general I don't very much like the "comparative angle," whether it's in the form of who was more beastly than who or who suffered more than the other–what I would call "comparative victimology."

Still, since the charge has so often been levelled against the Poles, I think it's worthwhile to mention a few other cases in addition to that of the Germans. Scholars who have studied the behavior of the Lithuanian population have concluded that no people participated more energetically in the extermination of their "local" Jews during World War II than the Lithuanians. It was to a very large extent the latter, rather than the German SS, who slaughtered about 95 percent of all Lithuanian Jews. Why this barbarism on the part of a people never known for its extreme anti-Semitism is another matter: for our purposes it is enough to note that this was so.

The Ukrainian example runs a close second. History knows many cases when victims turn into oppressors, or when they are at one at the same time both victims and perpetrators of monstrous injustices.

Be it as it may, Professor Aharon Weiss of Yad Vashem, an authority on the Holocaust in Ukraine, estimates that only 17,000 out of 820,000 Jews survived in western Ukraine, that is, two percent of the whole Jewish population in that area. While the Nazis bear "the full responsibility for these crimes...," he says, there is no doubt that had "the attitude of the population toward the Jews been different, the number of survivors would have been larger by far."[1]

Incidentally, the same holds true for Poland and Belorussia: had more Poles offered sympathy and support for the Jews–providing them with food and shelter, responding generously to their appeals for arms, admitting them into the ranks of the Home Army rather than, as so frequently happened, either ignoring them or in fact attacking them like enemies–more Jews would have survived. At the same time it must be remembered that in Poland, unlike in Ukraine and Lithuania, there was an organization dedicated to saving Jews–the *Zegota* (Council for Aid to the Jews)–and in Poland, too, the number of individuals who saved Jewish lives was higher than in the other three areas noted above.

What, then, characterizes Polish anti-Semitism? If it is, as I attempted to show, neither unique nor worse than anti-Semitism in many other countries, if it has been an expression of a chauvinism or xenophobia directed at other ethnic or religious groups as well, then why its notoriety? Why has it earned such an exceptionally sordid reputation and why is it that so many Jews regard it as more odious than Jew-hatred in other countries?

There are several reasons for the latter, some based more on perception than unalloyed facts. One was noted above: most American and all of the Ashkenazic Jews in Western Europe are but two or three generations removed from those millions of Jews in Poland, Ukraine, or Belorussia who had once constituted by far the largest Jewish communities in the world. They came to England and France and above all to the United States around the turn of the century, or ten or twenty years later, bearing with them the memories of suffering and persecution at the hands of the people in whose midst they had lived for generations–memories of daily humiliations, insults, pogroms, economic boycotts, discrimination in employment, and partial if not total bans on admission to universities and other institutions of higher learning.

It is those memories of by far the largest of all the Jewish emigrations from Eastern Europe that left their imprint on the succeeding generations of Jews and that have contributed, in my opinion, to the perception that the Poles–and next to them the Ukrainians–were the most implacable Jew haters in the world. It is interesting, for instance, that Romania, where Jews were treated no better than in Poland and where pogroms far bloodier than in Poland occurred (Kishinev in 1904, Jassy in 1941)–is not one of the countries singled out for its particularly brutal anti-Semitism.

The notoriety of Poland continued, of course, during its period of independence. And it persisted during the war, too. In fact, I would go as far as to say that the war was the acid test of the strength and virulence of Polish anti-Semitism–and that Poles did not pass it, to put it mildly, with flying colors. It would be absurd to claim that the Poles behaved more reprehensibly than the Nazis. Nor do I hold with those who maintain that the Nazis chose Poland for their gas ovens and crematoria because they counted on the passive if not active approval of it by the Polish population. There are plenty of better reasons why Poland, with the largest number of Jews in Europe, was chosen as the site of the largest death machine in the history of mankind.

But it is, again, precisely because Poland was the scene of the extermination of six million Jews that the attitude toward them by most of the local population, ranging from relative indifference to actual satisfaction that "Hitler was doing the job" for them was so appalling. In other countries, too, there were those who averted their eyes or tacitly approved of the carnage. But nowhere was it as conspicuous as in Poland.

To say that the size of the Jewish community in itself helped to shape the image of Poland as "the classic land of anti-Semitism" is not to deny that the image, or perception, is unrelated to reality. In fact—and this is one of the important points I wish to make—it is precisely the magnitude and history of the Jewish community in Poland that make it so distinctive, and that make the nature of Polish anti-Semitism so special as well.

To repeat: I did not say "unique," "worst," or "bloodiest." I said "distinctive" and "special." When I apply these terms to the Polish Jewish community, I have in mind not only size and numbers, but even more cultural and historical attributes. Poland—and I include here Ukraine, most of which had been part of Poland for centuries, as well as Lithuania, once part of the Polish Commonwealth—has been for centuries the heart and brain of most of Ashkenazy Jewry. It was in Poland that the most powerful religious movements, Hasidism and Mesnagdism, were born and flourished. It was in Poland, as I already mentioned earlier, that Jews created their own representative and legal institutions. Jewish book printing thrived in Holland and Germany, but flowered most bountifully in Poland. Poland was the birthplace of modern Yiddish literature and scholarship. It was in Poland that Zionism, Bundism, Folkism, Territorialism, and all the various other "isms," all the permutations of modern Jewish ideological and political movements, flourished. The *Haskala* arose in Germany, but developed more strongly in Poland than anywhere else. The same is true for modern Hebrew literature, and such twentieth century phenomena as Jewish schools having various ideological and linguistic orientations, youth organizations, sport leagues, and agricultural settlements.

It is precisely this background–the extraordinary strength and vitality of the Jewish community in Poland–that makes anti-Semitism in that country so striking. And it is precisely because at one time Poland *had* indeed been generous to and tolerant of its Jews as well as of other religious or ethnic minorities that the persistence *and growth* of anti-Jewish bigotry, from the eighteenth century on to this day, is so dismaying.

For in addition to what until the nineteenth century was the result of rampant religious beliefs–the image of Jews as the killers of Christ, the poisoners of wells, and people who use Christian children's blood to bake matzos–and in addition, too, to all the economic grievances against the Jews–that is, Jews as competitors or middlemen, or money lenders, or inn owners out to drive the honest Polish peasant into drunkenness and penury–in addition to all that, there came the development of anti-Semitism as a *political ideology.*

At bottom, of course, anti-Semitism as a political weapon or as an ideology is little more than a refurbished version of the Jew as the scapegoat for all of the country's ills and misfortunes. Why this came about when it did is not difficult to fathom. The nineteenth century saw the emergence of nationalism from its most humane form–that of a struggle for self-determination and equality for all nations–to its most malignant manifestations–the glorification of one's own people at the expense of and to the detriment of other peoples–i.e., chauvinism and xenophobia.

For the Poles, the nineteenth century was a trying and tragic era. They had lost their independence. They were oppressed by hostile powers. Their periodic insurrections invariably ended in failure and bitterness. Under those circumstances, it was easy for fervent nationalist movements to seek scapegoats: and what more compelling scapegoat than the Jew? The notion fell on fertile soil: the Jew had long been portrayed as the enemy of the Church, of the peasant, of the middle class; now, by extension, as it were, he became *the enemy* of the very essence of Polishness and of the Polish nation. The ultra-nationalist movements that preached this doctrine–in the first place the so-called National Democrats, who emerged in the late nineteenth century, exist, or their epigones exist, to this day. In independent Poland between the wars, their ideology–the notion that the Jew is an alien, a threat, and an excrescence on the Polish body politic, that he must be removed from Polish society either by means of exclusionary economic policies or by forced emigration, was embodied by the National Democrats ("Endeks"). Though never in power during the interwar period, the "Endeks"–and surely the anti-Semitic component of their ideology–dominated political life at that time. And it still remains active to this day.

One cannot but wonder about the tenacity of these attitudes in the face of the virtual absence of Jews in Poland–about seven thousand out of a prewar population of 3.5 million. In fact, of course, the notion of the physical expulsion of this handful of Jews is hardly entertained except by a few lunatics. Nevertheless, the idea that the Jews are the enemy of the Polish people, however many of them happen to be around, is still subscribed to by many Poles. What at one time had at least some grounding in reality–the Jews *had* comprised more than ten percent of the total pre-war population of Poland, and they did as a group present certain economic and political problems, like any ethnic or religious group in a multi-ethnic state–is now little more than a myth, a symptom of paranoia, a ghost or evil presence that no one can see but many are convinced is there, *somewhere;* and who is to claim that ghosts or evil spirits must exist to be believed in?

One could cite many examples, but let me mention only one: the presidential elections in Poland in December 1990,

   * One of the candidates, the incumbent premier Tadeusz Mazowiecki, who so often was tagged as a Jew (among other occasions, in posters showing his face with a superimposed Star of David), that the Secretary of the Polish Episcopate found it necessary (!) to issue a statement to the

effect that Mazowiecki's ancestors from at least the fifteenth century were all 'pure' Poles.

* Lech Walesa, who ran (successfully) for President, courted popularity by making numerous anti-Semitic remarks. At that time he (as much as his advisors) rejected such charges as figments of the imagination. Later on, while in Israel, he recognized the truth of the accusations and apologized for them.

* Another candidate, the previously unknown Canadian Pole Stan Tymanski who won 25 percent of the votes, ran on an explicitly anti-Semitic platform with accusations against Jewish 'enemies of Poland.'

More recently, the Polish weekly *Nie* (No. 26, 1992) carried a story about a meeting with voters in the town of Minsk Mazowiecki. One of the speakers was former prime minister Jan Olszewski, and the other was the head of the Peasant Party, Roman Bartoszcze. Both stated that most politicians are anti-national, Jews, and false patriots, and should be expelled from the country as soon as possible. The meeting, incidentally, was held in the presbytery of the local Catholic parish priest and the minutes were kept by two other priests.

The apologists for anti-Semitism claim that in the past anti-Semitic policies were altogether understandable if not justifiable by virtue of the fact that the Jews constituted a real "threat" to the Poles–a group that had refused to assimilate, spoke little Polish, and kept itself isolated culturally, religiously, and physically from the rest of society.

This view is no more than apologetics (in what way did the Jews pose a "threat" to the country, even if most of them spoke Yiddish rather than Polish?), but even if we accept it for the sake of argument, how does it explain the virulence of current anti-Semitism? Indeed, its existence offers the best evidence that anti-Semitism in Poland has its basis not in reality but in fears, myths, and collective paranoia, transmitted from generation to generation.

I noted before that while Polish anti-Semitism may not be unique, it is surely *distinctive,* and I should like to conclude this brief survey with a few more remarks on this subject.

Perhaps the most distinctive feature of anti-Semitism in Poland is the extent to which it has permeated, and to this day continues to permeate, various layers of the intelligentsia, from conservatives to liberals to democratic radicals. The origins and permutations of this phenomenon are as fascinating as they are complex, and I have already dealt with them elsewhere.[2] Suffice it to say that the stereotypes are so deeply rooted that many Poles are not even conscious of them–and indeed would reject any imputations of anti-Semitism as outrageous, all evidence to the contrary notwithstanding. Polish views and feelings on anti-Semitism encompass such a tangled web of rationalization, guilt, and rejection that few Poles can bring themselves to face it forthrightly, much less to condemn it in no uncertain fashion.

One person who exemplifies this ambivalence is the popular Polish writer Andrzej Szczypiorski, a man who has in fact spoken up against bigotry and national hatred. A few years ago he wrote the novel, *The Beautiful Mrs. Seidenman,*[3] to all appearances a veritable *philo-Semitic* work. Yet upon closer examination, it turns out to be replete with ambiguities and offensive stereotypes. The story is set in occupied Warsaw, both the Ghetto and the "Aryan" side, and the heroine, Mrs. Seidenman, is Jewish. She is portrayed as, in fact, a "good Pole," a person without the usual "Jewish traits" (that is to say, negative stereotypes)–to wit, "a golden haired beauty with azure eyes and a slender figure," a woman who "did not feel herself to be Jewish," and whose "heart welled up with gratitude to fate for having made her a Pole" (!). Of the four villains in the novel, two are Jews, one is German, and one is a Pole. Indeed the most repellent of all is the Jewish informer working for the Gestapo, while all the Poles with the exception of one (including that venerable cliché, the Virtuous Prostitute), are portrayed as men and women ready to sacrifice themselves for the sake of the beautiful Mrs. Seidenman. The novel has about as much verisimilitude as a socialist realist painting, and just about as much understanding for the Jewish experience during the Holocaust.

Another example is the celebrated Polish film director Andrzej Wajda, who peopled his *The Promised Land* (1975) with Jewish characters of an unredeemably repulsive nature. A few years ago he made a film about Janusz Korczak, the Polish-Jewish educator and author who went to his death together with the children of his orphanage in Warsaw in 1942. The film was meant to be a tribute to an extraordinary man. Yet all its Jewish characters (unlike the Polish ones) are either odious or nondescript or—at best—embody the noblest traits of "true Poles"—without, of course, ever uttering a word in Yiddish. When all this was pointed out to Wajda, he reacted with injured pride—no doubt sincerely.

For my final example, I turn to the literary scandal in the Polish press provoked by a 1990 book by a Polish scholar, Jadwiga Maurer.[4] The work made a very compelling case for the proposition that the mother of the great Polish nineteenth century poet Adam Mickiewicz had Jewish ancestors, and that Mickiewicz's wife also came from a family of converts. What lent particular piquancy to this "scandal" was not merely the allegations, which in fact had been made over the century by several writers, but the evidence assembled by Ms. Maurer demonstrating the extent to which so many Polish scholars, exercised by these allegations, went about denying, concealing, or explaining them away. The very idea that Poland's "Seer" (*Wieszcz*) could have had "Jewish blood" (however diluted), or could be joined in wedlock with somebody of such suspect lineage, was unthinkable.[5]

In conclusion, let me summarize the major contentions of this paper:

First, contrary to popular assumptions, Poland has not had a history of uninterrupted anti-Semitic hatred and policies.

Second, the record of Poland's treatment of its minorities has been mixed: worse than those of some other countries, better than that of some others.

Third, Poland's treatment of Jews in the twentieth century has been worse than its treatment of other minorities with the exception of the Ukrainians, who for a long time were subjected to more abuse than the Jews.

Fourth, the reputation of Poles as the principal offenders against the Jews is based on misperceptions. Unhappily, other nations, in particular the Lithuanians and Ukrainians–not to speak of course about the Germans–have had worse records in this respect.

Fifth, the distinctiveness of the Jewish community in Poland–its magnitude, its cultural and political vitality, and the fact that Poland was the scene of the greatest massacre of Jews in the history of mankind–renders anti-Semitism in that country particularly shocking. It is precisely because of the extraordinary accomplishments of Jewish life in pre-war Poland (and earlier), that makes the attitude to it on the part of the population and particularly of the elite so unforgivable. And it is precisely because there are virtually no Jews left in Poland today that anti-Semitism in that country is so grotesque.

Finally, though the intelligentsia in other countries has not been free of the taint of anti-Semitism, its resilience within the ranks of the Polish intelligentsia, all the efforts of many intellectuals to combat it notwithstanding, suggests that while the Jewish community in Poland is approaching extinction, the eclipse of the hatreds and the stereotypes in which it has so long been awash is still, unfortunately, not in sight.

NOTES

1. Aharon Weiss, "The Holocaust and the Ukrainian Victims" in *A Mosaic of Victims–Non Jews Persecuted and Murdered by the Nazis,* ed. Michael Berenbaum (New York: New York University Press, 1990), p. 113.

2. *Soviet Jewish Affairs,* London, vol. 20, no. 2-3, 1990.

3. New York: Grove, Weidenfeld, 1989.

4.   *Z matki obcej* (From an Alien Mother) (London: Polish Foundation, 1990).

5.   See Jadwiga Maurer, "The Omission of Jewish Topics in Mickiewicz Scholarship" in *Polin–A Journal of Polish Jewish Studies,* Oxford, no. 5, pp. 184-193.

Anti-Semitism and the Treatment of the Holocaust in Postcommunist Romania

Radu Ioanid

In the interwar period, Romania was among the European countries with the highest Jewish population: in 1930 756,930 Jews lived in Romania, constituting the third largest Jewish community in Europe (behind only those of Poland and the Soviet Union). The 1923 constitution, adopted under the pressure of the Western Powers, granting citizenship to almost all members of the ethnic minorities living in Romania, remained juridically in force until 1938. But even before 1938, theorists of the National Christian Defense League (*Liga Apărării Național Creștine*) the Iron Guard (*Garda de Fier*) systematically depicted the Jews as being "the ruling economic class," spies, communists, agents of Soviet Russia, and the principal enemies of the Romanian people.

After the destruction of the fragile political balance of post-World War I Europe, the Romanian government felt free to repeal the laws emancipating the Romanian Jews. On January 21, 1938, Royal Decree No. 169 signed by King Carol II and Prime Minister Octavian Goga provided a "revision" of the grant of citizenship to the Jews. The Constitutional Law of February 27, 1938 emphasized "the proclamation of the law of the blood" and also "the juridical and political distinction between Romanians having Romanian blood" and "other" Romanian citizens.

One month before General Ion Antonescu took power, the
government of Carol II, headed by Ion Gigurtu, passed severely
anti-Semitic legislation that was openly inspired by the Nuremberg racial laws. This legislation remained in force as a permanent reference for the legislators of the Antonescu–Horia Sima
and Antonescu periods. From August 1940 to May 1942 more
than one hundred anti-Semitic decrees and administrative deci-
sions were adopted in Romania, covering all aspects of economic, political, and social life.

Like many Romanian fascists and other anti-Semites, Antonescu was greatly disturbed by the existence of a relatively
large number of Jews in villages and towns, particularly in
northern and central Moldavia. In addition to the anti-Semitic
legislation against all Romanian Jews, Ion Antonescu put into
practice a second level of discrimination, based on geography,
that differentiated between the Romanian Jews of Old Romania
and those of northern Moldavia, Bessarabia, and Bukovina. The
lives of Romanian Jews during World War II were strongly
affected by this legislation: the Jews killed by the Romanian
fascist authorities were mainly from Bessarabia, Bukovina,
Transnistria, and Moldavia.

In July 1940, under the dictatorship of Carol II, even before
the first days of the Iron Guard government, a regular unit of the
Romanian army carried out an unprecedented pogrom during
which over 100 Jews died in the Moldavian town of Dorohoi. At
the end of January 1941, during the Iron Guard rebellion against
its former ally General Antonescu, Iron Guard members sav-
agely killed 120 Jews in Bucharest. In February 1941 Romanian
border guards at Burdujeni, on the frontier with the Soviet
Union, killed more more than 50 Jews.[1]

At the end of June 1941, over 8,000 Jews were killed in Jassy
(Iaşi) and in two death trains. The pogrom of Jassy, which started
on June 28, 1941, was organized by the leadership of *Serviciul
Special de Informaţii* (SSI-Special Information Service), the
Romanian agency in charge of espionage and counterespionage,
in close collaboration with Section II of the Romanian army's

general headquarters. There was also some German involvement in the organization of the pogrom.[2]

In terms of who bears the most blame, the Jassy pogrom can be considered to involve two distinct phases: the events in the city, and the death trains. In the city itself, Romanian and German military units, Romanian police, and gendarmerie units, former Iron Guard members, and local mobs perpetrated the killings. The heaviest responsibility lies with the local Romanian military authorities and with the Romanian and German commanders of the units that were in transit through Jassy toward the front line at that time. In the case of the death trains–there were two–the responsibility lies exclusively with the Romanian military authorities. Scenes of unbelievable cruelty took place in Jassy before the trains departed. Many Jews were killed with iron bars or machinegunned in the streets or in courtyards. The trains were sealed and many deportees perished because of lack of air and water. At least 2,594 Jews died in the two death trains. The survivors were kept by the Romanian authorities in two camps, Călărași and Podul Iloaei, for a few months and then set free.

Many other mass killings followed the events in Jassy, especially in Bessarabia and Bukovina, as well as the deportation of the entire Jewish population of Bessarabia and almost all Jews from Northern Bukovina. German involvement in the killing of Romanian Jews began after Romania entered the war in June 1941, but this involvement varied in magnitude. Sometimes, as in the cases of the mass killings in Bălți and Chișinău (Kishinev) *Einsatzgruppen* units and Romanian army and gendarmerie units acted together. On the other side of the Bug, where Romanian jurisdiction ended, the Germans killed Romanian Jews from Transnistria handed over by the Romanian administration. In the case of the mass killings in Odessa and in the Golta district, Romanian responsibility was overwhelming and the German one minimal.

The destruction of Romanian Jews was systematic in Bessarabia, Bukovina, and Transnistria, especially at the beginning of the war, and unsystematic in the Old Kingdom, i.e., within the pre-World War I borders of Romania. Almost the entire Jewish population of rural areas of Bessarabia and Bukovina was wiped out by the Romanian and German armies during the first weeks of the war. Before 1940 approximately 300,000 Jews lived in Bessarabia and Bukovina. Several sources indicate that some 130,000 retreated with the Red Army or were deported to Siberia by the Soviet authorities just before the beginning of the war. According to Raul Hilberg, over 27,000 Jews were killed in July and August 1941, mainly in Bessarabia and Bukovina (over 10,000 in July shootings, about 7,000 in August in transit camps, and about 10,000 in Transnistria). From 140,000 to 160,000 Jews were seized for deportation in Bessarabia, Bukovina, and Dorohoi, and at least 118,000 of them reached the eastern shore of the Dniester alive; two years later only 50,741 of the Bessarabian, Bukovinian, and Dorohoi deportees were left.³ Between 10,000 and 12,000 Jews were deported by the Romanian authorities to Transnistria from Dorohoi County in Old Romania, and only 6,000 came back; also deported from Old Romania to Transnistria were about 2,000 Jews in detention for "political crimes," i.e., people who had tried to escape forced labor, or families who had tried to emigrate to the Soviet Union before the war started. In Transnistria Romanian authorities were also responsible for the killing of approximately 150,000 indigenous Jews in the Odessa and Golta areas,⁴ and for the deportation of about 25,000 Gypsies from Old Romania to Transnistria, of whom only a few thousand returned.⁵

The deportation of all Jews from Bessarabia and Bukovina was ordered by Ion Antonescu. The vice president of the Romanian government, Mihai Antonescu, supervised the elaboration of the anti-Semitic laws and regulations implemented in Bessarabia and Bukovina. Both Antonescus considered the Jews of Bessarabia and Bukovina to be traitors, Soviet agents, and communists. The pretext was that these Jews had lived for one year under Soviet occupation in Bessarabia and Northern Bukovina and that some of them had welcomed the Red Army and showed hostility toward the retreating Romanian armies in 1940.

In fact, the old dream of Romanian nationalists to have these provinces free of Jews and other minorities seemed feasible at the beginning of World War II. Consequently in the fall of 1941, after the re-occupation of these provinces by the Romanian army, the military units and the police carried out the "transplantation" of the remaining Jews to Transnistria.

The summer and fall of 1942 represented a critical time for the Jews of the Old Kingdom and Southern Transylvania. During this period Romanian authorities decided on the deportation of all of them to the German death camps, and train schedules for the transports were established. But due to international pressure, the intervention of the leaders of the Romanian Jewish community, several Romanian politicians and clergymen, as well as the Royal Palace, Antonescu postponed the deportation to the spring of 1943. During November and December 1942, despite strong German pressures, Romanian authorities became more and more dilatory in this matter, as they began to realize that the Germans could lose the war.

In addition to defamation and violence, opportunism was an important feature of Romanian anti-Semitism. While at the beginning of the war the German authorities were dissatisfied by the ad hoc nature of the Romanian killing of the Jews with the country, in 1942 they were strongly displeased by the Romanian refusal to deport the Romanian Jews to the Nazi death camps.

During the summer of 1941 the Germans protested several times because the Romanian units did not bury their Jewish victims, thus creating the danger of epidemics and damaging the image of both armies. Another conflict arose in August 1941 when the Romanians tried to push thousands of Jews over the Bug river in an attempt to have them killed by *Einsatzgruppe* D; busy with the killing of the Jews from the Ukraine, the Germans pushed the Romanian Jews back to Transnistria.

General Antonescu, despite his anti-Semitism, allowed several thousand survivors to come back to Romania from Transnistria during the spring of 1944. A few thousand were allowed to emigrate to Palestine. For the Romanian authorities the Jews became a bargaining chip, a possibility to gain some sympathy from the Allies. Approximately 300,000 Romanian Jews survived the war.

It is important to emphasize the role of the Romanian army in the process of destruction. Through its *Biroul 10, Evrei* (Department 10, Jews) and through its military gendarmerie units, acting in coordination with the Ministry of the Interior which controlled the rural gendarmerie and the police, the Romanian army implemented the destruction of the Romanian Jews. The main features of the implementation of genocidal policies in Romania were defamation, outbursts of violence, disorder, robbery, geographical discrimination, and opportunism. Romanian authorities implemented the genocidal policies intensely at the beginning of the war and ended them gradually in 1943; most of the time there was no coordination between Romanian and German policies in this matter.

During the fall of 1944, the anti-Semitic laws were repealed. Several trials of Romanian war criminals followed and hundreds of them were condemned to prison or forced labor. For example, the Romanian war criminals involved in the Jassy pogrom were sentenced on June 26, 1948. During the trial 46 persons were found guilty and sentenced to heavy prison terms or forced labor. Members of the Romanian army or police made up almost half of these people. Among others, the court sentenced: General Gheorghe Stavrescu, commander of the 14th Division of the Romanian army; Colonel Dumitru Captaru, former Prefect of Jassy; Colonel Constantin Lupu, commander of the Jassy garrison; and several high-ranking officers of the SSI. The trials were used by the Romanian Communist Party (RCP) as a propaganda tool against its adversaries. Once solidly installed in power, the RCP first "forgot" about Romanian anti-Semitism and later encouraged it. When it is mentioned in Romanian history at all, the Holocaust in Romania is portrayed as being exclusively the result of actions of German Nazism or of Hungarian fascism. Especially during the rule of Nicolae Ceauşescu, a strong trend favoring the rehabilitation of Antonescu surfaced in Romanian historiography. Antonescu's responsibility in the destruction of

Romanian Jewry was ignored by Romanian historians and media; the fascist features of his regime were denied. Since the Hungarian authorities had deported most of the 150,000 Jews from Northern Transylvania to the German death camps of Poland (only 15,000 returned), the Holocaust in Romania became exclusively an anti-Hungarian propaganda tool.

After the fall of Ceauşescu a multi-party political system emerged in Romania. Most of the new political parties shared strong nationalistic and very often xenophobic features. Newly independent ex-Soviet Moldavia includes a large number of ethnic Romanians in its population, but for the time being refuses to unite with Romania. Romania has territorial problems with Ukraine: parts of Bessarabia and Northern Bukovina remained incorporated in the former Soviet republic. The fact that the numerically strong Hungarian minority in Romania quite often answers xenophobia with xenophobia provides added pretexts for anti-Hungarian propaganda. The disappearance of Yugoslavia is creating a certain tension between Romania and Hungary. All these problems fuel Romanian nationalism.

Ceauşescu, an anti-Semite, purged the main Romanian institutions of Jews. Many Jews left the country; today the Romanian Jewish community numbers 18,000 to 20,000 members, most of them elderly. A few Romanian Jews were instrumental in the fall of Ceauşescu and became ambassadors, senators, or ministers in the new regime, members of the new Romanian political class.

The recent wave of Romanian anti-Semitism started even before the 50th commemoration, in 1991, of the Jassy pogrom, but clearly gained in strength with this occasion. Before the commemoration, synagogues and Jewish cemeteries in Alba Iulia, Tîrgu Mureş, Galaţi, Oradea, Satu Mare, and Sighetul Marmaţiei were vandalized and, starting in February 1990, several Romanian newspapers published vehemently anti-Semitic articles. Among them were the pro-government newspapers *Adevărul* (Truth) and the opposition, National Peasant Party daily *Dreptatea* (Justice). *Dreptatea* also published several anti-Semitic articles identifying communism with Jews. The same newspaper attacked the United States for allegedly not helping

Romanian democracy, targeting George Bush, Henry Kissinger, and Lawrence Eagleburger. But in 1991, when a local leader of the National Peasant Party from Rădăuţi violently attacked Chief Rabbi Moses Rosen, he was strongly criticized by *Dreptatea* as being against the official line of the National Peasant Party (May 10, 1991). Iron Guard publications such as *Gazeta de Vest* (Western Gazette) began serializing the writings of C. Z. Codreanu, Horia Sima, and other Iron Guard leaders. Surprisingly, the Iron Guard today is less anti-Semitic than other political organizations in Romania; nevertheless the pogroms of the Iron Guard period are justified as defensive reactions against a pretended Jewish plot. *Gazeta de Vest* is close to *Mişcarea pentru România* (The Movement for Romania), led by the former student leader Marian Munteanu who has been described since 1990 as Iron Guard oriented.[6] A "scandal press" tabloid, *Oblio,* published *The Protocols of the Elders of Zion* in serial form. A denial of the Holocaust in Europe was published in *Arena Magazin,* with quotes from revisionists such as Robert Faurisson.[7] Extreme-right magazines such as *Europa* and *România Mare* (Greater Romania) published weekly attacks on Romanian Jews, accusing them of being communist agents and the main source of Romania's problems. Both *România Mare* and *Europa* systematically and vitriolically attacked Chief Rabbi Moses Rosen, Romanian Jews, the Hungarian minority in Romania, the American Joint Distribution Committee, the Mossad, the CIA, and George Bush. These neo-fascist publications warned their readers that the new authorities planned to colonize Romania with Soviet Jews. A retired Romanian officer with Lybian ties, Radu Nicolae, published several articles on this subject.

Both *România Mare* and *Europa* claim that the proportion of Jews in the government is overwhelming and that the Jews' ultimate aim is to transform Romania into a colony of Israel. Former Romanian Prime Minister Petru Roman, whose father was Jewish and who took a strong nationalistic stand, was often depicted in graffiti and at several rallies as a "kike," despite the fact that he hurried to submit his baptismal certificate to the press. A similar campaign developed against Silviu Brucan, a former RCP leader who turned against Ceauşescu and became a well-known dissident. A few Jewish publicists such as Radu F. Alexandru in *România Liberă* (Free Romania) and Vasile Grunea in *Mesagerul Transilvan* (Transylvanian Messenger) seemed to be standing quite alone in their attempts to oppose the wave of anti-Semitism. The distinguished historian Andrei Pippidi, who wrote in the opposition weekly *22* about the Holocaust and anti-Semitism in Romania and showed how the victims were being transformed by the anti-Semitic propaganda into perpetrators, was a lonely voice in the wilderness. During the fall of 1990, a forceful speech by Senator Gelu Voican Voiculescu in the Romanian parliament was published in the pro-government newspaper *Azi* (Today). The senator asked the government to take a stand against the anti-Semitic slogans issuing from the Romanian press, warning against the diversionist character of this campaign. He emphasized that for Romanian youth anti-Semitism was an abstract notion and that after the tragedy of World War II anti-Semitism was criminal behavior.[8] But the government did not take any kind of legal action against the authors of the anti-Semitic campaign.

It is interesting to note that exactly like the Ceauşescu ideologists who considered the Iron Guard to represent an alien ideology, an important fraction of Romania's anti-communists consider Romanian communism to be non-Romanian. According to them, communism was brought to Romania by the Red Army through its agents, above all the Jews. As Michael Shafir mentioned in his excellent study on contemporary anti-Semitism in Romania, "anti-Semitism contributes to the exoneration of the nation as a whole."[9]

The most tragic year of the Holocaust in Romania was 1941. On January 21, 1991 the Romanian Parliament organized a commemoration of the Bucharest pogrom. President of the Senate Alexandru Bârlădeanu and Chief Rabbi Moses Rosen were among the featured speakers. The commemoration did not stir notable public debate. Since then, however, there has been a campaign to rehabilitate Antonescu as a national hero, the liberator of Bessarabia and Northern Bukovina. The ruling and opposition forces were equally involved in this nationalistic campaign and equally ignored the historical truth that Antonescu was a dictator who suspended all political parties, that he declared war not only on the Soviet Union but also on the Western Powers, that he expressed his hate for democracy many times. They competed in praising Antonescu as the liberator of Bessarabia and Northern Bukovina. Streets and squares were named after him. In May 1991 the Romanian Parliament (including its few Jewish members) rose for a moment of silence in honor of Ion Antonescu. President Ion Iliescu disapproved this parliamentary initiative but both the press of the ruling party and the opposition press ignored his declaration. Only two newspapers reported his words, and they did so in order to criticize him.

The new Romanian political class reacted mildly if at all to the violent anti-Semitic campaign. On March 8, 1990, Prime Minister Roman promised Chief Rabbi Rosen that the government would not tolerate the resurgence of fascism; obviously, the promise has not been kept. During the spring of 1991 every issue of *România Mare* and *Europa* contained anti-Semitic articles. On June 5, 1991 the Romanian government condemned the anti-Semitic campaign in a weak statement. Also, President Iliescu and the leader of the National Peasant Party, Corneliu Coposu, denounced the increase of anti-Semitic propaganda. Former King Michael's publicly expressed wish to regain the Romanian throne complicated matters even further. It is clear that at least some of the leaders of the National Salvation Front (*Frontal Salvării Naţionale*) had a common interest with the extreme right to block the eventual return of the former king, who in a coup d'état in alliance with communists, national peasants, and liberals, had arrested Antonescu in August 1944. It was not the first time that the government and the extreme-right parties shared the same goals. A clash between the tiny Jewish community and the Romanian nationalists appeared unavoidable as anti-Semitism became an acceptable mode in political discourse.

Rabbi Moses Rosen is a controversial figure: he has been the Chief Rabbi of Romania since the late 1940s, and while he obviously has had to come to some accommodations with the communist regime, he has been associated with many of the Jewish community's advances. Since the early 1960s Romanian Jews have been able to emigrate to Israel or to the USA. After the 1967 Israeli-Arab War, Romania refused to break diplomatic relations with Israel. One year later Ceauşescu condemned the Soviet intervention in Czechoslovakia and relations with the USA improved; a nationalistic and anti-Soviet Romania was clearly being viewed favorably in Western diplomatic circles. By that time, the diminishing Jewish community in Romania had received a certain degree of autonomy and was allowed to benefit from American aid. Chief Rabbi Rosen, a member of Romania's rubber stamp parliament, acted several times as an intermediary between Ceauşescu's regime and Washington; and Israel literally purchased the Romanian Jews' right to emigrate from Ceauşescu. Despite a new and strong wave of Romanian anti-Semitism, the Chief Rabbi decided to commemorate the pogrom of Jassy openly and with as much press coverage as possible. Since the Holocaust in Romania has been systematically ignored and since the new Romanian authorities could be expected to act on this issue in an opportunistic way at best, Rosen's decision was clearly the right one.

At the commemoration, Romanians were told about the existence of the Holocaust in Romania for the first time in decades; facts widely known in the West had never been acknowledged in Romania after the late forties. As Chief Rabbi Rosen noted in his speech, echoing Elie Wiesel, Romanian Jews were murdered twice: once in the Holocaust and the second time through denial and lies. Through high-ranking officials, President Iliescu and Prime Minister Roman sent messages for the occasion. The President's conventional and weak message mentioned the Iron Guard (which had had only a marginal involvement in the pogrom), the legendary kindness of the Romanian people, and the fact that extremist actions during World War II were rare in Romania. The Prime Minister's message also avoided mention of the responsibility of Antonescu's regime in the mass murder of the Jews and quoted, in addition to

Rousseau, Kant, and Hegel, the Romanian philosopher and former Iron Guard ideologist Constantin Noica. Senator Gelu Voican Voiculescu and the President of the Senate, Alexandru Bârlădeanu, delivered courageous messages. Survivors from Romania and Israel shared their personal tragedies with the audience. Israel Singer, General Secretary of the World Jewish Congress, and Rabbi Arthur Schneier of the Appeal for Conscience Foundation denounced the current Romanian anti-Semitism. In his Jassy speech in which he deplored the Romanian Parliament's tribute to Antonescu, Elie Wiesel said: "I address myself to the leaders of this country; I hope you know that your representatives have great difficulties in mobilizing the world's sympathy and acquiring political and economic support for your country. Your image is not the best. You must know that. You must know that unless these anti-Semites are shamed in society, you will suffer. You will be isolated. The world is following with astonishment, dismay and outrage."[10] Elie Wiesel's speech was interrupted by a woman who repeatedly shouted "Lies!" from a front seat and added: "It's a lie! The Jews didn't die. We won't allow ourselves to be insulted by foreigners in our country."[11] Eventually the police hustled the woman away but refused to identify her. According to the Romanian daily *Libertatea* (Liberty), she was the daughter of the former Prefect of Jassy, Dumitru Captaru, condemned in 1948 to forced labor for life for his participation in the mass killing of Jews during the pogrom.

It is well known that during the Ceauşescu years *Securitate* (Security, the Romanian secret police) maintained close ties with a group a Ceauşescu's chauvinistic hagiographers belonging to the Union of Writers, including Corneliu Vadim Tudor and Eugen Barbu. *Securitate* also had strong ties with a wealthy extreme-right emigre and Iron Guard sympathizer, Iosif Constantin Drăgan, whom Ceauşescu often received and who maintained close relations with Tudor and Barbu. After the fall of Ceauşescu, Tudor and Barbu created first the extreme rightist weekly *România Mare* and then a political party with the same name. Other leaders of this party are Mircea Muşat, former high-ranking official of the Central Committee of the Romanian Communist Party in charge of the censorship of Romanian historiography, and several high-ranking retired anti-Semitic officers. The Romania Mare Party has very close relations with Drăgan, who controls the weekly *Europa* through the Italian publishing trust Europa Nuova. Drăgan is also the honorary president of the right-wing xenophobic political organization *Vatra Românească* (Romanian Hearth). Drăgan has been using *Europa* since 1990 as a forum for the rehabilitation of Ion Antonescu. *Europa* also mounted a systematic campaign defending the few dozen *Securitate* officers who are in prison and praising the *Securitate* and Ceauşescu. According to *Europa,* the fall of the Romanian dictator was the result of a conspiracy organized by the KGB, the CIA, Mossad, and the Hungarian intelligence services. The imprisoned former members of the RCP's Politburo are portrayed as victims of this plot.

At the end of June and during July 1991, both *România Mare* and *Europa* launched a rabidly anti-Semitic campaign denying the Romanian Holocaust. Most often the authors of these attacks were Tudor and Ilie Neacsu, the publishers/editors-in-chief of the respective publications. In order to support their campaign they enlisted several pseudo-historians such as Mircea Muşat and Maria Covaci, well known for their revisionist and pro-fascist writings published during the Ceauşescu years. Less well-known people such as Vasile Bobocescu, a high-school history teacher, joined this propaganda campaign, which also used writings by retired officers such as General Ion Munteanu, president of the Ion Antonescu Foundation and former director of the Romanian State Archives. Basically this campaign had three main themes:

1. Antonescu is a national hero and not a war criminal. Specially, it is asserted that he did not murder Jews, he saved them; and that when anti-Semitic incidents occurred this happened because of the overzealousness of "some Iron Guardists" or because of the "unpatriotic" attitude of the Jews.

2. There was no Holocaust in Romania. The responsibility for the pogrom of Jassy is attributed exclusively to the Germans, and the number of victims is radically minimized. The massacres during the summer of 1941, the deportations to Transnistria, and the massacres of local Jews in that area are ignored or attributed to the Nazis.

3. Chief Rabbi Rosen and the Romanian Jewish Community are destroying the image of Romania abroad through the Jassy commemoration and are the real authors of the new wave of anti-Semitism in Romania.

The press of the Romanian extreme right published dozens and dozens of articles containing these ideas. The same articles reminded their readers that "all prominent Romanian communists were Jews or had Jewish wives" and that fascist ideologists had "generous" ideas such as the "numerus clausus" measures affecting higher education. Anyone as much as questioning these assertions was labeled an enemy of the Romanian nation. Besides Chief Rabbi Rosen, the neo-fascists also aggressively attacked Senator Gelu Voican Voiculescu who had made a courageous speech at the Jassy commemoration, Răzvan Theodorescu, director of Romanian Television and president of the Romania-Israel Association, and Minister of Culture Andrei Plesu. *Europa* violently attacked Zvi Mazel, the Ambassador of Israel in Bucharest, lecturing and threatening him.[12]

Another extreme-right Romanian political organization, *Vatra Românească,* protested in strong terms the commemoration of the pogrom of Jassy. Heavily supported by *Securitate* officers and former middle-ranking RCP members, this organization's main aim is anti-Hungarian propaganda. Several political events such as the December 1990 rally in Alba Iulia proved that at least one faction of the ruling National Salvation Front also supported this organization. *Europa* and *România Mare* printed *Vatra Românească* protests against the Jassy commemoration. On July 3, 1991, the Steering Committee of the Bucharest branch of *Vatra Românească* protested against "the grave and groundless accusations Chief Rabbi Rosen raises against the Romanian people through a veritable campaign of anti-Romanian propaganda started by him right after the December revolution, which has recently climaxed with regard to the martyrdom of the Jews of Jassy." According to *Vatra Românească,* a "painful moment of meditation and human solidarity has been turned by Mr. Moses Rosen into a new opportunity for an extremely violent attack against the Romanian people." In the same statement *Vatra Românească* recalled "the courage and the human kindness of the Romanians who, with Marshal Antonescu in the lead, protected the Jewish community in Romania" and warned that "such actions will offer arguments and pretexts for the emergence of extremism in Romania."[13] In another statement issued on July 15, 1991, *Vatra Românească* again used the same "arguments" and selectively quoted the historians Randolph Braham and Israel Gutman and the former Neolog Rabbi of Cluj, Moshe Carmilly-Weinberger, to sustain its theses. This statement concluded: "For the time being, someone reading works devoted to World War II cannot see any proof that could support the thesis launched with so much enthusiasm by Rosen....We do not exclude the hypothesis of the vast anti-Romanian plot in the international press, a plot joined by certain Romanian journalists as well as Moses Rosen."[14]

The press supporting the ruling National Salvation Front did not behave much better. Since except for nationalism there is little ideology in Romania, the pro-government journalists mostly decided to ignore this issue. But sometimes they addressed the matter in ugly ways. Shortly before the Jassy commemoration, the daily *Dimineața* (Morning) published an article by Pierre W. Telleman-Pruncul, from Montreuil, France, which played down the number of the Jewish victims of the Romanian Holocaust, blamed the Jews for all the economic and political problems of twentieth-century Romania, and strongly praised Antonescu.[15] On July 11, 1991, in another newspaper supporting the National Salvation Front, *Adevărul,* Cristian Tudor Popescu attacked the Jassy commemoration and Elie Wiesel. The pro-government journalist argued that a Romanian soldier killed in the battle of Stalingrad has the same symbolic meaning as a Jew killed on the street in Jassy; he also argued that it was not useful at all to raise the issue of the Holocaust in Romania, and stated that despite many requests his newspaper refused to address the subject because it was not useful to "muddy the waters."[16]

In the main, the response of the democratic forces in Romania to this campaign proved to be weak and inconclusive. Among the exceptions was an article by the Jewish literary critic Zigu Ornea, published in a weekly that had succeeded in maintaining a high level of quality even under Ceauşescu, *România Literară* (Literary Romania). It emphasized the specificity of the Romanian Holocaust and the responsibility of Antonescu.[17] Another Jewish publicist, Andrei Oisteanu, published a chronicle of the Jassy pogrom based mainly on the reliable *Black Book* in *Cotidianul* (The Daily).[18] Some publications such as *Expres Magazin,* after condemning Chief Rabbi Rosen as totalitarian for trying to "impose his version of history" upon the Romanians, organized a "debate" on the existence of the Holocaust in Romania, publishing anti-Semitic opinions on this subject but also opinions of people trying to defend the historical truth.[19] A historian who is fairly well known in both Romania and the USA, Dinu Giurescu, approached the subject of the Holocaust in Romania with some prudence. He denied the uniqueness of the Holocaust and emphasized that Soviet authorities also deported Romanians from Bessarabia and Bukovina and that the Romanian communist regime threw many Romanians in jail. But Giurescu also did what other Romanian historians did not dare to do: he acknowledged that Ion Antonescu bears the main responsibility for the deportation of the Romanian Jews, and he acknowledged the mass executions as well as the fact that over 110,000 Jews were deported to Transnistria, of whom at least half were exterminated.[20]

After the commemoration of the Jassy pogrom the international perception of Romania declined still further. The American media extensively covered the Jassy commemoration. On July 30, 1991, a Joint Resolution of the House of Representatives and the Senate of the United States condemned the resurgent anti-Semitism and chauvinism in Romania. The Resolution mentioned that the Romanian Parliament, instead of condemning the extremist organizations and publications promulgating national chauvinism, ethnic hatred, and anti-Semitism, "recently stood in a moment of silence for the extreme nationalist Ion Antonescu who was responsible for the murder of approximately 250,000 Romanian Jews and was executed as a war criminal." The U.S. Congress condemned the passivity of the Romanian government an the anti-Semitic heckling of Elie Wiesel. The Resolution urged the Government of Romania to take steps against anti-Semitism and called on the President of the United States to ensure that Romania would make progress in combating anti-Semitism and protecting the rights and safety of its ethnic minorities, and that this progress would be a significant factor in determining levels of assistance to Romania. The reaction of the Romanian Parliament to the resolution of the U.S. Congress was symptomatic. A Front of National Salvation representative in the Parliament, Petre Turlea, declared that anti-Semitism should not be made unconstitutional in the new Romanian constitution. Gabriel Andreescu, a Liberal Party representative, declared that the Jews exploited Romania and that Moses Rosen was to blame for Romanian anti-Semitism. Another parliament member representing the same party, Aron Todoroni, declared that "Moses Rosen insulted the greatest man in Romanian history, Ion Antonescu." A representative of the National Peasant Party, C. Constantinescu Claps, declared that the Romanian Parliament should answer the "routine calumnies and lies in the American media which were used by the U.S. Congress." Martian Dan, the President of the Romanian Parliament, made an appeal for tolerance and asked whether anti-Semitism was an issue to be ignored.[21] The vice-president of the Liberal Party, Ionel V. Sandulescu, declared after a visit to the United States that Romanians would not let themselves be lectured because Antonescu belonged to world history forever.

The reaction of the Romanian government and president was again weak. Ion Iliescu condemned the weekly *România Mare,* emphasizing that he was a dedicated anti-fascist. At the same time, trying to position himself in the middle, he said: "...the mistake came from the other side as well. I talked to Moses Rosen and I reproached him for his attempt to promote the idea that the Holocaust started in Romania. This is not the historical truth. What he stated was taken advantage of by the anti-Semites, and therefore *România Mare* appeared as the people's defender.[22] When Prime Minister Petre Roman was asked when the Romanian government would take stronger measures against extremist, chauvinistic, and anti-Semitic publications, he answered: "You want to know when? Well, when we have a legal instrument for it."[23] On November 21, 1991, the Romanian Parliament adopted a new Romanian constitution, which a popular referendum confirmed in December of the same year. Article 30, Paragraph 7 prohibits provocation of ethnic, racial, class, or religious hatred and incitement to discrimination. Nevertheless, the anti-Semitic and chauvinistic campaign of *România Mare* and *Europa* continued.

Only a few encouraging signs have become visible since. In an article the journalist Cornel Nistorescu blamed the whole Romanian intelligentsia for keeping silent on the subject of the Romanian Holocaust. Referring to Raul Hilberg, Nistorescu stated that Antonescu and his cronies were responsible for the murder of the Romanian Jews.[24] Unfortunately, there were strong signs later that he was wavering in his position. A former revisionist journalist and a critic of Curzio Malaparte, Mihai Palin, completely changed his position and stated that the Holocaust in Romania had occurred and had been carried out by Romanians. But otherwise few Romanians of conscience have publicly resisted the current descent into neo-fascism and anti-Semitism.

After the commemoration of the pogrom of Jassy, Nobel Laureate Elie Wiesel returned to the United States sad and worried: "Anti-Semitism hurts Romania because of the blemish it brings to the nation."[25] He wrote that in Romania:

> *Zhidan* (Kike) was not limited to the fanatic mobs; it was shouted in the street, whispered in the train, heard in the street, in city parks, in government offices and in school courtyards too....Still, Jews fared

better in Romania than in what later became Hungary. Hungary's Fascist government handed over its Jews to Eichmann; Romania didn't but it did send many of them to Transnistria where they lived and died in terror and isolation....Romania's position today in the international community is visibly not the best. Not in the political sphere, and surely not in the intellectual one. Whether justified or not there is distrust toward what is happening now in Romania....Unless its leaders put an immediate end to this vicious, ugly and perilous anti-Semitic press campaign, unless they place the fanatic hate-mongers outside the accepted norms of society, Romania runs the risk of being isolated and condemned by the international community as few others have been....When the past is silenced, the future is jeopardized. When history is falsified, humanity is impoverished.[26]

Romanian anti-Semitism continued to run wild. *Expres* continued to attack Chief Rabbi Rosen violently and to publish anti-Semitic articles, while maintaining that the Romanians were not anti-Semitic, that Ion Antonescu was a national hero, that the anti-Semitic measures ordered by Mihai Antonescu were in fact only anti-communist measures. The post-World War II trials of Romanian war criminals guilty of the massacre of hundreds of thousands of Jews were systematically presented by *Expres* as "communist political trials," casting doubt on the fairness of these trials.[27] When a Canadian Ministry of Justice delegation visited Romania trying to find materials on presumed Romanian war criminals who had escaped to Canada, *Expres* was very fast in publishing not only the agreement with the Romanian Ministry of Justice regarding the delegation but also its own negative comments, the names and the hotel room numbers of the members of the delegation, and descriptions of how they dressed.[28]

Paul Everac, a novelist who had been quite popular during the Ceauşescu regime, launched a personal xenophobic campaign. He wrote that "the Jews are making noise about the Holocaust in order to buy Romanian factories at lower prices."[29] In a book published in 1992, Everac described the Jews as being "merciless and intolerant." According to Everac, the Jews were

the most important factor underlying socialism and communism, and the main promoters of present-day liberalism. Everac
wrote that the Jews make atheist propaganda while remaining
religious fanatics, and that they control the media and the armed
forces in the United States. Other enemies of Everac (and of the
Romanians, according to him) are the Hungarians, who are
"Asians who love metal, the horse and the sword," and the
Gypsies, who "are not very clean and not very honest" and whose
"demographic growth should be reduced by force."[30] Weekly
magazines such as *Totuşi Iubirea* (Nevertheless, Love) in its
issues of July 30-August 15, 1992, and *Baricada* (The Barri-
cade) in its July 28-August 3, 1992 issues published pro-Iron
Guard articles. *Europa* continued its violent anti-Semitic campaign. According to this publication the whole history of Romania is dominated by the struggle between (good) Romanians and
(bad) Jews. *Europa* stated again that the government of Prime
Minister Teodor Stolojan was opening the gates of Romania to
400,000 Jews, presumably formerly Soviets, as compensation
for the fact that they had been able to assassinate Ceauşescu [sic].
Europa also protested against the audience granted on his
birthday to Chief Rabbi Rosen by President Iliescu at Cotroceni
Palace.[31] The same kind of heinous campaign was continued by
România Mare. Aurel Dragoş Munteanu, the Romanian Ambassador in Washington, who is Jewish, was described as a Freemason agent who pressures President Iliescu in concert with Chief
Rabbi Rosen.[32] Also in *România Mare,* unbelievably vulgar
writings about the alleged circumcision of ex-Prime Minister
Petre Roman were published.[33] By this time the links between the
government and *România Mare* had become obvious; for example, in June 1992 *România Mare* published a photo showing
Prime Minister Stolojan and Minister of Defense Nicolae Spiroiu
drinking with Vadim Tudor at a banquet honoring the publication, while in July 1992 Minister of Education Mihai Golu
thanked Vadim Tudor for money donated to a high school in
Braşov.[34]

    The civilized world will probably not isolate Romania be-
cause of Romanian anti-Semitism, but will find it difficult to

ignore this matter completely. During the summer of 1992 various committees and subcommittees of the House of Representatives of the U.S. Congress, at the proposal of the Bush administration, recommended the reestablishment of most-favored-nation status for Romania. In a declaration published on August 6, 1992, the Romanian government reassured the U.S. Congress that the rights of minorities would be fully respected in Romania. The previous day the Romanian Ministry of Foreign Affairs had published a *Carte blanche* (White Book) listing all the articles and sections in the Romanian constitution that ensure equal rights to all national, ethnic, linguistic, or religious minorities in Romania. The document emphasized that any "show of racism infringes the exercise of the constitutional right of expression and information, and it is therefore the duty of the Prosecutor's Office to bring such cases before the courts of law so that the measures provided by the law might be taken."[35] Nevertheless, not one legal measure was taken against the authors of the anti-Semitic campaign. This was an important factor in the September 30, 1992 rejection by the U.S. House of Representatives of the reestablishment of most-favored-nation status for Romania. (The vote was as follows: 88 for, 283 against, and 61 not voting.)

It is indeed tragic that tolerance and civic courage appear to be foreign to most members of the Romanian intelligentsia and political elite. Unless the denial of complicity in the anti-Semitic atrocities comes to an end, Romanians will never be able to be truly free, and their hope for a more democratic political future will remain tarnished by lies and distortion.

NOTES

1. Matatias Carp, *Cartea Neagră* (Black Book) (Bucharest: Socec, 1947), vol. 3, p. 28.

2. Ibid., vol. 2, pp. 43-45.

3. Ibid., vol. 3, p. 442.

4. Ibid., vol. 3, p. 201; Raul Hilberg, *The Destruction of the European Jews* (New York: Holmes & Meyer, 1985), vol. 3, p. 759.

5. *Procesul marii trădări naționale* (The Trial of the Great National

Betrayal) (Bucharest: Eminescu, 1945), p. 65.

6. *In These Times*, Chicago, June 6-19, 1990.

7. *Arena Magazin*, Satu Mare, no. 28, 1991.

8. *Azi* (Today), Bucharest, no. 27, October 1990.

9. *RFE/RL Research Institute-Report on Eastern Europe*, Munich, vol. 2, no. 26, June 1991.

10. *The New York Times*, July 2, 1991.

11. Ibid., July 3, 1991.

12. *Europa*, Bucharest, no. 32, July 1991.

13. *Federal Broadcasting Information Service, FBIS-EUU-91-129*, Washington D.C., July 5, 1991, p. 27.

14. Ibid., July 15, 1991, p. 29.

15. "Ion Antonescu şi problema evreiască" (Antonescu and the Jewish Question), *Dimineaţa* (Morning), Bucharest, June 5, 1991.

16. "Mai gîndiţi-vă" (Think About It), *Adevărul* (Truth), Bucharest, July 11, 1991.

17. "Martiriul evreilor din România" (The Martyrdom of the Jews of Romania), *România Literară* (Literary Romania), Bucharest, July 4, 1991.

18. "Pogromul de la Iaşi" (The Jassy Pogrom), *Cotidianul* (The Daily), Bucharest, June 26, 1991.

19. *Expres Magazin*, Bucharest, no. 27, July 10-16, 1991, and no. 32, August 13-20, 1991.

20. "Adevăruri ce se cuvin neapărat rostite" (Truths That Must Be Recalled), *România Literară*, July 11, 1991.

21. *Adevărul*, Bucharest, July 27, 1991.

22. *Rompress:* Interview from *Expres Magazin*, August 15, 1991.

23. *Azi*, July 25, 1991.

24. "Tăcerea din jurul crimei" (Silence Surrounding the Crime), *Expres Magazin*, January 14-20, 1992.

25. *The Jewish Week*, New York, July 18, 1991.

26. Foreword to I. C. Butnaru's *The Silent Holocaust* (New York: Greenwood Press, 1992), pp. vi-viii.

27. *Expres Magazin*, April-July 1992.

28. Ibid., July 14-20, 1992.

29. *Libertatea* (Liberty), Bucharest, June 12-13, 1992.

30. *Reacţionarul* (The Reactionary), (Bucharest: Românul, 1992), pp. 111-124.

31. *Europa,* July 28-August 3, 1992.
32. *România Mare* (Greater Romania), Bucharest, May 15, 1992 and July 31, 1992.
33. Ibid., July 17, 1992.
34. Ibid.
35. *Federal Broadcasting Information Service FBIS-EUU-92-153,* August 7, 1992.

BIBLIOGRAPHY

Ancel, Jean, *Documents Concerning the Fate of Romanian Jewry During the Holocaust* (New York: The Klarsfeld Foundation, 1986), 12 vols.

Bitoaica, Dumitras G., *Statutul juridic al evreilor și legislația romanizării* [Legal Status of Jews and the Romanization Legislation] (Bucharest: Prometeu, 1942).

Carp, Matatias, *Cartea Neagră* [Black Book] (Bucharest: Socec, 1947), 3 vols.

Dallin, Alexander, *Odessa: A Case Study of Soviet Territory Under Foreign Rule* (Santa Monica, California: Rand Corporation Memorandum, 1957).

Dorian, Emil, *The Quality of Witness* (Philadelphia: The Jewish Publication Society of America, 1982).

Fisher, Julius, *Transnistria, the Forgotten Cemetery* (South Brunswick, NJ: Thomas Yoseloff, 1969).

Hilberg, Raul, *The Destruction of the European Jews* (New York: Holmes & Meyer, 1985), 3 vols.

Shafir, Michael, "Anti-Semitism Without Jews in Romania," *Report on Eastern Europe,* vol. 2, no. 26, June 28, 1991 (RFE/RL Research Institute, Munich).

U.S. National Archives and Records Administration, Washington, D.C.: OSS Files, Microfilm T 1175, Rolls 658 and 663.

Anti-Semitism and the Treatment of the Holocaust in Postcommunist Slovakia

Raphael Vago

The declaration of sovereignty of the Slovak parliament following the elections of June 5-6, 1992 symbolized the end of the "Velvet Revolution" that effectuated the dissolution of Czechoslovakia and reflected the intensification of the area's ongoing "return to history." The results of the elections in Slovakia clearly indicate that nationalism is the most pervasive postcommunist trend in Eastern Europe. Although the separation was nonviolent, the shock waves of resurgent Slovak nationalism are bound to have implications on the process of rehabilitating the wartime Slovak state. Since late 1989, Slovak nationalists have systematically used the Slovak puppet state led by Josef Tiso as a role model for fulfilling national dreams of independence and sovereignty. The extreme right wing, which did not emerge as a powerful force in the 1992 elections, could in the long run be riding higher, inasmuch as xenophobic, anti-Semitic, extreme-nationalist viewpoints are entering the mainstream of Slovakia's post-1989 political culture. Jews and Hungarians have increasingly been targeted as the main enemies of "Slovak independence." The combination of the grave economic crisis in Slovakia, the difficulties in splitting the assets and liabilities of Czechoslovakia, the very process of partitioning the country–which will certainly take a long time–are bound to intensify nationalism and bring to the fore new ways of expressing it. The correlation between the difficulties in facing the future and the return to a dark past is clear, and the case of Slovakia is yet another indication of a process evident in several East European states.

The Communist Legacy

The communist regime in Czechoslovakia left behind a difficult legacy in regard to anti-Semitism and the Holocaust, as became clearly evident after the Velvet Revolution in the reactions of wide segments of the public when the ignorance and falsification of history propagated by the communist regime became known. Czechoslovakia's post-World War II history is burdened by the extent to which anti-Semitism was used by the regime, culminating in the 1952 trials of Rudolf Slansky and other top communist officials.[1] For years the victims of the Holocaust were described as "Czechoslovak citizens"; the textbooks from which the new generation learned did not specify the extent of Jewish losses during the war and did not dwell on the anti-Semitic aspects of the Slovak state. The definitions of fascist and anti-Semite became blurred as new generations were taught about the evils of Nazism and fascism but not about the anti-Semitic nature of these regimes and movements.

As in the other Eastern European states, the communist regime of Czechoslovakia regarded the history of the Holocaust as taboo. Government and party officials have for years systematically refused to commemorate the memory of the Jewish victims at various sites in Czechoslovakia and in the death camps. One such request for a memorial plaque by the Jewish community in Prague was turned down by the authorities in 1973 with the argument that it would "insult the feeling of the working people in view of Israel's aggression" in the Yom Kippur War of 1973.[2]

Not only did the topic of the Holocaust become taboo, but a veil of silence was also drawn over other post-World War II events such as the anti-Semitic riots that occurred in 1945-48, especially in Slovakia, which resembled those in Poland and Hungary.

Coming as they did after a short-lived honeymoon in 1948 between Czechoslovakia on one side and the young State of Israel and Zionism on the other, the turn to the worse evidenced by the show trials left a very bitter legacy. A new trial of officials of the Jewish communities took place in 1956.[3]

In 1968, during what became known as the Prague Spring, there was a genuine attempt to cope with the past, especially in Slovakia. The leading intellectuals of the period opened the pages of popular as well as professional journals to discussion of the fate of Czechoslovak Jewry during the Holocaust, the role of the Slovak state in implementing the "final solution," and the cynical utilization of anti-Semitism by the regime. However, following the Soviet invasion and the "Husak consolidation," Czechoslovakia followed the Soviet line more than faithfully. State anti-Semitism became a major element of the anti-Zionist and anti-Israel policy of the regime. Publications dealing with Jewish matters, especially those relating to the Holocaust, were cut to a minimum. For public relations purposes, the regime allowed some Jewish-related presentations such as the exhibition on the Jewish past entitled "Precious Legacy" to be shown in various Western countries–but not in Israel; however, this did not entail a change in the anti-Semitic line.

Until the early 1980s, the Czechoslovak media pursued an open anti-Zionist and anti-Israel campaign, often using direct translations from the Soviet press. (Czechoslovakia and East Germany were the only Soviet Bloc countries to do so.) "Original" Czechoslovak contributions to this campaign included, for example, a series of articles published in 1979 in the weekly *Tribuna* which, echoing the Soviet line, drew a connection between the Nazis and the Zionists. The author of the series was Svatopluk Dolejs, reportedly the wartime editor of a Prague Nazi weekly, *Ariiski Boi* [Aryan Battle].[4]

While some Eastern European states such as Hungary and Poland were opening a keener discussion of the Holocaust and the wartime role and behavior of the respective nations, Czechoslovakia continued its policy of silence. Although more contacts were initiated with world Jewish organizations and there were symbolic gestures aimed at pleasing Jewish organizations with regard to the fate of Czech Jewry during the Holocaust, in Slovakia there were few if any signs of a keener discussion of the wartime role of the Slovak state. Slovakia may well have been the last of the Eastern European states to face the past, not starting the process in earnest until the collapse of the communist regime in late 1989.

Winds of Change Before the Velvet Revolution

In the last two years of the communist regime there were several indications that the pressure for reforms and pluralism had touched on issues relating to the Jewish past, and in particular to Jewish-Slovak relations and the responsibility of the wartime Slovak state for the fate of its Jewish population. The most significant development was the 1987 proclamation by 24 leading intellectuals, published in a *samizdat* journal that was well-known to the authorities and wide segments of the intelligentsia.[5] The declaration amounted to the first attempt by leading Slovak intellectuals to face their nation's recent past. The signatories, some of them members of the younger, postwar generation, included prominent figures about to play a leading role in post-1989 Slovakia. They asked for "forgiveness from all living relatives of the victims of inhumanity and all members of their nation, because so far no one in authority among us has done so." The document recalled the treatment of the Jews by the Tiso regime–an important point in light of the post-1989 attempts to rehabilitate the former president–and emphasized that the deportation of the Jews of Slovakia during the war "runs counter to the principles upon which we would like to build Slovakia's future–equality for all regardless of race, tolerance, freedom of worship, democracy, rule of law, and love of mankind." The document recalled the attempts of the communist regime to ignore the past and its stubborn refusal to allow decent commemorations in memory of the Jewish victims.

The declaration was openly criticized by the official press in a rather confused way,[6] leaving the impression that the regime could not ignore the voices of the leading Slovak dissidents but could not endorse them either. At the same time, by 1987 the Slovak press had published several articles that dealt more openly with the fate of Slovak Jewry and the role of the Slovak state. The growing attention focused on Slovak-Jewish relations and the fate of Slovak Jewry during the Holocaust was related not only to the pressure exerted by well-known dissident intellectuals and the attempts of the regime to present a more "liberal" and open-minded attitude on these issues, but also to the voices of Slovak emigrés in the West. In July 1987 the General Assembly of the Slovak World Congress, the leading organization of Slovak emigrés in the West, adopted a resolution in Toronto that presented a clear attempt to start a new phase in Slovak-Jewish relations. Inasmuch as the Slovak World Congress had been founded by, and had among its activists, former leading members of the pro-Nazi Hlinka movement and the wartime Tiso regime, the attempts by the Congress to provide a new look at the past with a view to the future could not have gone unnoticed by either the official circles or the dissidents' groups in Slovakia. The World Slovak Congress expressed its "sincere regrets for the misdeeds and injustices committed against our Jewish fellow citizens during the war years."[7] The declaration stressed the "democratically minded, compassionate, and peaceable" nature of the Slovak nation in terms that recalled similar attempts in Eastern Europe, especially in Romania, to whitewash the role of the respective nation during the Holocaust by stressing the intrinsic nature of such positive national qualities. The timing of the declaration should be seen in the context of the attempts by the Congress to change its tarnished image and acquire more respectability by opening a dialogue with Jewish organizations. In view of the subsequent dramatic changes in Czechoslovakia, not anticipated at the time, and the role of the emigré organizations in fostering the new spirit of Slovak nationalism after the Velvet Revolution, the declaration by the Slovak World Congress takes on greater significance as an indicator of the attitudes among the younger generation of Slovak emigrés active in the

West before 1989, some of whom continued their activities in post-1989 Slovakia.

With the growing pressure within Czechoslovakia for reforms, more voices were added to those calling for a more open look at issues relating to the Jewish past, especially the Holocaust, and the fate of the Jewish community in Czechoslovakia in 1989. A Charter 77 document, dated April 1989,[8] sharply criticized the attitude of the communist regime regarding the remembrance of the Jewish victims of the Holocaust, from the hiding of the true facts in textbooks to the absence of memorial plaques and organized sites commemorating the Jewish victims. The document also discussed the neglect of Jewish cemeteries, synagogues, and museums linked to the Jewish past. It especially singled out the lack of information provided at sites such as Theresienstadt and the restrictions on access to documents relating to the Holocaust. The "destruction of the religious and cultural life" of the Jewish community was mentioned several times in the document, which provided ample examples of a premeditated policy aiming at the distortion of historical truth.

Before the first shocks of the earthquake in 1989, the small Jewish community of Czechoslovakia, numbering less than 12,000 and involved in a rapid process of "decommunizing" and reorganizing its top leadership, did not raise its voice. A group of younger and middle-aged members of the community criticized its leadership in February 1989, blaming it for not utilizing to the fullest the limited means and facilities provided by the regime for furthering Jewish life in the country.[9] The targets of the sharp criticism were Bohumil Heller, Chairman of the Council of Jewish Religious Communities in the Czech Socialist Republic, and Frantisek Kraus, Secretary General of the Council. The criticism was leveled principally at the operating procedures of the community's leadership and its ability to cope with the revival of Jewish identity in a period of political uncertainty.

While pressure from within the Jewish community against the established leadership did not directly include issues linked to the ways in which the Holocaust is treated and signs of anti-

Semitism, the revitalization of the community immediately after the regime's collapse facilitated a stronger Jewish response to the emergence of anti-Semitism and historical revisionism.

From Slovak Separatism to Anti-Semitism

The second postcommunist elections in Czechoslovakia were held in June 1992. The victory of Vladimir Meciar's Movement for a Democratic Slovakia reflected the strong nationalistic wave sweeping Slovakia two and a half years after the collapse of the communist regime. Slovak political life at this time was marked by a growing polarization and radicalization in which extremist formulas of the right wing found their way into the mainstream of political life. Anti-Semitism and the process of historical revisionism, in this case the rehabilitation of Josef Tiso, became major elements in Slovakia's post-1989 political life. There were a number of anti-Semitic incidents, usually attributed to "small groups of psychologically unbalanced skinheads"–this was, for example, the reaction of Prime Minister Vladimir Meciar to the vandalization of the Jewish cemetery in Nitra in November 1990. Additionally, anti-Semitic accusations became a standard feature of the new-old political culture of the republic. There were two main elements in the rise of political anti-Semitism: accusations against moderate politicians and public figures who were, or were suspected of being, of Jewish origin, and the growing equating of Jews with "the enemies of the nation."

The campaign against "Jews" controlling the new regime echoed similar accusations from other Eastern European states including Poland and Romania, or the accusations in Hungary against the alleged "Jewish nature" of the Alliance of Free Democrats (*Szabad Demokraták Szövetsége*), a major left-of-center party. The sensationalist Prague daily *Stredocesky Express* (Central Czech Express) published an article in October 1990 claiming that the country was still ruled by communists who in fact had masterminded their own removal by such clever means as fostering the Charter 77 movement–which, according to this article, was a "Jewish Freemasonry Lodge" and acted in conjunction with Russia's KGB, the United States' CIA, the Czech secret service, and of course Israel's Mossad.

The coalition of communists, many of them offspring of well-known communist leaders, were said to be the very people, mostly Jews, who tried to block the national aspirations of the Slovak people. This point resembled very similar accusations in Romania, where the children of former communists were cited as "living proof" for the theory of "communist continuity." In fact, the growing accusations in Slovakia about a Jewish conspiracy were picked up by the anti-Semitic, racist, and fascist press of other countries. For example, the *Christian Defense League Report* published in the U.S.A. quoted the "revelations" of the Prague newspaper with its comments that "pro-Jewish stooge President Havel of the Bohemian [Czech] nation has recently made statements against those who would protect themselves from Jewish manipulators."[10] In addition, Jews were blamed for every failure of Slovak nationalists to advance their legitimate demands. Thus, in the same *CDL Report* there is a statement that "in November 1990, Slovak nationalists tried to get a bill passed in the Slovak parliament in Bratislava regarding separate languages for the Slovaks and the Czechs. The bill was scuttled due to efforts by the Jews and their allies."

In postcommunist Eastern Europe there are numerous extremist publications that are produced and distributed by dubious and often unknown sources. In Slovakia the clearing house for extremist propaganda is AGRES Publishing House, the publisher of most of the anti-Semitic pamphlets, brochures, and books. AGRES's publications include a pamphlet defending Iraq's policies during the Gulf War; this was characteristic of Eastern European extremist publications, which presented Iraq's case as part of their anti-Semitic and anti-Israel propaganda. An article in the *Prague Post*[11] raised the possibility that Arab money was financing extremist publications and publishers, including AGRES.

It was AGRES that published the vicious anti-Semitic *The Protocols of the Elders of Zion* as well as the anti-Zionist pamphlet *Geneza Sionizmu* [The Genesis of Zionism].[12] Despite the bitter Czech-Slovak debate between the nationalists on both sides, anti-Semitism seems to hold an appeal for the extremists on both sides of the debate.

Between 1989 and 1992 there clearly was a great deal of cooperation between AGRES and Czech right-wing nationalists and anti-Semites. Starting in 1991 the leading Czech anti-Semitic newspaper, *Politika,* has had a joint publishing agreement with AGRES, which in fact became the publishing house that specialized in Czech anti-Semitic, anti-Zionist, and anti-Israeli literature. Martin A. Savel, one of the directors of AGRES, was very active in defending the publication of *The Protocols of the Elders of Zion* and other anti-Semitic material when it was confiscated on orders of the District Attorney of Bratislava to keep it from being displayed and available for purchase, in hundreds of copies, at the Book Fair held in Olomouc in March 1992.[13] In the course of his argument, Savel maintained that the books had been confiscated under the direct orders of the Israeli government acting through its embassy in Prague. AGRES also published pieces by the Czech right-wing extremist Vojtech Doleisi, who specializes in one of the new myths of the post-1989 extremists in Eastern Europe: that the Velvet Revolution was the result of a conspiracy among the KGB, the Western intelligence services, and the Jews.

While there was no mass political movement in Czechoslovakia that directly blamed the Jews for "ruling" the Federation, in this period of proliferating newspapers and magazines freed from the restrictions of communism many publications competed against each other in the area of sensational "revelations," most of them dealing with an alleged conspiracy against the Slovak people. Characteristic of such attacks was the article in *Novy Slovak* [New Slovak], a well known ultra-nationalist newspaper, claiming that "Slovak political life is permeated by people of non-Slovak origin."[14] The logic of the article was very clear–the "non-Slovaks" who had penetrated Slovak political life were Jews and Czechs working collaboratively to destabilize Slovakia. The Jews–and in this case the main target was Fedor Gal, the chairman of the liberal wing of Public Against Violence, the Slovak counterpart of the Hungarian Democratic Forum (*Magyar Demokrata Fórum,* a right-of-center party)–were said to be "Czechoslovakists," meaning that they were opposed to the aspirations of the Slovak people, and to include Havel, Foreign Minister Jiri Dienstbier, and then Minister of Finance Vaclav Klaus. The article in *Novy Slovak,* entitled "Gal's Camarilla and the Talmud," used a combination of political and religious anti-Semitic formulas, such as, for example: "The Talmud, that diabolical teaching, allows the cheating of a Christian–or a Slovak." It should be noted that the obsessive reference to the Talmud's "diabolical teachings" was not unique to Slovakia; this mode was widely used in Romania in such newspapers as *România Mare* [Greater Romania] and *Europa.*

Following the vitriolic accusations and even physical violence, Fedor Gal resigned in May 1991 and left Slovakia with his family. He was the first casualty of political anti-Semitism in the newly independent postcommunist Slovakia. Inasmuch as the campaign against Gal was led by Vladimir Meciar's Movement for a Democratic Slovakia, the way this movement (which emerged victorious in the June 1992 elections) used nationalism in the campaign is highly significant. A very bitter recounting of the campaign against Fedor Gal has been published by his son Robert Gal. He emphasized that one of the accusations against his father originated by the Movement for a Democratic Slovakia was that Fedor Gal had dared to bring up the question of the Slovak national state's guilt in the fate of Slovak Jewry during the Holocaust. Reflecting on that accusation, Robert Gal wrote that in the existing atmosphere not only whoever speaks out "against the alleged purity of the Slovak nation, which is absolutely innocent, is guilty, but so is whoever doubts its innocence."[15]

During 1991 several incidents were reported in which members of the Federal Assembly received anti-Semitic documents in the mail that accused the "ruling trio" of Havel, Dienstbier, and Klaus of "conspiring with world Zionist and Freemason organizations." Thomas Masaryk, the founder of Czechoslovakia, was described as an enemy of the Slovaks and a friend of the Jews, and the United Nations was presented as a body "controlled by Jews."

Leading former dissidents of Jewish origin were especially targeted in a campaign of slander and threats of violence. Such a campaign was conducted, for example, against Miroslav Kusy, one of the best known pre-1989 dissidents and the representative of President Havel's office in Slovakia. The harassment of Kusy included the placement in several newspapers of advertisements in his name offering *The Protocols of the Elders of Zion* for sale.

Czechoslovakia's Ambassador to the United States, Rita Klimova, the daughter of a former editor of the Communist Party newspaper *Rude Pravo* [Red Justice], was frequently criticized by anti-Semites in Slovakia and cited as "proof" of Jewish control of the regime. In late 1991 Mrs. Klimova was attacked by representatives of all shades of opinion in Slovakia as a result of a statement by her in the U.S.A. on expressions of anti-Semitism in her country; she was accused of having slandered Slovakia by allegations of anti-Semitism. President Havel came to her defense, explaining that she had spoken not of "anti-Semitic demonstrations" but of "demonstrations of anti-Semitism" which, as stressed by Havel, were unfortunately visible in Slovakia as well as elsewhere.[16]

Immediately after November 1989 there was an increase in the number of anti-Semitic incidents. Some of them were acts of vandalism such as that in the Jewish cemetery in Nitra, where swastikas had been painted on gravestones, or the numerous graffiti in Bratislava that were no different from those in other Eastern European cities including Warsaw, Budapest, or Bucharest. However, shortly after the Velvet Revolution a more disturbing sign emerged: a surge of right-wing extremism in both parts of the Czechoslovak state. There were daily reports of attacks on foreign workers–sad leftovers from the days of "socialist internationalism"–and Gypsies, and in Slovakia also on Hungarians who were accused of attempts to dismember Slovakia. The separatist movement in Slovakia, which gradually encompassed almost all shades of opinion across the political spectrum, started to use an offensive language that was bound to have an immediate impact on expressions of anti-Semitism and other forms of xenophobia, especially against Hungarians and Gypsies.

With an internal split within Public Against Violence as well as the trend toward center to center-right movements, some led by former communists, the polemical language became more vitriolic and attacks on "aliens" sabotaging Slovak national rebirth became a standard feature of Slovak politics. As mentioned earlier, conspiracy theories were abundant and often propagated by high-level officials of the Slovak Republic. During a mass demonstration in Bratislava on March 14, 1991, commemorating the formation of the Slovak National State, some of the banners bore very explicit anti-Czech and anti-Semitic messages such as "Out with the Jews," "Czechs back to Prague on foot," and "Jewish pigs." Slovak Minister of the Interior Ladislav Pittner provided some original explanations for the racist and fascist character of the demonstration. He declared: "I do not exclude the possibility that, in addition to former members of the state security organizations and chauvinistic Czechs, foreign sponsors may also have participated in organizing the demonstration, namely the foreign sponsors who were already interested last year in the painting of anti-Semitic slogans in Slovakia. In the intelligence service we had indications that Western intelligence services were financing those slogans in order to destabilize the situation here."[17]

The accusation that "foreign" elements were interested in spreading anti-Semitism, of course, had to be coupled with an economic reason. As Pittner explained, "Why would Western capital not be interested in buying factories in Czechoslovakia cheaply? And when would it buy them? When there is disorder here to scare away other prospective buyers." One may wonder about the true extent of the collapse of the old regime in view of the fact that in 1991 the Slovak Minister of the Interior was still using classical Stalinist arguments.

The resurgence of anti-Semitism is undoubtedly linked to the deep economic crisis in Slovakia. Facing large-scale unemployment, Slovak politicians openly criticized U.S.-Israeli pressure aimed at the suspension of deliveries to Syria of tanks built in Slovakia. One Slovak newspaper calculated the expected loss to the Slovak economy of such a suspension, and asked: "Who will pay for it? The United States, the wealthiest country in the world, wealthy Israel (sic), or poor Czechoslovakia, currently in a deep depression caused by the transformation of its economy?"[18]

In this context it should be mentioned that Havel's positive attitude to Israel, his state visit in April 1990, and the return visit by President Herzog in October 1991 that included a stop in Slovakia have often been mentioned as examples of "Israeli pressure" on Slovakia on the issue of the sale of tanks to Syria. One must take into consideration the vulnerable state of the Slovak economy, which faced the double task of implementing market reforms and, after June 1992, preparing the economy for an eventual break-up of the Federation. It is not surprising that "economic anti-Semitism" could easily find its way into the mainstream of politics, both through conspiracy theories holding that anti-Semitism was a Western capitalist provocation and because of the pressure to limit the heavy-armaments industry, which unfortunately was a basic component of a major part of Slovakia's socialist economy.

The Holocaust and the Planned Rehabilitation of Josef Tiso

Historical revisionism and the rehabilitation of those guilty of war crimes is certainly not a phenomenon unique to Slovakia–it is a phenomenon that appears in all of Eastern Europe. Since 1989, the rehabilitation of Josef Tiso, Slovakia's leader during World War II who was executed in 1947, and the whitewashing of the role of the Slovak state during the war became one of the major issues dominating political and public debate in Slovakia. The attempts by Soviet emigrés in the West, led by the Slovak National Council, to change the image of Tiso and his movement have been going on for years. The main thesis of the pro-Tiso argument is that in fact he "used his presidential exemption power to save as many as he could."[19] Under this thesis Slovakia is portrayed as a haven for Slovak and Central European Jews between September 1942 and August 1944. The argument focuses on Tiso's "moderate" line as compared to the one pursued by the extremists, and disregards the fascist-clerical nature of the Hlinka movement with its clearly racist, anti-Semitic ideology.

Within the country, the attempts to rehabilitate the wartime Slovak puppet state, on lines similar to those advanced for years by the emigrés, started very soon after the collapse of the communist regime. Within a short time something resembling a cult had developed around the person and views of Tiso, who was portrayed as a victim of underserved persecution–a victim of communists, Jews, and enemies of the idea of an independent Slovakia. This was very similar to what was happening in Romania with regard to General Ion Antonescu. The first major public incident in Czechoslovakia relating to the Tiso rehabilitation was the unveiling of a commemorative plaque in Banovce in July 1990. Large segments of Czechoslovakia's public and political circles condemned this action that honored the memory of the war criminal responsible for the deportation and murder of more than 80,000 Slovak Jews. President Havel strongly condemned the unveiling of the plaque, which indeed was removed several days later.

The attempts to rehabilitate Tiso and everything he stood for rapidly became more organized and coordinated. A good indication of this is the evolution of the manner in which March 14, the anniversary of the birth of "independent Slovakia" in 1939, has been commemorated since 1990. In 1991, some 10,000 extremists demonstrated in Bratislava, insulting Havel and carrying signs proclaiming slogans such as "Long live Tiso" and "Only Hitler was able to teach the Czechs and those Jewish pigs a lesson." At the time Prime Minister Meciar spoke out strongly against the clearly revisionist, pro-Tiso, nationalist demonstration; however, no practical conclusions were drawn from the nationalistic, anti-Semitic upsurge and the attempt to rehabilitate Tiso. As mentioned earlier, the Slovak Minister of the Interior attributed the extremist and anti-Semitic slogans to "foreign agents."

The various political parties, including the Christian Democratic Movement, the coalition partner of Public Against Violence, called for "an objective evaluation of the past." It is very indicative of the radicalization of Slovak political life that in the June 1992 elections the Christian Democratic Movement, led by Prime Minister Jan Carnogursky, lost to Meciar's Movement for a Democratic Slovakia.

The "objective evaluation of the past," in fact, became a strong pressure, bluntly rejected by the liberal media, to rehabilitate the wartime Slovak state. The "Jewish question" became a side issue that was rather conveniently pushed aside by the nationalists. The Jewish aspect, in fact, only came to the forefront of discussions when leading intellectuals rejected the attempts to mythologize "the Slovak national state" as well as the Tiso cult. Several major arguments were advanced very forcefully by the new Slovak politicians. One was that the wartime Slovak state had been the historical fulfillment of Slovak aspirations for independence. Thus, they held that one should not concentrate so much on the ideology and nature of the regime but rather focus on its essence as the embodiment of age-old national aspirations. It followed from this principle that anyone attempting to criticize the Slovak state and subject its activities, for example with regard to the Jewish question, to more close examination was acting against the interests of the Slovak nation. In post-1989 Slovakia it very soon became politically correct to identify with the past for the sake of a bright national future. The legal status of the wartime Slovak state became an important pillar in the rehabilitation of Tiso and his regime, since its legal existence proved, or was supposed to prove, the legality of the Slovak state and thus could provide a legal basis for a possible new, post-1989 independent Slovakia. Even some moderate politicians adhered to the theory of "continuity" and accepted the legality of Slovak wartime "independence" under Tiso. Thus Frantisek Miklosko, the chairman of the Slovak National Council, stressed that the Slovaks had had a proper and firm legal basis for declaring independence in March 1939.[20] Miklosko, who at the time (1991) was also a member of the executive committee of Public Against Violence, recognized that his movement was adopting an "unambiguous attitude" toward the Slovak state, although "...we distanced ourselves from it. There were deportations of Jews; there was the rule of a single party...." In this case, even among the most moderate Slovak politicians who openly distanced themselves from the character of the Tiso regime, the temptation to support the legal basis for the state was too great to resist. It should be noted, though, that the arguments supporting the legal continuity between the wartime Slovak state and the process started after 1989 were rejected by some well-known historians.[21]

From the ultranationalist small fringe groups to the major political parties, defending the legacy of the Slovak state became a primary objective. Such a near-obsession among Slovak politicians did not allow the emergence of a sharp public debate on the nature of the wartime state and its true legacy in regard to the fate of the Jews. Nevertheless, there were some very critical voices urging that "the main objective today is to do away with the whole legacy of the Slovak state and not to revive it."[22] According to one such view, "the unwanted Slovak state, imposed upon us by Hitler, was founded on Nazi ideology...." Furthermore, "nationalism, jingoism, and racism are being revived; there are renewed longings for unity, for some kind of totalitarian system, for a leader who would think and act for all of us and lead us toward a brighter future."[23]

Among the various viewpoints represented among those who are intent on rehabilitating Tiso and his regime, several shades of opinion can be distinguished. They range from "moderate revisionism" to the denial of the Holocaust, a range of views which is also evident in similar rehabilitation efforts in other formerly communist states of Eastern Europe.

The "moderate revisionists" clearly echo some of the arguments used by Slovak emigrés in the West. As the Slovak National Council leadership preached for years in the West, they do not deny the Holocaust; rather, they emphasize what they describe as "the rescue of Slovak Jews" by the Tiso regime. According to this line of argument, not only were the Germans to blame for the suffering that did occur but the Slovak wartime regime rescued Jews who might have perished under a direct German occupation.[24] Thus there is reinforcement of the argument that Tiso's regime was a positive one, inasmuch as among its other virtues it is said to have saved Jews by its very existence. As is the case in Romania, where the rehabilitation of Ion Antonescu runs parallel with that of Tiso, Slovak nationalists use the Holocaust to legitimize the role of their wartime regime, and their arguments concentrate on scenarios showing that more Jews might have been killed under different historical circumstances.

Compared to this more sophisticated approach, that of the Holocaust deniers is extremely easy to follow. Their extremist propaganda not only adds a chapter to the general history of the Holocaust denial but is also indicative of the linkage between anti-Semitism, historical revisionism, and Slovak nationalism. One of the most vocal deniers is Stanislav Panis, head of the Slovak National Unity Party. In various forums including the communications media, he has expounded a line which exactly repeats the arguments of the Holocaust revisionists in the West. In March 1992, during interviews on Norwegian as well as Czechoslovak television, he argued that the extermination of the Slovak Jews never took place and that it would have been technically impossible for the Germans to accomplish it.[25]

Another well-known revisionist is Frantisek Vnuk, one of the leaders of the Slovak Christian Democratic Party. Vnuk specializes in books on the Tiso era and has published, among

others, a biography of Alexander (Šano) Mach, the Minister of
the Interior in the wartime Slovak state. In several publications
and interviews he accused the Jews of slandering Slovakia by
blaming the Slovaks for deeds he claimed had never been
committed. His attempts to deny the Holocaust are often mixed
with anti-Israeli propaganda; for example, Vnuk wrote that the
same people who accused the Slovaks of "never committed" war
crimes were the very same people who were responsible for "the
violation of Palestinian rights."[26]

The role of the Church in the Slovak state is also conveniently being reevaluated. Since 1989, a process is taking place in
Slovakia that is in line with the viewpoint of the Slovak World
Congress, which in its publications systematically disregarded
the Christian anti-Semitism of Tiso's ideology and in recent
years emphasized the role of Church members who saved Jews.
The clearly observable religious revival in the country, yet
another accompanying feature of postcommunism, is being
reinforced by the rehabilitation of the Church. In this case too,
the views of the more moderate leaders are essential to reinforce
those of the extreme right wing. It seems that misinterpretations
by moderates fuel the extremist viewpoint, providing the extremists with legitimation. Frantisek Miklosko, the chairman of
the Slovak National Council, regards the term "clerical-fascist
state" as an artificial term that "was supposed to aid gradual
liquidation of the Church over 40 years;" the Slovak state "simply
had to rely on the Church, because in those days the Church
represented the only moral force."[27] One frequent argument
advanced by moderates such as Miklosko is that, in fact, the role
of the Church in the Slovak state was not as strong as has been
suggested, since "in addition to President Tiso, only two clerics
served in the Slovak parliament, one of whom was posthumously
honored with an award by the representatives of the Jewish
memorial organization Yad Vashem for rescuing Jews."
Miklosko's view that "the role of the Church in the Slovak state
has been slanted and distorted over the past 40 years" makes any
meaningful discussion of the true essence of the role of the
Church during the Tiso regime much more difficult.

Thus, even politicians who cannot be accused of fostering nationalism are in fact contributing to the revival of the Slovak fascist state's legacy. By identifying the clerical-fascist model as a "communist" model, they imply that anyone opposing the communist regime should view the role of the Slovak Church differently, in a manner that supports Tiso's position. As one critic of this position expounded, the Church in Slovakia could claim, based on Vojtech Tuka's statements, that "they fused Hitler's methods with Hlinka's spirit; thus they created a hybrid whose theory and practice sharply differed. In theory they remained Christians, but in practice they were Nazis. Never before has Christianity in our country been so discredited as in those days."[28] The wholesale whitewashing of the role of the Church in the Slovak state, along with the anti-Semitic Christianity that so deeply infused Tiso's dogma, creates a major obstacle to a meaningful debate on the issue in post-1989 Slovakia.

Attempts by high-ranking clergy to whitewash the Tiso regime by alleging Jewish collaboration with Tiso could only divert attention from a discussion of the policies and attitudes of the religious establishment in Slovakia during the Holocaust. There have been several disturbing signs since 1989 indicating that the Catholic Church and its leadership are not doing enough to foster a Jewish-Slovak reconciliation based on a confrontation with the Church's past. Church documents during 1989 to 1991 show that the higher levels of the Church in Slovakia failed to cope with the issues of the Holocaust and anti-Semitism, as the Polish episcopate has done despite the sensitivity of Polish-Jewish relations. In July 1990, Cardinal Corec participated in a ceremony to dedicate a plaque in memory of Tiso at Banovce, and local clergy participated in the unveiling of a second plaque in Tiso's birthplace.[29] There is no doubt that the highest echelons of the Catholic Church cannot be accused of anti-Semitism and Cardinal Corec himself supports pro-Jewish activities; nevertheless, the Church's current passivity in coping with the Holocaust and the revival of anti-Semitism seems clearly linked to the attempts to rehabilitate Tiso. Presumably there is a feeling that

Tiso's own background and the post-1989 identification between Slovak nationalism and religion are more important than facing aspects of the Church's own past.

The Slovak National Uprising of 1944 has also been the target of reappraisal. Deconstruction of a communist "myth" of the events and their significance has been going on since 1989. In this connection, the legacy of the communists is of course problematic as well, since communist historiography distorted aspects of the Banska Bystrica 1944 uprising and took credit for the communists' leading role. Today, this uprising is a main bone of contention between those who see it as one of "Slovakia's most progressive historical manifestations" and an attempt to save Slovakia from bearing "the mark of Cain or Hitler's stigma on its forehead"[30] on the one hand, and those who identify it with communism on the other. A positive view of the 1944 uprising is essential for the "theory of continuity" of the Slovak state during World War II. Thus, one of the small extremist political movements, the Slovak National Unity Party, has applied to change its name to Hlinka's Slovak People's Party (*Hlinkova Slovensak Lidova Strana*). The request for the name change, in a letter to the Slovak National Council, claimed that the 1944 decree to outlaw the fascist movement had been "issued on the territory of the sovereign Slovak republic by an illegal group of rebels consisting mostly of criminal, communist-oriented elements who opposed the Slovak state in the guise of the anti-fascist struggle."[31]

On the Future of Slovakia and the Future of the Past

With the changes in Czechoslovakia's structure, Slovakia has embarked on a road that will not only make it difficult to cope with the problems of the present but also will certainly make it more difficult for the Slovaks to face their own past. In Slovakia, as elsewhere in Eastern Europe, the future and the past are closely linked. Slovakia's "return to history" involves the legacy of wartime Slovak nationalism and its responsibility for the deportations and the death of some 80,000 of Czechoslovakia's 140,000 Jews. In contrast to the Czech Republic, it is highly likely that Slovakia, with its relative lack of civic culture, will head toward a more authoritarian system in which nationalism will play a major role. Slovakia is not a nation state, since at least 17 percent of its people are minorities, primarily Hungarians and Gypsies. The minuscule Jewish population is not under any direct threat; the issue is that of "anti-Semitism without Jews," for which Slovakia represents a clear example. The need for scapegoats, the search for "aliens" who oppose the national will, the myths of Judeo-communism on the one side and the Jewish plutocracy on the other, are all part of the nationalist revival in contemporary Slovakia.

The attempts to rehabilitate Tiso and his ideas and to whitewash the role of the wartime Slovak state in determining the fate of Slovak Jewry have become part of the political mainstream. It is, of course, highly significant that the opening since 1989 is providing opportunities for research and discussions among scholars; an example is the Symposium on the Tragedy of Slovak Hungarian Jewry held in March 1992 in Banska Bystrica.[32] Nevertheless, the main questions remain the extent to which the Slovak nation is willing and able to confront its past, and the extent to which the new means and forms of free expression will be used to highlight the historical truth.

As a 1992 study again documented, "anti-Semitism in Slovakia is a serious matter that must not be evaded or downplayed."[33] Fedor Gal, perhaps the first political victim of this round of Slovak anti-Semitism, has been just one of those who warned that the breakup of Czechoslovakia creates a fertile ground for nationalist chauvinism—and the first to feel the impact are always the Jews.[34] Anti-Semitism without Jews seems to have taken roots in postcommunist Czechoslovakia; even if it does not represent a widespread phenomenon, it poses a clear danger to the moral stability of the two new states emerging from the Czechoslovak state. Nostalgia for the past that is accompanied by a distortion of the historical truth will only be indicative of the retrograde aspect of Slovak nationalism in the past-1989 era. Truly, state-condoned anti-Semitism now represents a greater danger for the nation's own future than for the small Jewish community.

It is a sad coincidence that at the same time when a complaint against the publication of *The Protocols of the Elders of Zion* was rejected by a court in Bratislava in the name of "freedom of expression," the moral voice of President Havel was also rejected–perhaps also in the name of "freedom of expression"–by the Slovak voters in the 1993 elections.

NOTES

1.   Like Slansky, most of the 11 communist leaders executed on December 3, 1952 were of Jewish origin. They were accused, among other things, of having had links to Israel.

2.   For some aspects of the policy of the communist regime on commemorating the victims of the Holocaust, see the Charter 77 document of April 1989 published in *Soviet Jewish Affairs*, London, vol. 20, no. 1, 1990, pp. 58-65.

3.   Following the Sinai campaign, the Czechoslovak authorities intensified their campaign against alleged pro-Israeli and Zionist tendencies in the Jewish communal leadership. Twenty-seven community leaders were arrested during the end of 1956 and beginning of 1957 as "Western spies" and were accused of "Zionist activities." See *American Jewish Yearbook 1958*, Philadelphia, vol. 59, 1958, p. 334; *Encyclopedia Judaica*, vol. 15, p. 1202. On Czechoslovak Jewry after World War II see Avigdor Dagan, "The Jews of Czechoslovakia after World War II," *Gesher*, no. 2-3, 1969 (in Hebrew).

4.   Reported in Radio Free Europe's *Czechoslovak Situation Report*, no. 6, February 14, 1979.

5.   For a translation and analysis of the document, see Yeshayahu A. Jelinek, "Slovaks and the Holocaust: Attempts at Reconciliation," *Soviet Jewish Affairs*, vol. 19, no. 1, 1989, pp. 57-68. The "proclamation of the twenty-four" was also published in *Cross Currents*, vol. 9, 1990.

6.   Jelinek, op. cit., p. 67.

7.   Ibid., p. 61.

8. See footnote 2.

9. *Soviet Jewish Affairs*, vol. 20, no. 1, 1990, pp. 58-65.

10. *Christian Defense League Report*, no. 136, January 1991, p. 3.

11. See *Anti-Semitic Publications and Holocaust Denial in Slovakia—July 1992* (Tel-Aviv: Tel-Aviv University, Project for the Study of Anti-Semitism, 1992), p. 1.

12. Yeshayahu A. Jelinek, "Slovaks and the Holocaust: An End to Reconciliation?", *East European Jewish Affairs*, vol. 22, no. 1, 1992, p. 18.

13. See *Anti-Semitic Publications and Holocaust Denial*, op. cit., p. 2.

14. M. Mozer in *Novy Slovak*, 14, 1991, quoted in Joint Publications Research Service's *JPRS-EER*, Washington, May 2, 1991.

15. Robert Gal in *Kulturny Zivot* (Cultural Life), Bratislava, December 31, 1991, published in English in *JPRS-EER*, December 27, 1991. For the campaign against Fedor Gal, see also "Antisemitism in Central and Eastern Europe," *Research Reports of the Institute of Jewish Affairs*, London, nos. 4-6, 1991.

16. Ambassador Klimova explained the origins of the misunderstanding in the Prague daily *Lidove Noviny* (People's Newspaper), October 30, 1991.

17. *Respekt*, Prague, March 31, 1991. Translation in *JPRS-EER*, May 8, 1991.

18. *Narodna Obroda* (National Rebirth), Bratislava, October 16, 1991.

19. Ibid.

20. The interview with Miklosko was published in *Respekt*, October 6, 1991. Translation in *JPRS-EER*, October 25, 1991.

21. See, for example, Jan Mlynarik in *Respekt*, October 6, 191. Translation in *JPRS-EER*, October 25, 1991.

22. Teodor Munz in *Kulturny Zivot*, August 26, 1991. Translation in *JPRS-EER*, September 30, 1991.

23. Ibid.

24. Yeshayahu A. Jelinek, "Historical and Actual Minority Problems in Czecho-Slovakia," *Patterns of Prejudice*, London, vol. 17, no. 1, 1993, p. 103.

25. *Anti-Semitic Publications and Holocaust Denial*, op. cit., p. 1.

26. *Koridor*, April 22, 1992 as quoted in *Prague Post*, May 19-25, 1992.

27. Interview with Miklosko, op. cit.

28. Munz, op. cit.

29. Jelinek, *Slovaks and the Holocaust*, op. cit., p. 1.

30. Munz, op. cit.

31. Reported by Radio Prague in *Summary of World Broadcasts* (SWB-EE), November 7, 1991.

32. For conferences on anti-Semitism in Czechoslovakia, see *Jerusalem Post*, February 21 and March 23, 1992; *SICSA Report* (Newsletter of the Vidal Sassoon International Center for the Study of Antisemitism, The Hebrew University of Jerusalem), no. 7, Spring 1992.

33. Zora Butorova and Martin Butora, *Wariness Towards Jews and 'Post-Communist Panic' in Slovakia* (New York: American Jewish Committee, December 1992).

34. *The Jewish Chronicle*, London, January 1, 1993.

Anti-Semitism and the Treatment of the Holocaust in the USSR/CIS

William Korey

Orwellian inversion has rarely been illuminated as effectively as in a Soviet literary experience about which Arthur Miller, the distinguished Pulitzer Prize playwright, had written a quarter of a century ago.

A prominent Soviet author had written a children's book titled *The Story of the Bible.* The editors, though enthusiastic about the book, were unhappy with the author's treatment of certain concepts, such as "God" and "Jewish People." As the editors put it, "God is a mythological construction, and in any strict sense mentioning God is really unnecessary." But what disturbed the editors even more than the reference to God were the repeated comments about "the Jewish People." "Why is that necessary?" the editors asked. When the author began to answer that "the Bible, you see is...," he was cut off with the following:

> Why not simply call them "the People"? After all, it comes to the same thing, and in fact it generalizes and enhances the significance of the whole story. Call them "the People."

Not only was the title changed to read *Myths of the People,* but the Jews suddenly, as if by magic, disappeared as a historical entity. They had been plunged down the "memory hole" of history.

The episode was no isolated incident. A close study of the Soviet history textbooks published at the time and used in the Russian Republic's elementary and secondary schools in the 1970s and much of the 1980s revealed that Jews were virtually invisible, whether in Russian history or in world history. (The other Union Republics of the USSR replicated the Moscow teaching pattern.) Not only were Jews rarely referred to; Jewish culture was never treated and the contribution of Jews to civilization was completely neglected. Both ancient and present-day Israel, if mentioned at all, were discussed in a highly critical and condescending manner.

The suppression of Jewish historical identity was very much an expression of the official Soviet anti-Semitism that had characterized the USSR since World War II. Jewish institutions were obliterated with the obvious intention of pulverizing Jewish consciousness. At the same time, an anti-Jewish quota system was imposed in employment and higher education. Virulent anti-Jewish propaganda, masquerading first as anti-"cosmopolitanism" and later as anti-Zionism, was unleashed by the Kremlin to saturate the reading (and, at times, viewing) public.

Not that the Kremlin ever admitted to its racist, anti-Jewish policy. The contrary was the case. Premier Aleksei Kosygin in 1967 hammered home the Orwellian thesis that "there has never been and thee is no anti-Semitism in the Soviet Union." Nearly 20 years later, a glasnost-oriented Communist Party General Secretary, Mikhail Gorbachev, was to repeat the theme. Queried in February 1986 by the French communist newspaper *L'Humanité* about anti-Jewish bigotry in the USSR, he responded that anti-Semitism was "impossible in the USSR" because it was "prohibited by law and constitutes a crime."

Gorbachev was referring to Article 36 of the USSR Constitution and Article 74 of the Russian Criminal Code–replicated in the criminal codes of other Union Republics. The constitution prohibited the advocacy of racial or national hostility and the criminal code made the "inciting (of) national discord" a crime punishable by incarceration of up to several years. But no one in the Soviet Union has ever been charged with anti-Semitic behavior, let alone convicted and sentenced, after the 1920s up to the early 1990s.

Pulverization of group consciousness was no easy task. It was insufficient to blot out the Jewish past from history textbooks. Imprinted deeply on the memory of every Jewish family was the trauma of the Nazi Holocaust, the greatest tragedy ever inflicted upon the Jewish people throughout its long history. Moreover, there was hardly a Jewish family in Soviet Russia that was spared the consequences of Hitler's genocidal plans. Expunging the Holocaust from the record of the past was hardly a simple matter, but unless it were done the profound anguish of the memory was certain to stir a throbbing national consciousness. Martyrdom, after all, is a powerful stimulus to a group's sense of its own identity.

The expunging of the Holocaust began with the liquidation of a major source work, the famous *Black Book* which documented the fate of Soviet Jewry under the Nazis. Prepared during and immediately after World War II by the prominent Jewish writers Ilya Ehrenburg and Vasily Grossman with the assistance of 27 others, the work encompassed sixty-five detailed reports totalling 1,200 typescript pages. Ehrenburg would later recall how the diaries, letters, and eyewitness accounts which documented the painful horrors of the Holocaust in the Soviet Union gave him the feeling "that I was in the ghetto...and they were driving me towards the ravine or ditch." Close to two million Soviet Jews were murdered or disappeared.

The monumental work was printed in 1946. But not a single copy of the *Black Book* reached state libraries, let alone Soviet bookstores. The entire edition was taken directly to warehouses. Original type molds were smashed by Stalin. (A hidden copy of the manuscript safely reached Palestine and, eventually, was translated and published in Hebrew and English.)

A veritable blackout was to engulf the Holocaust in Soviet Russia. Textbooks in the primary and secondary schools taught nothing about the massacre of Jews. Indeed, anti-Semitism was not even mentioned as a vital element of Nazi ideology or of such notorious concentration camps as Auschwitz. A Congress of Jewish Organizations meeting in Moscow in December 1989, bemoaned the fact that "there are no historical studies and publications in the USSR devoted to the genocide of Jews; in the schoolbooks, the tragedy of the Jewish people is not mentioned."

The policy of total silence was initiated in late 1948 when the curtain was rung down by Stalin on all Jewish communal institutions, and the Jewish Anti-Fascist Committee was liquidated. Prior to that development, Moscow had published works on Jewish partisans and on the Jewish resistance movement in the Minsk ghetto. Later, a translation of *The Diary of Anne Frank* provided a deviation from what had become the norm.

In 1987, after Gorbachev spoke of the need to fill in the "blank spots" of history, a leading Jewish activist from Leningrad, Semyon Dyskin, wrote to the Central Committee of the Soviet Communist Party formally complaining that works about the Holocaust had not been published in the USSR. His letter strikingly noted that there was no Russian word for the English word "Holocaust" or the Hebrew word "Shoah." At the same time, heroic Jewish resistance to the Nazis was stunningly suppressed. Dyskin asked: "Where can the Soviet reader obtain information about the historic struggle of the Jews against Fascism?" Or "about the revolt of the Warsaw ghetto and about the unprecedented uprising in the Treblinka concentration camp where a small group of Jews managed to destroy the camp and escape to bring the incredible and horrible truth to the world?"

The Soviet attempt to obliterate the Holocaust in the memories of Jews as well as non-Jews was especially pronounced in the case of Babi Yar, near Kiev, the site and symbol of Soviet Jewry's greatest tragedy during the Nazi era. Almost from the beginning, Soviet authorities sought to blur this record. Six months after Kiev's liberation, the official government report on the massacre referred to Nazi crimes against Soviet citizens generally rather than against Jews specifically.

Plans were made by some Soviet officials shortly after the war for a monument to be built at Babi Yar. A well-known architect, A. V. Vlasov, designed a memorial and the artist B. Ovchinnikov worked out appropriate sketches for a sculptured frieze. But these plans were quietly shelved. In March 1949, a Ukrainian-Jewish poet, Savva Golovanivsky, who had written sympathetically about the victims at Babi Yar, was denounced for "defamation of the Soviet nation." For more than a decade, Babi Yar and its ghastly history were blanketed in silence. Meanwhile, Kiev city officials began to advance proposals to flood the site, fill it with earth and turn it into a park on which a stadium would be erected.

These plans prompted sensitive intellectuals, momentarily encouraged by an official cultural "thaw," to react with revulsion. Viktor Nekrasov, a prominent Ukrainian novelist and writer, wrote in *Literaturnaia Gazeta* on October 10, 1959: "Is this possible? Who could have thought of such a thing? To fill a...deep ravine and on the site of such a colossal tragedy to make merry and play football?"

A much larger community, extending far beyond Soviet borders, was stirred by poet Yevgeny Yevtushenko in September 1961, almost twenty years to the day after the Babi Yar tragedy. In a poem recited to 1,200 students in Moscow on September 16 and published three days later in *Literaturnaia Gazeta,* Yevtushenko bewailed the fact that "no monument stands over Babi Yar," where, he declared, a major episode in the history of Jewish martyrdom had taken place. Before long, the official response was issued: eight days after it was published, the poem was severely criticized by two prominent literary ideologists, Aleksei Markov and Dmitri Starikov. Later, the issue was taken up by no less an authority than Premier Nikita Khrushchev. At a conference of writers and artists held in the Kremlin on March 7 and 8, 1963, he contended that the poet had displayed an "ignorance of historical facts," and declared: "Events are depicted in the poem as if only the Jewish population fell victim to the fascist crime, while in fact at the hands of the

Hitlerite butchers there perished not a few Russians, Ukrainians, and Soviet peoples of other nationalities."

The attacks on Yevtushenko were joined by attacks on the famous composer Dmitri Shostakovich, whose 13th Symphony constituted in part a musical and choral setting for Yevtushenko's "Babi Yar." A day before the premiere, the top party ideologist, Leonid Ilyichev, told an assemblage of party leaders and leading Soviet intellectuals that Shostakovich had chosen an undesirable theme for his symphony. First performed on December 18, 1962 and given a tumultuous reception, the symphony was not reviewed by major press organs. A critic writing in a Minsk newspaper, *Sovetskaia Byelorussiia,* in April 1963 denounced the symphony for elevating "a petty incident to the rank almost of national tragedy."

In the summer of 1976, a memorial was finally erected at Babi Yar–but it was scarcely the one Soviet Jews and Yevtushenko and his associates in the Soviet intelligentsia had hoped for and had demanded. Indeed, it was built about a mile from the actual site of the massacre. The huge bronze monument, built at a cost of nearly $2,000,000, contained nothing even remotely suggesting the Jewish agony. It is capped by a frieze that includes eleven distinctive figures, none of which is symbolic of Jewry. Instead, like dozens of other Soviet memorials that dotted Eastern Europe from the Brandenburg Gate to the Urals, the frieze highlighted traditional heroes. As characterized by *Novosti,* "Proudly raising their heads, implacable and unconquered, the imprisoned soldier and the partisan are struck by the volley of bullets. Even in their last moments, they terrify the enemy with their hatred."

At the base of the memorial was an inscription which made no reference to the Jewish trauma. It read: "Here in 1941-43 the German Fascist invaders executed over 100,000 citizens of Kiev and prisoners of war." The effacement of Babi Yar as a symbol of the Holocaust was breached but once–in October 1980, when the Moscow Jewish Drama Ensemble was allowed to perform in a tiny theater an original play about Babi Yar, entitled "Ladies'

Tailor," by Alexsandr Borshchagovsky. Powerful and moving, the play was permitted only a one-week run. A Soviet Ukrainian 70-minute documentary film about Babi Yar, released in 1981, mentioned Jews but once–and equated Zionists with Nazis.

The official Soviet anti-Zionist propaganda climaxed the campaign of silence and distortion about Babi Yar with a particularly obscene allegation. A two-part *Pravda* article on February 18 and February 19, 1971 by a notorious peddler of hate, Vladimir Bolshakov, charged that "Zionists" had actually colluded with the Nazis in the Babi Yar massacre. During the propaganda drive, other professional hate mongers added to the ignorance by challenging the size of the Holocaust. Lev Korneyev, in his Party-lauded book, *The Class Essence of Zionism*, published in 1982, claimed that the number of Jewish martyrs was far less than six million.

So vast over space and time was the blanket of silence and distortion that the population of the former USSR came to have an especially high level of ignorance about the Holocaust. In 1991, Tatyana Zaslavskaya's highly respected Soviet Center for Public Opinion and Market Research conducted a survey of attitudes and ascertained that 74 percent of the Soviet public had absolutely no idea of how many Jews died in the Holocaust. Probably nowhere else in Europe could one find such a stunning absence of knowledge concerning a profound moral issue of our age.

The official Kremlin-orchestrated anti-Zionist campaign that had saturated the public with Judeophobia was brought to a halt in 1986. State organs and media, with some exceptions, no longer published the propagators of hate. Nonetheless the campaign had left a strong impact. In 1987 populist and "street" anti-Semitism emerged which assumed the name of *Pamyat* (Memory) (or *Otechestvo* or *Spasenie*) and targeted the Jews as responsible for all the ills of Soviet society.

Not until July 1990 did the Kremlin come to recognize what the vast anti-Zionist propaganda had produced. *Pravda* on July 22 put it succinctly:

Considerable damage was done by a group of authors who, while
pretending to fight Zionism, began to resurrect many notions of anti-
Semitic propaganda of the Black Hundreds and of fascist origin; hiding
under Marxist philosophy, they came out with coarse attacks on Jewish
culture, on Judaism, on Jews in general.

It was scarcely surprising that three of the most prolific
writers in the official anti-Zionist campaign of the 1970s and
1980s–Yevgeny Yevseev, Vladimir Begun, and Aleksandr
Romanenko–had become the favorites of *Pamyat* once that
campaign had been ended by Gorbachev in February 1986. The
same applied to the notorious lecturer, Valery Yemelyanov.

But how far was the impact of the past to be neutralized?
Izvestiia on July 12, 1990 revealed that Vladimir Kryuchkov,
head of the KGB, was far from holding a totally negative view
about *Pamyat* and its activities. He reportedly found one *Pamyat*
group–unnamed–to be "very useful" and "really patriotic." No
wonder, then, that the author of the remarkable *Pravda* article in
July predicted that the exodus of Soviet Jews in 1991 would
double or even triple.

Pamyat was by no means inconsequential in the public mind,
at least in Moscow. A poll sponsored by *Der Spiegel,* the
prominent West German journal, and conducted in April 1989
with the Institute of Sociology of the USSR Academy of Sciences, found that *Pamyat's* recognition factor was remarkably
high. Nearly 80 percent of Muscovites had heard of it, as
compared with only 58 percent who had heard of the Berlin Wall.
Seventeen percent of those polled reacted "very positively" or
"positively" to *Pamyat.* Another 14 percent considered the
organization "partly positive." While 47 percent judged *Pamyat*
"negatively" or "very negatively," a sizable 23 percent of the
respondents, answered "don't know."

The pro-*Pamyat* individuals, according to poll data, appeared to come largely from the working class and those with
limited education. *Komsomol* (Communist Youth) members
were more likely to be sympathetic that non-members. The most
striking correlation related to attitudes about Gorbachev and

perestroika. Pamyat sympathizers tended to oppose Gorbachev, to be less critical of the prevailing Soviet system, and to be more pessimistic about the future. A perceptive Western commentator observed that the poll illuminated a major cluster of interrelated attitudes in Moscow: "authoritarianism, anti-Westernism, anti-Semitism, and extremist Russian nationalism."

Evaluating the strength and impact of *Pamyat* and other extremist groups is difficult. Candidates backed by them in the elections for the Congress of People's Deputies in 1990 failed to win a single seat, but they racked up a vote ranging from seven to 11 percent of the total, depending upon the region. In absolute terms, however, the number of followers or supporters runs into the millions. Such figures may not be surprising. According to Fyodor Burlatsky, a prominent analyst close to Gorbachev, if a multiparty system were established in Russia, *Pamyat* "would grow in size to 10 million in one year."

In a 1990 poll in Moscow, conducted for the American Jewish Committee by the Institute of Sociology of the Academy of Sciences, 17 percent of respondents thought that "most people in the Soviet Union are anti-Jewish" and 60 percent thought that "some are anti-Jewish." More striking was the percentage—48—who believed that "anti-Jewish feeling is on the rise."

Far more significant than membership numbers or voter percentage were three prominent Soviet monthly publications that expressed and serviced conservative and Russian nationalist opinion—*Nash sovremennik* (*Our Contemporary*), *Molodaia gvardiia* (*Young Guard*), and *Moskva*. Under *glasnost* these periodicals have expanded greatly, with a combined circulation of 1,500,000. Articles appearing in them, not infrequently by some of the nation's leading writers, have endorsed *Pamyat* and have promoted anti-Semitism.

Anti-Semitism embraces a broad segment of the intellectual community: the *pochvenniki* (nativists), who see Soviet salvation in the Russian folk tradition. Western culture is perceived as a corrupting influence which must be rejected in favor of an ancient set or mores rooted in the Orthodox and peasant tradition. While the *zapadniki* (Westerners) seek to advance democratization and humanism, the *pochvenniki* aim to exclude "alien" elements, which are often viewed as emanating from a "powerful Zionist center." This view was articulated, for example, in a work by Igor Shafarevich, a mathematician and scholar. His book, *Russophobia,* presents the Jews as having always been the enemy of the Russian people.

Especially troubling was the willingness of powerful conservative forces in the Communist Party to exploit anti-Semites and anti-Semitism in their struggle against *perestroika.* The most outstanding example was the appearance of a long letter-article in the important Central Committee daily, *Sovetskaia Rossiia,* on March 15, 1988, written by Nina Andreyeva. A glowing paean to Stalin and Stalinism, it could not fail to be perceived as an indirect assault upon Gorbachev's initiatives. Strikingly, Andreyeva targeted "cosmopolitanism," the Stalinist code word for Jewry, as responsible for the undermining of Soviet patriotism.

That Andreyeva's thinking is riddled with anti-Jewish bigotry is apparent in an interview she gave to a Western newsman. In her perception, Jews are everywhere and dominate Soviet intellectual life. "Certain international Zionist organizations staffed by clever conspirators," she said, are engaged in "carrying out their work here" to the disadvantage of Russians.

Fear and anxiety pervaded the discussions of the December 1989 Congress of Jewish Organizations representing over 125 Jewish groups from seventy cities throughout the Soviet Union. The key presentation to the conclave highlighted "the sharp upsurge of public anti-Semitism," which "poses a great danger" and which has "literally drowned" the country in a flood of bigotry. Projected was a nightmare vision of "pogroms (as) a feasible reality of the nearest future."

To leaders and organizers of the Congress, the Soviet scene, with its economic "recession," political "instability," and "growing discontent," recalled nothing less than "the political atmosphere in Germany at the beginning of the 1930s, just before the Nazis seized power." Their Cassandra-like warning echoed throughout the proceedings: "Let us not forget the horrible lesson of the Holocaust." Hardly a speaker avoided the throbbing emotional issue, even as some 60 *Pamyat* toughs picketed outside the meeting hall with cries of "Yid" and "Jewish prostitute."

In a poll conducted by Moscow researchers connected with sociologist Tatyana Zaslavskaya, 72 percent of Moscow's Jewish leaders and 94 percent of Leningrad's Jewish leaders said that they could envisage an explosion of anti-Semitic emotions in the "nearest future."

The response of the Soviet authorities to the *Pamyat* and anti-Semitic challenge has been extraordinarily timid despite their linkage to anti-*perestroika* forces of powerful neo-Stalinist bureaucratic circles in the party and potent chauvinist forces both in and out of the party.

Support extended to *Pamyat* by nationalist intellectual elements was matched by the assistance rendered by the military leadership. Arrangements were made for the official distribution of such publications as *Nash sovremennik* and *Molodaia gvardiia* at all military posts. A principal military organ, *Military-Historical Journal,* was a continuing channel for chauvinist views that often bordered on racism. It even went so far as to publish in 1990 portions of Adolf Hitler's *Mein Kampf,* and had announced plans to publish the notorious *Protocols of the Elders of Zion* in 1991. The editor, Stanislav Kunyayev, publicly admitted that he found the "Protocols" theme of a Jewish conspiracy for world mastery to be valid.

There can be little question but that had the putsch of August 19-21, 1991 succeeded, a revival of official anti-Semitism would have followed. The leadership of the attempted coup comprised precisely those military, nationalist, and reactionary party elements that fostered an outlook of bigotry. Evidence from Party files that became available after the coup showed how Party officials had secretly and deliberately exploited anti-Semitic stereotypes during public election campaigns.

The political and diplomatic context within which anti-Semitism and the treatment of the Holocaust was to be viewed in

William Korey

Europe changed radically since 1990 in consequence of the Helsinki process. At a meeting of the Helsinki signatories (CSCE–Conference on Security and Cooperation in Europe) in Copenhagen in June 1990, dealing with the "human dimension," a formal document was adopted which "clearly and unequivocally" condemned "anti-Semitism" along with "racial and ethnic hatred." The signatories agreed "to intensify the efforts to combat these phenomena...."

The action was unprecedented. No international or regional treaty or agreement or declaration had ever specifically condemned anti-Semitism. Even the Genocide Treaty of 1948 makes no reference to that term, although the Jewish Holocaust was precisely what prompted the adoption of the treaty. Motivation for the changed attitude resulted from the shock of European leaders with the results of the 1989 revolutions in East Central Europe which brought in their wake waves of hatred directed against Jews as well as Gypsies and migrants.

In addition to the requirement that CSCE governments are to condemn anti-Semitism, the Copenhagen agreement requires them to adopt laws against acts that "constitute incitement to violence" based upon anti-Semitism. Where such laws already exist, governments are called upon to implement them. Finally, CSCE governments are required to ensure that the "objectives of education" include fighting against bigotry and promoting "understanding and tolerance."

These government obligations were further sanctioned at a summit meeting of the CSCE heads of state in Paris in November 1990. Adopted at this meeting was the historic "Charter for a New Europe" which gave emphasis to the Copenhagen decision. At subsequent CSCE meetings in Geneva (July 1991) and Moscow (September-October 1991), further attention was paid to the struggle against anti-Semitism, especially in educational terms.

A second unprecedented decision taken by CSCE related to the Holocaust. In May 1990, while meeting in Cracow, Poland, on the subject of "cultural heritage," the CSCE governments agreed to "preserve and protect...sites of remembrance, including most notably extermination camps," as well as "related archives" concerning the recent past's "tragic experiences" (i.e., the Holocaust). Explanation for the decision immediately followed: "Such steps need to be taken in order that those [Holocaust] experiences may be remembered, may help to teach present and future generations of these events, and thus ensure that they are never repeated."

With respect to the decision at Copenhagen to vigorously oppose anti-Semitism, it should be emphasized that the Soviet delegate agreed to the language of the document and, indeed, was an avid supporter of it. Still, the Soviet chief of state, Mikhail Gorbachev, was reluctant to use his office as a "bully pulpit" to condemn a burgeoning anti-Semitism, even when deputies of the Congress of People's Deputies appealed to him to do so and specifically urged him to allow the Congress to adopt a resolution, already signed by 200 deputies, that would denounce anti-Semitism.

At the same time, *Pravda* did take the unusual step on July 22, 1990–one month after Copenhagen–to print the long article that disclosed the extent of anti-Semitism in Moscow's immediate past history and that was harshly critical of it. Equally important, that some month the government finally brought a case under Article 74 of the Russian criminal code against a *Pamyat* extremist leader–K. Smirnov-Ostashvili–whose group had used violence against Jewish writers earlier in the year. In October, the *Pamyat* leader was found guilty and imprisoned. Yet the public prosecutor, Andrei Makarov, related that he was met with systematic opposition from the authorities, and he expressed strong doubts that similar trials would ever take place again.

Gorbachev finally got around to a severe public condemnation of anti-Semitism in October 1991. The occasion was a special ceremony of world Jewry at Babi Yar commemorating the martyrdom at the ravine one-half century earlier (September 29, 1941). The Soviet President sent a special message to the function, which was read by his associate Aleksandr Yakovlev. Gorbachev acknowledged, for the first time, that hatred of Jews in "everyday life" persists in the Soviet Union. After tracing "venomous sprouts of anti-Semitism" in the USSR to World War II, he expressed regret that the failure of his regime to oppose and resist bigotry was leading to the emigration of hundreds of thousands of "gifted and enterprising citizens."

For the first time, too, a Kremlin leader took account of what Babi Yar and the Holocaust meant for Jews. He spoke of the massacre of "almost six million Jews, representatives of the great nation dispersed over the whole planet" and he added that "Babi Yar shows that Jews were among the first Nazi victims both in our country and in all of Europe."

While the message was very much welcomed by those concerned with the deepening anti-Semitism in the USSR, it was also recognized that it was coming rather late in the day. By October, Gorbachev's popularity was continuing to plunge as the economy worsened and inter-ethnic strains widened. It was altogether tragic that by the time he finally chose to address a potent moral issue, he had become politically impotent. The Soviet empire was rapidly unravelling. By December, it collapsed together with the presidency which he had occupied. In an attempt to preserve the empire, the USSR itself was transformed into the Commonwealth of Independent States–CIS.

As for the Babi Yar ceremony itself, it was not Gorbachev's doing nor that of the USSR. On the contrary, the initiatives came from the increasingly autonomous Ukraine whose complete independence was to be proclaimed in December 1991. Its principal nationalist movement, RUKH, had already taken a strong public position against anti-Semitism, and by the summer of 1991 Ukrainian government leaders had already embarked upon rectifying the distortions about Babi Yar. Ukraine's Deputy Prime Minister Serhiy Komissarenko declared that "for far too long the truth about Babi Yar has been hushed up and distorted." Frankly and explicitly declaring the ravine to be "a symbol of Jewish martyrdom," Komissarenko announced that a cornerstone would be laid in October precisely "at the site of the massacre;" and the new monument to be built there "will tell the true story of Babi Yar."

A week of ceremonies was projected beginning on September 29, with the city of Kiev observing a "Day of Memory and Sorrow" in which the city flags would fly at half-staff. Public prayers, various programs, and an academic conference on the Holocaust would take place, climaxed by a special day set aside for world Jewry on October 6 for the intoning of the Kaddish. Especially significant was a plan to arrange student exchange programs focusing on the Holocaust with Israeli and American students.

Within Russia, the evidence of a resurgent anti-Jewish bigotry could hardly be denied. A public opinion survey conducted by Zaslavskaya's research center, published in September 1991, showed that of some 4200 in the polled sample, 40 percent manifested some degree of negative hostility toward Jews while 50 percent believed that the USSR "should be more resolute in fighting Zionism." A high Russian Embassy official in Washington told American Jewish leaders in December 1991 that Russians "are beginning to look for who is guilty" with respect to the profound economic difficulties. And, he warned, "this is not a good situation for minorities...." He added that "the Government is losing control of many processes."

Recent mass nationalist demonstrations in Moscow marked by virulent Jew-baiting placards, posters and screaming, have focussed world attention once again on a burgeoning anti-Semitism in Russia. Two sources of the resurgent bigotry merit special concern: revived Russian chauvinist nationalism and traditional scapegoating. Breakouts of nationalism such as the one that occurred as a psychological response to the breakup of the USSR and the Soviet empire in Eastern Europe have always had anti-Semitism as a coefficient. Whether under tsars or commissars, Jew-baiting was a mechanism for creating solidarity among Russians.

Even with a democratic regime in place, the mechanism doesn't cease to function. A very perceptive Soviet analyst, Andrei Kortunov, has explained that "the road from communism to democracy is much longer than the road from communism to nationalism, because nationalism and communism have a lot in common." What both ideologies do, Kortunov added, is to "liberate people from personal responsibility" and, instead, unite people around "some sacred goals." In the case of Russian nationalism the goal is to return to being a great state.

The mass base has been provided by xenophobic *Pamyat* and various splinter groups. A recent article in the liberal daily, *Komsomolskaia Pravda,* placed a searching spotlight on one such group–Russian National Unity [RNU], headed by Aleksandr Barkashov. This black-shirted group is in constant military training. Within two hours, it can bring several thousand marchers onto Moscow streets. RNU's "enemy" is clearly delineated in the Russian organ: "World Zionism is trying, by means of its puppets–the U.S. and other Western countries–to tear Russia to pieces and destroy it as a unified force blocking world Jewish hegemony." Says Barkashov: "I simply feel it in my bones...our time is approaching."

Scapegoating, flowing from the grave economic difficulties, reinforces anti-Jewish stereotypes. On the one hand, Jews are held responsible for the communist revolution and for collectivization, both of which led to the current trauma. On the other hand, Jews are imagined to be the agents of the new market capitalism and, therefore, of social inequality and shortages. (The fact that numerous Jews are involved in the unfolding capitalist enterprises in Russia feeds the imagery.)

The paradox of Jews being blamed for both Marxism and capitalism is characteristics of scapegoating: logic is turned on its head. Vaclav Havel, the distinguished Czech playwright and president [of the Czech Republic] recently described the function of scapegoating, which he, incidentally, applied to East Europe generally : "...they feel frustration that nothing is as good as they wish or as they thought it would be after the revolution; and they are searching for a culprit–preferably a simple, comprehensive and easily defined one, and that means a collective one. Thus...some say it is the Freemasons who are to blame for all our troubles; others say it is the Jews...." Havel put it just right. His remarks help explain why Soviet Jews are leaving for Israel by the thousands and others hold on to their Israeli passport affidavit as their insurance policy.

Russian President Boris Yeltsin has avoided speaking out strongly on the subject of anti-Semitism. While he acknowledged its existence in the course of a special ABC-TV telebridge program on September 5, 1991, he seemed to minimize its significance. More striking–and disturbing–was his downplaying of *Pamyat* as a serious threat and his odd admission that he had ongoing contacts with the hate group.

How strong anti-Semitism is elsewhere in the former Soviet Union is not known with any degree of precision. As late as the spring of 1991 (prior to its independence), Belarus demonstrated a high degree of Judeophobia in Communist Party organs. Ukraine and Moldova have each had a long history of anti-Semitism, but whether the past is prologue for the emergent future is yet to be ascertained. Ukraine, as indicated, is making determined efforts in another direction.

Concerning the six Moslem republics of Uzbekistan, Kazakhistan, Kyrgyzstan, Turkmenistan, Tadjikistan, and Azerbaijan, the evidence is not definitive. Jews in this area total 203,000, not an inconsequential figure. That the overwhelming majority are considering exodus is suggested by the number who have requested and received *vizovs* or affidavits from an Israeli relative. An astonishing 184,500 Jews of the 203,000 have obtained *vizovs*. This represents a hefty 91 percent.

While overt indications of anti-Semitism in the Moslem area have been minimal, two current features of the scene warrant attention and concern. One is a growing native nationalism in various areas directed against Russia and the Russian-speaking population. Included in the Russian-speaking population are the Ashkenazi Jews who constitute three-quarters of the total Jewish population residing in the Moslem republics.

The local anti-Russian nationalism has been greatly intensified by the Islamic renaissance, a process of Islamization that has given nationalism a religious or ideological dimension. Not surprisingly Iran's fundamentalism, crossing the porous borders, is already a factor in the Islamic renaissance and could become a disturbing one. Islamization has already had troubling consequences. During the Persian Gulf War, two Moslem Republics–Azerbaijan and Uzbekistan–publicly expressed formal sympathy with the suffering of the Arabs of Iraq. This despite the pro-American and pro-UN policy of the then Gorbachev central government. Nor did it go unnoticed that a 1992 visitor to the area was PLO chief Yasir Arafat. Other high-level visitors have come from Syria, Saudi Arabia, and Iran.

This is not to say that an anti-Israel and anti-Jewish policy has already taken hold in the capitals of Moslem republics. The contrary is the case. Sympathy for Israel is to be found among the population at large and among the ruling elite. Some speculate that the attitude flows from a belief that Israel's economic capabilities can be placed at their disposal. Related to this perception is a hope of recruiting Jewish capital for investments.

As for Jewish emigration, there has been no hint of a cutoff. In addition, each of these republics has pledged to adhere to the Helsinki human rights standards, which includes the right to leave any country including one's own. On the basis of these pledges, all have very recently been admitted into the Helsinki process. At review meetings of the process, which occur on a regular basis, the Moslem republics can be held to account for any violation of Helsinki obligations–and these obligations also extend to combatting anti-Semitism.

Anti-Semitism and the Treatment of the Holocaust in Postcommunist Yugoslavia

Radmila Milentijevic

The demise of communism and the disintegration of the one-party system in Eastern Europe that opened the way to democracy and a market economy has been marred by political instability, economic chaos, and social unrest. The vacuum created by the collapse of the communist order has been, for the most part, filled by a virulent nationalism. These conditions have been marked by the reemergence of anti-Semitism. Yugoslavia represents a more extreme case of this general situation, with its Jewish community engulfed by the forces that brought on the disintegration of the country.

Yugoslavia was established at the end of World War I[1] on the ruins of the Habsburg and Ottoman empires. As Professor Joseph Rothschild so aptly observed, "By virtue of every relevant criterion–history, political traditions, socioeconomic standards, legal systems, religion, and culture–Yugoslavia was the most complicated of the new states in interwar East Central Europe, being composed of the largest and most varied number of pre-1918 units."[2] The peoples who came to comprise the new state had during the prior centuries been subsumed within Byzantine, Ottoman, Hungarian, Germanic, and Italian cultures and institutions.

The Jewish community in Yugoslavia was as varied and complex as the country itself.[3] The creation of Yugoslavia brought together the Sephardic Jews of the former Ottoman lands and the Ashkenazic Jews of the former Habsburg territories. Sephardic Jews came to the Balkans in the sixteenth century, following their expulsion from Christian Spain in 1492. Welcomed by the Sultan into the Ottoman Empire, they established their communities in Serbia, Bosnia, Macedonia, and along the Dalmatian coast, flourishing both economically and culturally. But with the decay of the empire, the conditions of the Jews within it also deteriorated, so that by the nineteenth century Ottoman Jewry was but a pale reflection of its former strength. The Sephardic communities remained traditional: they spoke Ladino; their society was closely knit and separated from the outside world.

By contrast, the Ashkenazic communities in the Habsburg lands were all of recent origin. Until the end of the eighteenth century, Jews had been banned from residence in the Habsburg lands of present-day Yugoslavia, except for Zemun, a town across the Sava river from Belgrade. During the nineteenth century a larger number of Ashkenazim from various parts of the Habsburg Empire established their communities in Croatia and the Vojvodina. The majority of the Ashkenazic Jews who spoke German or Hungarian were reformist and integrationist, but a small number among them adhered to strictly Orthodox beliefs and practices.

On the whole, the border between the Habsburgs and the Ottomans was the line of demarcation between the Ashkenazic and Sephardic Jews. The Ashkenazim, who constituted two thirds of Yugoslav Jewry in the interwar period, lived in the more westernized and urbanized parts of the country, while the Sephardim were situated mainly in the poorer and less developed areas. The Sephardim emphasized their history and tradition, whereas the Ashkenazim considered themselves advanced and enlightened. Zagreb was the center of Ashkenazic culture, Sarajevo of the Sephardic. Belgrade was a city where the Sephardic and Ashkenazic communities existed side by side.

By the late nineteenth century the Jews living in the territories that later became Yugoslavia had achieved legal emancipation, and by 1918 they formally enjoyed full equality with other citizens. In the Kingdom of the Serbs, Croats, and Slovenes they were legally defined as a religious rather than a national minority. Like national minorities, the Jews were entitled by law to their own religious, educational, and social institutions.

In 1921, the Jews numbered 64,746 out of a total Yugoslav population of 12 million. By 1939, this number had risen to 71,342 in a country of 15.7 million.[4] Virtually the entire Jewish population was concentrated in urban centers. Indeed, the urban nature of the Jewish community in a predominantly rural and agricultural society made the Jews a distinct socioeconomic group in interwar Yugoslavia, as did the fact that the Jews averaged a higher level of education than the Yugoslav population as a whole. These factors distinguished the Jews from other groups in society and discouraged their full integration.

At the same time, the Jews, particularly the Sephardim, managed to adapt themselves successfully to their environment and achieve acceptance. They increasingly adopted Serbo-Croatian as their common language, so that by 1939 all the Jewish newspapers, except for a few in the Vojvodina that were published in Hungarian or German, appeared in Serbo-Croatian.[5]

The traditional Sephardic communities in Serbia, Bosnia, and Macedonia, the fairly recent integrationist oriented Ashkenazic communities in Croatia and Vojvodina, and the Orthodox community united in 1919 to form the Federation of Jewish Religious Communities. Shortly thereafter, the Orthodox seceded to create their own Union of Orthodox Jewish Religious Communities. The Law on the Religious Community of Jews enacted in 1929 recognized the Jewish community and its organizational framework.[6] Within this framework a multiplicity of institutions covering a wide range of activities flourished on both the local and national levels, reflecting a vibrant and active Jewish society in Yugoslavia.

The multinational complexion of interwar Yugoslavia, which hindered the progress of integration, facilitated the acceptance of a Jewish national identity. Zionism provided an alternative for Jews who believed that they could never integrate themselves fully into the surrounding culture. In Yugoslavia this applied more to the Ashkenazim than to the Sephardim. Among the Sephardim in Serbia the concept of a Serb of the Mosaic faith prevailed. The Sephardim of Bosnia advocated Diaspora nationalism. Retaining the heritage of the Ottoman millet system in a multiethnic society among Muslim Bosnians, Catholic Croats, and Eastern Orthodox Serbs, they long considered themselves Jews by nationality, with a dual loyalty to Palestine and to their Diaspora homeland.

The approach to Jewish nationalism brought the Bosnian Sephardim into sharp conflict with the proponents of Zionism. With its center in Zagreb, the Zionist Federation was the strongest organized force within the Yugoslav Jewish community, drawing its growing support primarily from the middle classes both among the Ashkenazim and the Sephardim. By the 1930s, the Zionists had won over the local communities, the Federation of Jewish Religious Communities, and almost the entire Jewish youth movement, and had a virtual monopoly of the Jewish press.[7]

The political scene of interwar Yugoslavia reflected the political heritage of the South Slavs and the diversity of their history. The main Yugoslav political parties were regional in character and depended upon the support of one particular nationality. The largest Serbian party, the Radicals, was the most sympathetic of all Yugoslav political parties to the Jewish cause. Its leader, Nikola Pasic, projected himself as a great friend of the Jews and thereby gained the loyal support of many Serbian Jews. In 1927 a Jew, Semaja Demajo, was elected to the *Skupstina* (Parliament) as a Radical Party deputy. In Croatia the mass party was the Croatian Peasant Party, led by Stjepan Radic, a charismatic leader who occasionally resorted to anti-Semitic demagoguery. In this atmosphere, Jews did not play an active part in Croatian politics at the national level but they did put forth Jewish lists in municipal elections.

A sizable number of younger Yugoslav Jews played an active role in the illegal communist party that functioned underground after 1921. During the 1930s more and more Jewish students joined the ranks of communist sympathizers.

Throughout the 1920s and 1930s the Yugoslav government was essentially controlled by the Serbs, and government policy toward the Jews reflected the Serbian viewpoint. The Serbs displayed sympathy for the Zionist cause, and the Serbian government was among the first to express its official support for the Balfour Declaration in 1917. The Karadjordjevic royal family maintained a cordial relationship with the Jewish community. The Yugoslav chief rabbi, Isaac Alcalay, was an intimate friend of the royal family and a confidant of the king.

The official position of the government was that no "Jewish question" existed in Yugoslavia. The Jewish community was repeatedly assured that the government would protect its Jews. Nevertheless, sporadic anti-Semitic incidents occurred in various parts of the country. The petition by the Zagreb medical students in 1920 demanding a *numerus clausus* for all "native" Jews and the expulsion of all "foreign" Jews; the Yugoslav Muslim Organization's boycott against Jewish stores in Bosnia in 1925; and the blood libel accusation in a predominantly Hungarian town in the Vojvodina, which was promptly squelched by the courts, were all instances of anti-Semitic behavior. In the 1930s anti-Semitism surfaced more frequently, especially in the press, often linked to Nazi propaganda. Following the publication in 1933 in Munich of an appeal by Croatian nationalists for a boycott of Jewish shops in Zagreb, anti-Semitic articles became common in certain newspapers. *Die Erwache,* the organ of the Serbian fascist party of Dimitrije Ljotic, was the most flagrant proponent of Nazi racist ideology. Attempting to stem this tide, the Federation of Jewish Religious Communities condemned anti-Semitism in Yugoslavia; however, it was unsuccessful in its effort to have the *Protocols of the Elders of Zion* banned from Yugoslavia and equally unsuccessful in its efforts against the anti-Semitic press.

The growing pressure on the Jewish community was dramatized in Croatia in 1938, when 821 Jews reportedly converted to the Roman Catholic faith; the vast majority of them were undoubtedly Ashkenazim. The Jewish press published the names of 205 Jews from Zagreb and 82 from elsewhere who had left Judaism in order to escape the deteriorating situation of European Jewry. Although this conversion epidemic was of short duration and its impact only serious in Zagreb, it was indicative of the ominous times to come.

Yugoslavia was slipping under the domination of Germany and the government found itself increasingly under pressure to conform to Nazi policy. In spite of this, Yugoslavia was a country that offered shelter to some 55,000 Jewish refugees from Nazi-occupied countries to the end of 1939. Prior to the invasion of Poland it resisted the introduction of anti-Jewish laws, but soon after succumbed to Nazi pressure. On October 5, 1940, the Cvetkovic-Macek government promulgated laws that effectively revoked emancipation.[8] The Federation of Jewish Religious Communities reacted to the passage of this legislation with a declaration of faith in Yugoslavia and the Jewish people. But Yugoslavia had become a victim of the Nazi war machine. The Jews could not defend themselves, and Yugoslavia was no longer capable of protecting them. Yugoslav Jewry was to suffer the fate of the rest of European Jewry.

On March 25, 1941, Yugoslavia signed a pact with Hitler. Two days later a successful *coup d'état* in Belgrade brought to the throne young King Peter II and a new government which hastened to assure the Third Reich of its intention to adhere to the pact. Nevertheless on April 6 Hitler launched an attack on Yugoslavia with intensive bombing of Belgrade. Joined by Italy, Hungary, and Bulgaria, the Axis forces overran the country in less than two weeks and Yugoslavia was partitioned. Germany occupied northern Slovenia and the Banat; Hungary annexed the rest of the Vojvodina; Bulgaria received Macedonia; Italy acquired southern Slovenia, the Dalmatian coast, and certain interior regions including Kosovo. From the remaining territory a Fascist Independent State of Croatia (NDH) that included Bosnia and Herzegovina was proclaimed and a small puppet state of Serbia was established.

The dismemberment of Yugoslavia, the harsh policies of the occupation forces, and the genocidal policies of the fascist government of Croatia generated powerful resistance movements, both nationalist and communist. A bloody civil war ensued, in the course of which more than a million and a half people, or 10 percent of the total population of Yugoslavia, perished.

Although the treatment of the Jews varied slightly from region to region and the plans for their destruction differed accordingly, the ultimate result was the same everywhere: the almost total annihilation of the Yugoslav Jewish community.

The Jews in Serbia were the first to be subjected to the Nazi Final Solution. In Serbia, the Germans at first seem to have planned to rule through a regime of occupation, without any Serbian authority. But, alarmed by the resistance movement, they enlisted some Serbian support for the preservation of order and in August General Milan Nedic formed a puppet government. Although relying on Nedic for suppressing resistance and supplying labor levies for Germany, the Germans held the policy of the destruction of the Jews in Serbia in their own hands. Beginning on May 30, 1941, the German military command launched a series of preliminary measures that included defining who was a Jew, removing of Jews from public service and the professions, forbidding the Serbian population from hiding Jews, ordering Jews to wear yellow stars, and introducing forced labor for the Jews. Arrests of Jews began in July, supposedly in retaliation for communist activities. In August several concentration camps were set up and systematic roundups of Jewish men were carried out in Serbia and the Banat. In October some 4,000 Jewish men were shot by the Germans. Women and children were interned at the Sajmiste camp near Zemun, and in the summer of 1942 more than 6,000 of them perished in mobile gas vans. By August 1942 the Nazis had achieved the goal of the "Final Solution" in Serbia and declared Belgrade to be the first major city in Europe to be free of Jews.[9]

In Croatia, implementation of the anti-Jewish policy was conducted by the Croatian fascist government led by the Ustashe. There, with discriminatory regulations issued on April 30, 1941, roundups of Croatian and Bosnian Jews began in earnest in the summer of 1941 and concentration camps mushroomed all over Croatia. Sarajevo's Jewry disappeared by August 1942. Zagreb's Jews managed to remain largely unconfined as late as 1944, when they were herded into the notorious torture camp of Jasenovac. There a large number of Croatian Jews, along with hundreds of thousands of Serbs, lost their lives. The Jewish inmates who survived Jasenovac were deported to Auschwitz and other death camps outside Yugoslavia.[10]

Jews in the Hungarian-occupied territories shared a similar fate. In January 1942 several thousand Jews and Serbs were shot in Novi Sad and other towns of the Vojvodina, and some 4,000 Jews were sent to hard labor in the copper mines of Bor, the Ukraine, and Hungary. Like the Hungarian Jews, the rest of the Vojvodina Jews remained at liberty until after the Germans occupied Hungary on March 19, 1944. Shortly thereafter almost all of them were deported to Auschwitz.[11] In Macedonia the Bulgarian authorities rounded up some 8,000 Jews from Bitolj, Skopje, and other towns in March 1943 and shipped them to Treblinka. Macedonian Jews were thus annihilated almost completely.[12] The bulk of Slovenia's 1,000 Jews fled, partly to Croatia and Serbia and partly to Hungary, where they all perished. Those Jews who remained in Slovenia were completely exterminated.[13] The Jews in the Italian occupation zone fared relatively better. There the Jews were eventually interned in Italian camps and the Italian authorities saved them from deportation to Germany. After the capitulation of Italy, those Jews who fell into German hands were transported to death camps. The more fortunate ones managed to reach Southern Italy, where they remained until liberation.[14]

Altogether, the Holocaust wiped out an estimated 60,000 Yugoslav Jews, or 80 percent of the prewar Jewish population of the country. At the end of the war, fewer than 15,000 Yugoslav Jews remained alive; 12,495 of them were on Yugoslav soil. With the creation of the State of Israel, Tito permitted Jews to emigrate there. By 1952, 7,578 Jews had departed for Israel, leaving behind them a Jewish community in Yugoslavia of no more than 6,500. Some 4,000 of these Jews lived in Belgrade, Zagreb, and Sarajevo.[15]

The Jews who remained in Yugoslavia after the war were mainly professionals or civil servants. During the interwar period, a significant number of younger Jews had joined the communist movement. An estimated 3,000 Jews fought with Tito's partisans. Those who survived now assumed high positions in the government, with the foremost Jewish communist leader, Mosa (Moshe) Pijade, becoming the Vice President of Yugoslavia under Tito. The surviving Jewish population, a mere 10 percent of its prewar strength, managed to rebuild their lives; the Jewish community succeeded in reconstructing itself. Belgrade, Zagreb, and Sarajevo emerged again as the three strongest and most active centers of Jewish national life.

Although the Jewish community in postwar Yugoslavia was officially recognized as both a national and a religious community, it had lost control over matters of Jewish status and jurisdiction over Jewish affairs. Consequently, Jewish communal life focused on cultural activities in an effort to preserve the heritage of Jewish culture, and on social services as exemplified by the Home for the Aged in Zagreb.

The Jewish community and its leadership supported Tito and his brand of communism. The importance for the community of fostering close official ties with the government surfaced in 1969 in a case that involved the State of Israel. Although Yugoslavia had been one of the first countries to recognize the State of Israel in 1948, Tito severed diplomatic relations with Israel after the Six-Day War. Subsequently the Yugoslav press, reflecting the official government policy, revealed a pronounced bias against Israel and supported the Arab cause. Thus, when in 1969 the London *Jewish Chronicle* published an article under the headline "Yugoslav Papers Become Anti-Semitic," the Federation of Jewish Communities of Yugoslavia rejected the accusations of the *Chronicle* as sensationalist and accused it of not serving the best interests of Jewry in Yugoslavia or of Jewry in general. It insisted that "the Yugoslav state...has always taken a correct stand on the national question in general and especially has maintained a correct relationship with the Jewish community."[16] Generally the Holocaust was viewed in line with the official government position, which made no distinction between the victims of genocide and the other victims of fascism.

With the rebirth of nationalism and the liberalization of the press following Tito's death, signs of anti-Semitism became discernible. Nevertheless, in 1987 a well-known leader in the Jewish community in Zagreb, Slavko Goldstein, could still state that "anti-Semitism in Croatia does not exist."[17] Within the next three years, however, the situation would change dramatically. The critical turning point occurred with the publication in 1988 of *Wastelands of Historical Truth* by Franjo Tudjman, a former communist, partisan, and general in the Yugoslav Army, who became the President of Croatia in May 1991. With this work Tudjman set the stage for the debate and politics of anti-Semitism, genocide, and the Holocaust within the context of a program for achieving Croatia's independence as an organic nation state.

Tudjman's central objective is the exoneration of the Croatian people from responsibility for genocide in the Independent State of Croatia. The concentration camp of Jasenovac is his point of departure. This house of death for several hundred thousand Serbs, Jews, and Gypsies had come to symbolize both the magnitude and the heinousness of the Ustashe crimes. For Tudjman, however, Jasenovac was a myth blown out of all proportion, which had to be demolished because it had been used to support the theory of "the genocidal nature of every and any Croatian nationalism." He asks: "Isn't the purpose of the Jasenovac myth exaggerated to create a black legend of the historical guilt of the entire Croatian people, for which they must still make retribution?"[18]

Tudjman contends that the concept of a "Final Solution" of the Jewish question did not originally entail the destruction of European Jewry, but rather its territorial resettlement. The military failures on the Soviet front, however, forced the Third Reich to adopt instead a "Final Solution" through gradual extermination.[19] In connection with this extermination Tudjman claims that one million is an "impartial judgment" of the number of Jews who perished, explaining that: "The declared estimated loss of up to six million dead is based too much on emotionally biased testimonies as well as on one-sided and exaggerated data resulting from postwar settling of accounts on war crimes and squaring of accounts with the defeated perpetrators of war crimes."[20]

Tudjman is annoyed that the Jews continue, almost fifty years after the event, to complain about the Holocaust:

> And all this is happening in the mid-eighties, when world Jewry continues to have the need to remind us of its victims during the 'Holocaust,' even by trying to prevent former UN Secretary Kurt Waldheim from being elected as President of Austria! There were no genuine reasons for this, seeing as, during the Second World War (with the rank of a minor officer of the German Army), he was neither an inflicter of 'war crimes' nor in a position to make decisions as to their execution. But just as one can be deaf and blind as to what is happening under one's very nose on the orders of Israeli generals and their Government, so this also testifies to the fact that historical narrowmindedness and stupidity fully prevail, and Jewry is obviously no exception to this.
>
> And precisely because of this, the example of the Jewish people was and has remained historically instructive in many ways. After all that it endured in history, especially its terrible suffering during the Second World War, the Jewish people will, within a very short time, initiate such a cruel genocidal policy that it can justifiedly be called 'Judeo-Nazism.'[21]

Pointing to the "Judeo-Nazi" policy of the State of Israel toward the Palestinians, Tudjman asks: "What does this small historical step from Nazi-Fascism to Judeo-Fascism indicate?" In Tudjman's view, it apparently indicates there is actually very little difference between yesterday's Nazis and today's Jews. His argument leads him into a diatribe against the Old Testament with the intent of revealing the particularly virulent genocidal nature of the Jewish people: "As expressed by the Biblical God

Jahveh: 'genocidal violence...is to be used whenever necessary for the survival or renewal of the kingdom of the chosen people....The enemies of the chosen people are also God's enemies...which justifies hatred and the holy war of Israel against its hateful enemies."[22]

With the stage thus set, Tudjman turns to the central point of his book, Jasenovac. Dismissing Serbian claims of 700,000 victims, as well as the figure of 60,000 advanced by the Croat historians, Tudjman claims that no more than 30,000 to 40,000 inmates perished in Jasenovac. Even the figure of 40,000 over-states the Ustashe crime, according to Tudjman, since in his view the liquidation apparatus was largely controlled by the Jews. Quoting the report of an inmate from Bosnia, Tudjman offers this description of the Jews in Jasenovac:

> [Jews]...managed to grab all the more important jobs in the prisoner hierarchy, so as to maintain their privileges...they continuously and cleverly intrigued against the Serbs....As the Ustashe had more confidence in the Jews, the Serbs, in addition to suffering at the hands of the Ustashe, also suffered at the hands of the Jews....The Jew remains a Jew, even in the Jasenovac camp. In the camp, they kept all their defects except that they were more visible. Selfishness, craftiness, unreliability, stinginess, deceit and secrecy are their main characteristics.[23]

The obvious conclusion Tudjman draws from his sources is that the mass murder of the Serbs by the Croats during World War II is not an issue, since not that many Serbs were killed, and those who were, were killed primarily by the Jews. As for the Jews, very few of them perished at the hands of the Croats, since most of them were deported to camps outside Croatia, while others escaped to the Italian zone of occupation. So the case of the Holocaust in the Independent State of Croatia is dismissed.

Published by the prestigious Matica Hrvatska, *Wastelands of Historical Truth* was widely read. It went through a second printing in 1989, and a third in 1990.

Meanwhile in other parts of Yugoslavia there were signs of a growing interest in anti-Semitism. In Ljubljana, the capital of

Slovenia, the influential tabloid *Tribune* began the serialization of the *Protocols of the Elders of Zion*. The Federation of Jewish Communities immediately filed a lawsuit in Slovenia to ban the publication. The Federation was joined by the tiny Jewish Community in Ljubljana, in whose name Mladen Schwartz filed a separate suit. But the effort was unsuccessful and *Tribune* concluded the publication of the *Protocols* in March 1990.[24] Another anti-Semitic work, *The Secret World of Free Masons* by Macedonian author Mihailo Popovski, was published in Belgrade and Skopje, the Macedonian capital. The Federation sought legal remedy again, and was successful in getting the court in Belgrade to ban the distribution of the book on the grounds that it "inflamed national, religious, and racial hatreds."[25] The court in Skopje used the decision of the court in Belgrade as a precedent to ban the book there on the same grounds.[26]

Aside from the obvious appeal of communism as a conspiracy to be blamed on foreign elements, i.e., the Jews, there were no other visible indications of anti-Semitic behavior in other republics of Yugoslavia. The Jewish communities in Slovenia, Macedonia and Montenegro remained very small. In Sarajevo the Jewish community of more than 1,000 maintained a tradition of harmonious relations in that city of four faiths. In Belgrade ties between the Jewish community and the Serbs continued to be strong. A Serbian-Jewish Friendship Society which agitated for close ties with Israel was founded in 1989, and the fraternization between the cities of Rehovot and Valjevo was celebrated. In October 1990 the municipal government and the Jewish community in Belgrade unveiled a monument to Jewish victims of Nazi genocide in the Old Jewish Quarter of Dorcol, on the banks of the Danube.

In Croatia Tudjman had legitimized anti-Semitism and the denial of the Holocaust. By 1990 Croatia was fast moving toward independence. New political parties emerged, gearing their efforts toward the elections scheduled for late April 1990. Many former Ustashe now returned from exile were actively engaged in the political process. They included Ivo Omrcanin, a leading Ustashe propagandist and minister in the Pavelic government, and Sime Djodan, who later became Minister of Defense in Tudjman's government. The leading political party, the Croatian Democratic Union or HDZ, led by Tudjman, ran on an ultra-nationalist platform. It attracted some of the leading Ustashe into its leadership, including Djodan and Omrcanin, who now agitated throughout Croatia.

Slavko Goldstein, President of the Jewish community in Zagreb, registered a strong protest against Tudjman's book[27] and Ljubo Weiss, in an "Open Letter to Franjo Tudjman," subjected the book to a lengthy critical analysis.[28] These protests passed largely unnoticed, however, and things remained quiet until the electoral campaign forced the issue into the open. Speaking at the founding meeting of the HDZ in the city of Split on January 13, 1990, Djodan accused the Serbs and the Jews of conducting relentless campaigns against the Croatian people in foreign countries. Djodan's speech was reported on TV Zagreb and was published in *Nedeljna Dalmacija* (Dalmatian Weekly).[29] Responding to the TV report in *Vjesnik* (The Herald), Nenad Pogres, President of the Zagreb Jewish Community, lashed out at Djodan. Tying Djodan's statements directly to Tudjman, Pogres demanded accountability for the course the HDZ was taking, which was of particular concern should the party win the elections.[30]

On January 31, Miso Montiljo, President of the Mosa Pijade Chorus and Vice President of the Jewish Community in Zagreb, responded at length in *Vecernji List* (The Evening Journal). Djodan's statement reminded Montiljo of similar statements from the dark period of the Independent State of Croatia during World War II when 80 percent of Yugoslavia's Jews were killed. Insisting that the Jews in Croatia had never said anything against the Croatian people but only cooperated with them, Montiljo discerned ominous signs in the fact that no one in the audience had reacted critically to Djodan's speech. Reminding Djodan of the significant contributions of the Croatian Jews, Montiljo condemned anti-Semitism.[31] Djodan answered Montiljo in *Magazin* shortly thereafter, insisting that he had only presented the facts about the alliance of certain Jews with the Chetniks (Serbian nationalists led by Draža Mihailović during the Second World War) who claimed that the Croatian people were the only genocidal people in the world. Djodan asserted that: "There is no anti-Semitism [in Croatia]....This hollow and worn-out phrase hardly means anything today, when the Semitic peoples are killing each other....That is where one should look for anti-Semitism." Significantly, particularly since the Jewish community in Zagreb was the stronghold of Zionism during the interwar period and also because the Jews were recognized as a nationality under communist Yugoslavia's constitution, Djodan acknowledged the contributions to Croatian culture of certain "Croats of Jewish origin," who, he stated, "were eager Croats," but expressed doubts whether Montiljo could count himself among them.[32]

If Djodan sounded heavy-handed and threatening, the Croatian Jews were in for an even bigger disappointment when in March *Slobodan Tjednik* (Free Daily) published an interview with Omrcanin. There Omrcanin denied the Holocaust in Jasenovac, asserting that the Serbian, Jewish, and Gypsy deaths were an invention of Bolshevik propaganda. To the extent that genocide took place, he claimed, the Jews were the executioners. He made the Jews responsible for the massacres of Serbs in Glina and elsewhere.[33] Omrcanin could have been quoting from Tudjman's book. A few days later, in an interview in *Novosti,* Goldstein protested: "I must withdraw my statement that in Croatia anti-Semitism does not exist." Omrcanin, Goldstein charged, spread nothing but lies. "He has loaded all the Ustashe crimes of Jasenovac on the backs of the Jews....I have not read an uglier article in our press since 1945."[34] Omrcanin's speech prompted the Federation of Jewish Communities to condemn it and announce its decision to file criminal charges against *Slobodan Tjednik* and Omrcanin.[35]

As the election campaign proceeded the voices of anti-Semitism were strengthened by the pronouncements of Tudjman himself. At the HDZ Congress in February 1990, Tudjman stated that the Fascist Independent State of Croatia expressed the historic aspirations of the Croatian people.[36] Speaking on April

17 at a HDZ meeting in Dubrava, a suburb of Zagreb, he proudly declared: "Fortunately, my wife is neither a Serb nor a Jew."[37]

Ljubo Weiss eloquently defended the Jewish community in Croatia in two interviews appearing in *Vecernji List* in April and May, stating that: "The Jews will not succumb to manipulation. We are loyal to the society in which we live, but we are above all Jews....Here in Croatia anti-Semitism is reflected in the book *Wastelands* by Dr. Franjo Tudjman, in the unrestrained statements of Sima Djodan in Split, and, most drastically, in the pronouncements of Ivo Omrcanin in *Slobodan Tjednik*....[Here] anti-Semitism seriously threatens Jewish culture." Weiss concluded his message with an appeal to the public for help at the very time when the election brought Tudjman to power in a landslide victory.[38]

Now that Tudjman had a clear mandate, one might have expected that anti-Semitism would give way to a more compromising approach to the Jewish community. Instead, the Croatian government announced plans to change the name of the Square of the Victims of Fascism in Zagreb to the Square of Croatian Rulers. The news created an uproar among Croatian Jews, bringing strong protests from the Jewish community in Zagreb, the Federation of Jewish Communities of Yugoslavia, the Survivors of Jasenovac and Stara Gradiska (The Old Gradiska), the War Veterans, and the media.[39] For the Jews this action appeared calculated to erase the memory of the victims of fascism and with it the memory of the genocide against the Jews, Serbs, and Gypsies. Simon Wiesenthal, on behalf of the Federation of Jews Persecuted by Nazism, lodged his protest, but to no avail.[40] Moreover, nationalist circles in Croatia initiated a campaign for the erection of monuments for all victims of the Second World War, irrespective of whether they were victims of Nazism or Nazi collaborators.

The anti-Semitic and anti-Serbian policy of the Croatian government caused the American Ambassador Warren Zimmerman, at a meeting with the Croatian government officials in July, to "express serious concern for the Serbs who live in Croatia, as well as for the Jews."[41] In response to an inquiry from the Croatian Bureau of Information, Zimmerman confirmed his statement about the Serbs and Jews being endangered in Croatia, which provoked the Zagreb tabloids *Start* and *Slobodan Tjednik* to call him "an American-Zionist agent and a Jew."[42]

For the rest of 1990 the Jewish community in Zagreb continued to fight anti-Semitism in Croatia, efforts to erase the memory of the Holocaust, and the revival of fascism, while the Zagreb weeklies *Danas* and *Start* published essays by Ivo Goldstein and Slavko Goldstein calling attention to events with anti-Semitic underpinnings and dealing with the theme of genocide. Articles such as "And History is Not Being Repeated, Not Being Repeated, Not Being Repeated" in another Zagreb tabloid, *Novi Forum,* exposed to its readers 48 legal acts against the Jews legislated by the Independent State of Croatia from April to October 1941.[43] However, while anti-Semitic pronouncements and acts, such as the desecration of the old Jewish cemetery in the city of Split, continued, Tudjman apparently decided to change his stand and distance himself from them. To pacify the Jewish community, he promised assistance for the construction of a Jewish Cultural Center at the site of the destroyed synagogue in Zagreb. On his visit to the United States in September 1990, he also met with representatives of the Anti-Defamation League and declared willingness to take action against anti-Semitism. In fact a more dramatic change was contemplated.

Tudjman's anti-Serbian policy had ignited a Serbian revolt in the *Krajina* (the Border) which began on August 17, 1990. The Serbs were advancing and clearing their areas from Croatian control. The Croats were retreating. In order to concentrate all efforts against the Serbs, a decision seems to have been made to abandon the anti-Jewish policy for the time being in order to secure the support of the Jewish community for the defense of the Croatian government. Consequently, in the course of 1991 several members of the Jewish community in Zagreb accepted high positions in Tudjman's government. Probably pressure coupled with other factors worked to assemble a team that included

Mihailo Montiljo, Nenad Porges, Srdjan Matic, and Lea Bauman, among others. The foremost among them, Montiljo, became Deputy Minister of Foreign Affairs.

As this group now moved to a campaign in defense of the
Croatian government, the Serbs and the Yugoslav army became
the targets. On October 7, 1991, an appeal to the entire world
Jewish community was signed by the Vice President of the
Zagreb Jewish community, Srdjan Matic, in the name of its
President, Nenad Porges. Claiming to speak for all Jewish
communities in Croatia, Matic declared that Croatia had been
brutally attacked by military forces, led by the Yugoslav army,
which were indiscriminately killing civilians and destroying
property, hospitals, schools and cultural monuments. Matic
denied any discrimination against Jews, asserting that the Jewish
community in Croatia enjoyed all the rights of citizens. Moreover, he wrote, the government of Croatia had denounced all
neo-fascists and extremists who threatened Croatian democracy.
Matic declared full support for the government of Croatia, and
called on the people of Yugoslavia "to oppose aggression against
Croatia and on world Jewry to help bring peace to Croatia."[44]

Seeing this action as proof that Tudjman's government had
co-opted the Jewish community in Zagreb, the Belgrade Jewish
community assembled on October 20 to call upon the World
Jewish Congress "to protect the Jewish communities in Yugoslavia from attempts to convert them into instruments of political
propaganda."[45] Simultaneously, the Jewish War Veterans, Former Concentration Camp Inmates and Prisoners of War in
Belgrade addressed an appeal to the General Assembly of the
World Veterans Federation. Signed by Aleksandar Demajo,
President of the Veterans, Concentration Camp Inmates and
Prisoners of War organization of the Jewish community of
Belgrade, this document unveiled a blistering attack on Tudjman's
government. "We condemn this war," declared Demajo, "but we
recognize the appearance of extremists and totalitarian nationalism at home, and German expansionism." Noting that in the past
nationalism and chauvinism had led to anti-Semitism and persecution of the Jews, Demajo pointed to Croatia as a place where

such a situation existed, citing examples such as the renaming of the Square of Victims of Fascism, the return from abroad of a number of leading *Ustashi,* the high positions held by anti-Semites in the Croatian government, the bomb explosions on August 19 at the Jewish community building and the Jewish cemetery in Zagreb, and the desecration of the Memorial Center in the Jasenovac death camp which had been stripped of all evidence of the genocide committed there. Above all, Demajo pointed at Tudjman and his book, *Wastelands of Historical Truth,* holding Tudjman to be the most anti-Semitic of all, who called the Jews Judeo-Nazis and saw historical continuity between modern Croatia and the former Fascist Independent State of Croatia. Citing examples to prove that the current Croatia primarily jeopardized the positions and rights of Serbs, Demajo defended the Serbs as the people who had fought together with the Jews against fascism. Holding Germany, Austria, and the Vatican responsible for the civil war in Yugoslavia, and the European democracies responsible for the fate of the Yugoslav people, Demajo concluded with a call on world veterans to "heed this appeal by Jews who have survived...the fascist genocide."[46]

What was clear from this activity is that the leading Jews in Zagreb and Belgrade were being embroiled in the Croatian-Serbian conflict and that this involvement was growing deeper. Hardly were the above messages dispatched, when, on October 24, a piece by Lea Bauman appeared in *The Independent,* published in London. Identifying herself as a member of the Jewish community in Zagreb and an official of the Ministry of Information in Croatia, Bauman accused the Serbs of being responsible for the Holocaust of the Jews in Serbia during World War II. "Sixty thousand Jews were exterminated," she said, and "the actual killing was done by the Serbs."[47] Four days later, a dismayed Demajo replied in *The Independent.* "Not 60,000 but 14,500 Jews were killed in Serbia [and] it was the Germans and not the Serbs who killed the Jews in Serbia." Demajo also accused Bauman of using the Jews and their tragedy as a tool of war propaganda for the government of Croatia against their Serbian adversaries.[48]

On the same day Lea Bauman's allegations of the Serbian responsibility for the genocide against the Jews appeared in *The Independent,* the Chief Rabbi of Yugoslavia, Cadik Danon, appealed to the Pope in Rome to call on all Roman Catholics of the world to pray for "all the victims of the crime of genocide committed in Croatia during the Second World War." The Chief Rabbi expressed his conviction that this would significantly contribute to calming the passions in Yugoslavia.[49] Just as the Chief Rabbi was appealing to the Pope to admit the Holocaust in Jasenovac, the Jewish community in Zagreb cabled a message to the Patriarch of the Serbian Orthodox Church, Pavle, charging that on October 24 and 25 "artillery shells aimed intentionally by the Yugoslav Peoples Army hit the synagogue in Dubrovnik, the second oldest in Europe." On November 1, the Federation of Jewish Communities in Yugoslavia "declared this statement to be false," basing its conclusions on the reports of journalists and foreign diplomats who had the opportunity to visit Dubrovnik and who asserted that the old synagogue had not been damaged. Signed by the Federation's Honorary President Lavroslav Kadelburg and Secretary Luci Petrovic, this statement was addressed to all Jewish organizations in the world and the media.[50]

As this war of words continued unabated, it was clear that not the entire Jewish community in Zagreb stood behind Tudjman's government. Thus the organ of the Zagreb community carried an article entitled, "Are the Croatian Jews Endangered?" and answered in convincingly affirmative terms.[51] It was also apparent that many in the Jewish leadership were concerned about the consequences of this rift on the relationship between the two largest Jewish communities in Yugoslavia. Consequently, the representatives of the two communities met in Budapest on December 1, 1991, in an attempt to address the problem. There they agreed that "all Jewish communities must refrain from political statements and appeals dealing with the ethnic conflicts and civil war in Yugoslavia."[52]

Reporting on the outcome of the meeting in Budapest to a special assembly of the Jewish community in Belgrade, its president Jasa Almuli described what apparently was a stormy and difficult meeting in Budapest. The assembly decided to adhere to the earlier agreement not to become involved in the civil war in Yugoslavia, as long as the Jewish Community in Zagreb also honored the agreement.[53]

And did the Jewish community in Zagreb live up to the Budapest agreement? The unanimous answer of the Executive Board of the Federation of Jewish Communities in Yugoslavia, which met later in December, was that it did not. The Board noted that the Jewish Community in Zagreb in its Bulletin of December reprinted the contested appeal of October 7; that on the front page of the Bulletin the community's president Nenad Porges published a statement insisting that in Nedic's Serbia the Serbs killed the Jews: and, moreover, that he had sent an appeal to President Bush asking for his intervention to stave off the destruction of Croatia.[54]

As the above debates illustrate, the Jewish community had taken the decisive step of following the civil war road in Yugoslavia, with the Zagreb Jews supporting the Croats and the Belgrade Jews supporting the Serbs. And where did Tudjman stand now that he had been able to secure the support of some of the leading Jews in Zagreb? In an interview with *Vecernji List* on January 1, 1992, Tudjman was asked about the alleged anti-Semitism expressed in his book and during the electoral campaign. Ascribing such allegations to nationalistic Serbs and some Jews, he stated:

> Had I written the book as President of Croatia, I would have, for pragmatic reasons, left out certain things. But even as the book stands, there is no reason for dissatisfaction. Nevertheless, I have the understanding of the American Jews and of most Jews of the Zagreb Jewish Community.[55]

In thus reconfirming the central thesis of his *Wastelands of Historical Truth,* Tudjman dismissed the question of the Holocaust in the fascist Independent State of Croatia and, at the same time, conferred renewed legitimacy on anti-Semitism in Croatia under his rule.

The Jews in Croatia who rallied in support of the Croatian government's policies presumably had to consent implicitly to Tudjman's anti-Semitism. But this circumstance was the continuation of their experience in Croatia historically—a condition which they had learned to live with. In Serbia, by contrast, the Jewish community which came to the side of the Serbian government did not have to contend with the issue of anti-Semitism. Indeed, following the ban on the distribution of *The Secret World of Free Masons,* no expression of anti-Semitic behavior was registered until an article appeared in the January 15, 1992 issue of *Pravoslavlje* (Orthodoxy), the official journal of the Serbian Orthodox Church. The author (identified by the initials O. E.) of the lead article entitled "The Jews Are Again Crucifying Christ," raised the question of "why state propaganda in Serbia does not want to mention discrimination against Christians and the overall condemnation of the official Serbian policy in Israel?" Without dealing with the question raised, the author unveiled a picture of virulent anti-Christian feeling and behavior which, according to him, threatened to expel Christianity from Israel altogether. Although the examples of the persecution of Christians and destruction of Christian monuments were the work of the most Orthodox Jews, the author generalized from these examples to infer that this behavior permeates the entire political structure and society in Israel.[56] The article apparently provoked a strong reaction from the Jewish and the Serbian community alike causing the Patriarch of the Serbian Orthodox Church to dismiss the chief editor of *Pravoslavlje* for having allowed the article to be published. This incident notwithstanding, in Serbia historically anti-Semitism was not a factor in politics or in society.

The situation leads to the conclusion that the history of the Jews in former Yugoslavia continues, as in the past, to be intertwined with the histories of the peoples with whom they live. To that extent, the Jews in Croatia and the Jews in Serbia fully share in the destinies of the Serbian and the Croatian peoples.

NOTES

1. The country was proclaimed on December 1, 1918 as the Kingdom of the Serbs, Croats and Slovenes. In 1929 it was renamed the Kingdom of Yugoslavia.

2. Joseph Rothschild, *East Central Europe Between the Two World Wars* (Seattle and London: University of Washington Press), p. 201.

3. Harriet Pass Freidenreich, *The Jews of Yugoslavia* (Philadelphia: The Jewish Publication Society of America, 1979) is the best study on the subject to date.

4. Freidenreich, p. 58.

5. Ibid., pp. 62-64.

6. Ibid., pp. 71-72; *Zakon o verskoj zajednici Jevreja u Kraljevini Jugoslavije* (Law on the Religious Community of Jews in the Kingdom of Yugoslavia) (Belgrade: Stamparija Feniks, 1930).

7. Freidenreich, pp. 153-59.

8. "Uredbe i o uredbama protiv Jevreja" (The Regulations and About the Regulations Against the Jews), *Jevrejski glas* (Jewish Voice), vol. 13, no. 31 (October 16, 1940), pp. 1-3.

9. Zdenko Lowenthal, ed., *The Crimes of the Fascist Occupants and Their Collaborators against Jews in Yugoslavia* (Belgrade: Federation of Jewish Communities of Federal People's Republic of Yugoslavia, 1957), pp. 1-9; see a much more detailed account in Serbian, pp. 1-53.

10. Ibid., pp. 10-20 (English), 54-114 (Serbian).

11. Ibid., pp. 26-37 (English), 136-188 (Serbian).

12. Ibid., pp. 38-39 (English), 189-195 (Serbian).

13. Ibid., p. 21 (English), 115-116 (Serbian).

14. Ibid., pp. 22-25 (English), 117-135 (Serbian).

15. Freidenreich, pp. 192-93.

16. Ibid., p. 208.

17. Slavko Goldstein's interview in *Novosti* (The News), March 19, 1990.

18. Franjo Tudjman, *Bespuca povijesne zbiljnosti* (Wastelands of Historical Truth) (Zagreb: Nakladni zavod matice hrvatske, 1990), pp. 9-23.

19. Ibid., pp. 152-53.
20. Ibid., pp. 155-58.
21. Ibid., pp. 160-61.
22. Ibid., pp. 172-73.
23. Ibid., pp. 317-18.
24. *Jevrejski pregled* (The Jewish Review), March-June 1990, p. 28.
25. Ibid., July-December 1990, p. 34.
26. Ibid.
27. *The Jewish Review*, January-February 1990, p. 8.
28. Ljubo Weiss, "An Open Letter to Franjo Tudjman" (parts 1-3) in *Arhiv Federacije jevrejskih zajednica Jugoslavije.*
29. *Nedeljna Dalmacija* (Dalmatian Weekly), January 14, 1990.
30. *Vjesnik* (The Harold), January 19, 1990, p. 10.
31. *Vecernji list* (The Evening Journal), January 31, 1990.
32. *Magazin*, February 25, 1990.
33. *Slobodan tjednik*, March 14, 1990.
34. *Novosti*, March 19, 1990.
35. *Jevrejski pregled*, March-June 1990, pp. 26-27.
36. *Politika*, May 27, 1990.'
37. Ljubo Weiss, "Tako je nacista govorio" (This is the Way the Nazi Spoke), *Borba* (The Struggle), May 9, 1990; *Jevrejski pregled*, March-June 1990, p. 28.
38. *Vecernji list*, April 30, 1990 and May 2, 1990.
39. *Jevrejski pregled*, March-June 1990, pp. 19-24.
40. Ibid., pp. 21-22.
41. *Nin*, July 6, 1990, p. 17.
42. *Jevrejski pregled*, March-June 1990, p. 29; July-December 1990, pp. 33-34.
43. *The Jewish Review*, July-December 1990, p. 7.
44. "Apel nasoj zidovskoj braci i sestrama" (Appeal to Our Jewish Brothers and Sisters), *Arhiv Federacije jevrejskih zajednica Jugoslavije.*
45. Minutes of the Meeting of the Jewish Community of Belgrade, August 20, 1991, *Arhiv Jevrejske opstine, Beograd.*
46. "Message from Jewish War Veterans, Former Concentration Camp Inmates and Prisoners of War," October 20, 1991, *Arhiv Jevrejske opstine, Beograd.*
47. *The Independent*, London, October 24, 1991.

48. Ibid., October 29, 1991.

49. "Appeal by the Rabbi of Yugoslavia Addressed to Pope John Paul," October 24, 1991, *Arhiv Jevrejske opstine Beograd.*

50. "To All Jewish Organizations and Media," November 1, 1991, *Arhiv Saveza jevrejskih opstina Jugoslavije.*

51. Marc Singer, "Kroatische Juden gefahrdet?," *Gemeinde,* November 1, 1991, p. 10.

52. Minutes of the Special Membership Meeting of the Jewish Community of Belgrade, December 7, 1991, p. 4.

53. Minutes of the Meeting of the Working Committee of the Federation of Jewish Communities in Yugoslavia, December 23, 1991, *Arhiv Jevrejske opstine Beograd.*

54. Ibid.

55. *Vecernji list,* January 2, 1992, p. 2.

56. O. E., "Jevreji ponovo raspinju Hrista" (The Jews Are Again Crucifying Christ), *Pravoslavlje* (Orthodoxy), no. 596, January 15, 1992, p. 2.

CONTRIBUTORS

RUTH BETTINA BIRN received her doctorate from the University of Stuttgart. A specialist on the Higher SS and Police Leaders of the Nazi era, Dr. Birn is Chief Historian of the War Crimes Section of the Department of Justice in Ottawa, Canada. She was also associated with the Office of Special Investigations of the U.S. Department of Justice and the Special Investigations Unit of Australia.

RANDOLPH L. BRAHAM is Distinguished Professor Emeritus of Political Science, The City College and the Graduate Center of The City University of New York, where he serves as Director of the Rosenthal Institute for Holocaust Studies. He is the author of numerous works in comparative politics and the Holocaust, including the revised and enlarged edition of *The Politics of Genocide. The Holocaust in Hungary* (1994).

ABRAHAM BRUMBERG has written widely on Russian, East European, and Jewish affairs. He is the former editor in chief of *Problems of Communism*, the editor of and contributor to *Poland: Genesis of a Revolution* (1983) and other books. He is also the author of articles in *Foreign Affairs, The New York Review of Books, The Economist, The New Republic, Soviet-Jewish Affairs*, and many other journals.

FREDERICK B. CHARY is Professor of History and Chairman of the Department of History and Philosophy at Indiana University Northwest. With a doctorate from the University of Pittsburgh, he is recognized as the leading authority on modern Bulgarian history in general and of Bulgarian Jewry in particular. Dr. Chary is the author of *The Bulgarian Jews and the Final Solution, 1940-1944* (1972) and numerous articles on modern Bulgarian and Balkan history.

251

ISTVÁN DEÁK is Professor of History at Columbia University in New York. He is the author of numerous works, including *Weimar Germany's Left-Wing Intellectuals: A Political History of the Weltbühne and Its Circle* (1969), *The Lawful Revolution: Louis Kossuth and the Hungarians, 1848-1849* (1979), and *Beyond Nationalism: A Social and Political History of the Habsburg Officer Corps, 1848-1918* (1990). He is also the author of many scholarly articles and is a regular contributor to *The New York Review of Books*. In 1989, Professor Deák was elected into the Hungarian Academy of Sciences in Budapest.

FRED HAHN is Professor Emeritus of History at Trenton State College. He also taught at the University of Frankfurt and served as an associate of the Institute of East Central Europe at Columbia University. He is the author of several works, including *Marxist and Utopian Socialists* (1963), *History of Russia* (1965) and *Stürmer* (1971), and of numerous scholarly articles. He is vice president and a member of the editorial board of the Society for the History of Czechoslovak Jews and a member of International PEN.

RADU IOANID is an associate of the U.S. Holocaust Memorial Museum in Washington, D.C. He is the author of *The Sword of the Archangel. Fascist Ideology in Romania* (1990) and *Urbanizarea în România. Implicații sociale și economice* (Urbanization in Romania: Social and Economic Implications; 1978). He also authored several scholarly articles.

WILLIAM KOREY, former Director of International Policy Research for B'nai B'rith, is the author of several works, including *The Soviet Cage: Anti-Semitism in Russia* (1973) and *The Promise We Keep: Human Rights, the Helsinki Process and American Foreign Policy* (1993). He also authored a large number of articles which appeared in such prestigious journals as *Foreign Affairs, Foreign Policy, Commentary*, and *Problems of Communism*.

ANDRÁS KOVÁCS is on the faculty of Eötvös Loránd University of Budapest. A prolific writer, he contributed chapters to many books and published a large number of scholarly articles in such journals as *Magyar*

Filozófiai Szemle (Hungarian Philosophical Review), *Világosság* (Light), *Valóság* (Reality), and the *Budapest Review of Books*.

RADMILA MILENTIJEVIC is Professor Emeritus of History, The City College of The City University of New York. Her articles and reviews appeared in such journals as *Canadian Review of Studies in Nationalism, Library Journal,* and the *American Historical Review.*

RAPHAEL VAGO is a Senior Lecturer in History at Tel Aviv University. He is the author of *The Grandchildren of Trianon: Hungary and the Hungarians in the Communist Countries* (1989) and of chapters in several books. His reviews and articles appeared in such journals as *Slavic and Soviet Studies, Soviet Jewish Affairs, Hungarian Studies Review,* and *East European Quarterly.* Dr. Vago is a frequent commentator on East European affairs.